ARISTOTLE'S VOICE

Rhetoric,
Theory,
and Writing
in America

Jasper Neel

Southern Illinois University Press • Carbondale and Edwardsville

Designed by Robyn Laur Clark
Production supervised by Natalia Nadraga

Library of Congress Cataloging-in-Publication Data

Neel, Jasper P.
    Aristotle's voice : rhetoric, theory, and writing in America /
Jasper Neel.
        p.   cm.
    Includes bibliographical references and index.
    1. English language—Rhetoric—Study and teaching—United
States. 2. English language—Rhetoric—Study and teaching—
Theory, etc. 3. Aristotle. Rhetoric. I. Title.
    PE1405.U6N44   1994
    808'.042'07073—dc20   94-9931
    ISBN 0-8093-1933-0   CIP

The paper used in this publication meets the minimum require-
ments of American National Standard for Information Sciences—
Permanence of Paper for Printed Library Materials, ANSI
Z39.48-1984. ∞

For Jessie W. and Jasper Peaster Neel, Jr.

With Love and Gratitude

Exodus 20.12   Proverbs 22.6

CONTENTS

ACKNOWLEDGMENTS

I gratefully acknowledge permission to quote the essays "An Analysis of Images and Structure Within Andrew Marvell's 'On a Drop of Dew,'" by Kelly J. Mays, and "Thank You Miss Alice Walker: *The Color Purple*," by Earnestine Johnson, Copyright © 1986, from *Student Writers at Work: The Bedford Prizes*, by Nancy Sommers and Donald McQuade, editors; reprinted by permission of St. Martin's Press, Incorporated.

Like all authors, I have many, many people to thank. I will limit myself to those most directly associated with this book. First, I wish to thank Jacque Voegeli, former dean of arts and science at Vanderbilt, who gave me a leave so that I could finish the book, and who gave me released time so that I could learn Greek. He also paid a tutor who spent a summer helping me read through twenty chapters of the *Rhetoric* in Greek. I must also thank my colleagues Carter Philips (a classics professor here at Vanderbilt) and Margot Avakian (a Ph.D. candidate in classics) who helped me learn my (exceedingly rudimentary) Greek.

Once again, I must thank Sharon Crowley. Southern Illinois University Press always seems to have the good sense to send my books to her, and she always knows both what is wrong with something I have written and how to fix it. I wish also to thank Andrea Lunsford. Her suggestions greatly helped as I tried to decide how to begin and end this book.

Most importantly, I must thank my wife, Faye Richardson Neel, without whose encouragement I would never have tried to write books in the first place. Writers—even (perhaps especially!) those with modest aspirations and accomplishments—are surely the hardest people in the world to live with. Anyone who lives gracefully and supportively with a writer deserves a seat very near God.

ARISTOTLE'S VOICE

Michelangelo's *Captive* (Atlas), Accademia, Florence.
Courtesy of Alinari/Art Resource, NY

PROLOGUE
The Situations of Writing

This is not a book about Aristotle, nor is it a book about rhetoric. Admittedly, I could not have written *this* book without the scholarly site named "Aristotle," nor could I have written it without the scholarly conversation named "rhetoric." But for me, "Aristotle" and "rhetoric" function as nothing more than locations. They allow me to foreground my own situation and to study (as an outsider) the operation of the professional discourse closest to my own. Up front, let me agree with those who excavate the site named "Aristotle" and those who speak the conversation named "rhetoric." Each group is right. I truly do not understand "Aristotle"; I truly do not know "rhetoric." Since I am nothing but a sophist, any good Aristotelian (and perhaps any good rhetorician) would understand right away that I do not know anything at all.

I do, however, have a lot of experience: forty-six years of personal experience and (if I count my four years as a TA) twenty-two years of teaching experience. The institutions where I have taught represent, in order, the flagship public university in the state of Tennessee; a medium-size, private, church-related university in Texas; a huge, private, research university in New York City; a brand new, very small, rural, public, commuter college in South Carolina; a large, regional, public university near Chicago; the Canadian equivalent of MIT; and a small, highly selective, private university in Nashville. I have also done a three-year stint as director of English Programs at MLA. Throughout all twenty-two years and all eight jobs, three questions have remained constant. As a set, these questions have constituted the "strange attractor" in the "chaos" of

1

my intellectual and professional lives: (1) What does it mean to teach writing? (2) What should one know *before* teaching writing? (3) If there is any such thing as "research in the teaching of writing," what is it?

I have learned to answer these three questions by contextualizing them in a specific situation. For example, I now answer question one (What does it mean to teach writing?) by saying this: It depends on the situation. A kindergarten teacher teaching students to form the letters of the alphabet, a middle-school teacher trying to help at-risk students who have ceased writing altogether, an English teacher in an expensive prep school assigning essays on *The Scarlet Letter*, a basic writing teacher working with adult learners at an urban community college, a college junior working as a peer tutor in a writing lab, an M.A. candidate teaching general composition at a regional university, a postdoctoral lecturer teaching business writing while desperately seeking a permanent position in literature, an assistant professor of literature administering a drop-in writing center, an associate professor of rhet/comp teaching a graduate seminar in composition theory, a writing program administrator running a WAC training program for non-English faculty, a part-time instructor teaching technical writing in a college of engineering, a paid consultant teaching report writing for a multinational corporation—all these people (not to mention the dozens of other people in dozens of other situations) are "teaching writing." As a result, "teaching writing" means a specific situation in which one or more teachers meets periodically over a defined period of time with a group of learners—even though some of the learners may have no intention whatsoever of "learning" anything, even though teachers and learners may "meet" only electronically or only through the mail.

Like question one, question two (What should one know *before* teaching writing?) can never do more than foreground a situation. The answer must always go something like this: It depends on the situation. Who, for example, is going to do the teaching? Who is going to do the learning? Who is empowered to perform the speech act, "You're hired," thereby creating a teacher? Who is empowered to perform the speech act, "You're admitted," thereby creating students? Until each of these questions has been answered, no one can begin to list or describe the necessary prior knowledge or training. And even after these questions have been answered the nature of the required "prior knowledge" depends on contingencies of time, availability of resources, and likelihood of reward (both monetary and personal).

And the answer to question three (What *is* research in the teaching of writing?) goes like this: It depends on the situation. Even if one changes the label from "teaching of writing" to "composition studies," the research can never be more than a situated undertaking. No object of study can appear on the horizon until someone accepts the responsibility of teaching someone else how to write; no research methodology can begin to reveal knowledge until a situation arises in which someone needs to know something before beginning to teach writing.

One might, of course, quibble about my order. One might claim that the answer to question three enables the posing of question two. Until one has done research on the teaching of writing, one cannot define the prior knowledge that a teacher of writing must have before offering a course. My response (the response that I learned from Aristotle) is that question three, if posed before question two, becomes entirely *too* prior. Anyone who tries to answer question three before answering question two sets out on a Platonic journey toward truth. Although such a journey may both improve the researcher's soul and dramatically enhance the researcher's scholarly credentials, it will not lead to the beginning of classes some Monday morning in late August. And since the teaching of writing cannot, in my opinion, ever be separated from the real and practical beginning of classes in the very near future, question three must await the answer to question two so that it can have a specific situation.

All this "situating" leads me to the purpose of this book. I offer the book as nothing more than a crude manual for those composition teachers who wish to study themselves and their pedagogy. Naturally, this book does not offer anything like a whole theory, nor does it even pretend to explain anything that might be called a "discipline." I suppose I would describe the book by making two analogies—one visual, the other (anti)intellectual. The visual analogy refers to Michelangelo's "partially completed" Atlas, which appears at the beginning of this Prologue. This sculpture was intended for the tomb of Pope Julius II. It is one of a group of four sculptures referred to as the "captives." Each of these sculptures bears the name *Captive* because none of the four is "complete"; each remains partially imprisoned in stone. Of the four, the Atlas, in my opinion, has the greatest power. The figure seems forever caught trying to escape from the unformed block. The figure's struggle to wrest itself into full being is palpable, especially as the left arm strains to pull the head free. The viewer feels the elation of trying imaginatively to "help" the artwork become whole and free, but this elation can never extract itself from the stone's unrelenting hold on the unfinished form. Thus in an odd way, the "unfinished" sculpture itself becomes an artwork. Its aesthetic power derives from its "unfinished" commentary, a commentary not only on art but also on life. The sculpture is not an oscillation between imagined explosion into full human form and imagined implosion into unshaped stone; rather, the sculpture transcends this very oscillation, forcing a theoretical commentary on art itself. As a result of this commentary, the modifiers "partially completed" must be written in inverted commas because the state of partial completion is what makes the sculpture complete.

This book is a manual for a professional life that resembles such sculpture. It suggests a professional life forever caught in the process of becoming. Such a professional self-definition leaves itself incomplete but then, without changing a thing, transforms its static and unfinished condition into a complete, though never-ending, dynamic reconfiguration. This reconfiguration operates continually as an escape from, descent into, and commentary on itself. The teacher of writing and the researcher who studies the teaching of writing exist jointly in a manner much like one of Michelangelo's "captive" sculptures. Neither "thing" can be itself without its counterpart. So closely joined are the "two" that they are not two at all. Just as the art remains forever embedded in and indistinguishable from the raw material from which it has been (is being) shaped, the writing teacher (composition studies researcher) both studies the teaching of writing and constitutes the thing being studied.

The intellectual analogy (whether "anti" or not) merely summarizes an obvious process of personal history. What, I ask myself, shapes my pedagogy when I conceive a course? And what shaped whatever shapes my pedagogy? These two questions allow the teacher's education to play both the conceptual role of architect and the productive role of construction crew. In a specific way, the teacher's entire intellectual and personal history forms the walls, windows, and doorway of the "classroom." Research specific to the teaching of writing constitutes most of the "room's" furnishings. Once the students appear on the scene, the "room" expands greatly, often taking wildly eccentric shapes, but the "room" itself always begins in the intellectual and personal life of the teacher, who sets the syllabus, chooses the texts, bears responsibility for classroom activity, and assigns grades. Each teacher/researcher's situation leads, therefore, to a double intellectual undertaking. In one gesture, the researcher tries always to foreground and understand his or her own intellectual and personal history. Or, said differently, the mind attempts the well-known philosophical impossibility of understanding itself. In the other gesture, the researcher tries to understand whatever the researcher's mind claims as an influence. Thus research in the teaching of writing is forever contaminated by itself. Whatever the teacher brings to the classroom constitutes the "research" that enables that particular class, yet what goes on in the classroom constitutes the "object of study" on which the researcher conducts research. (One could, of course, argue that the intellectual and personal histories of the students are as important as those of the teacher. Speaking politically, this claim is undeniably true; speaking pedagogically, however, it is a red herring because the teacher, having been "authorized," remains forever limited by the dimensions and boundaries of that particular teacher's capabilities. Although the teacher must surely try to meet the students where they are and help them learn what they are capable of and willing to learn, no teacher can ever transcend his or her own boundaries of knowability. The best the teacher can do is to foreground those boundaries, always trying to make them as broad and flexible as possible.)

This book is a manual for such (anti)intellectual speculation. I call it (anti)intellectual because I have worked with enough apprentice teachers to know that no intellectual history, no imaginable set of influences necessarily predicts success in the classroom. My kind of research tends toward the anecdotal, the accidental, and the nonreplicable; thus, by any normal definition of the term *research*, my research is not research at all. No one, as I have said, will be able to extract any "knowledge" from these pages.

The obvious question one might pose to this book (or to me as its "author") is "Why so much time on Aristotle?" After all, Aristotle has been dead 2,316 years (give or take a few months), and *a lot* has happened in all that time. Surely one can neither credit nor blame Aristotle for the successes and failures of American composition teachers. The leap from fourth-century Athens to twentieth-century America is too great. One could spend time more productively by tracing the full history from Aristotle's death to yesterday morning. Then, at least, one would know how much blame to allot, how much praise to allot, and where to make the allotments. Or, merely for sake of expediency, would it not be sufficient to begin in eighteenth-century Scotland and trace the history of contemporary rhetorical theory from Edinburgh and Aberdeen, making sure to account for all the political, philosophical, social, aesthetic, and scientific advances that have shaped the contemporary discipline called rhetoric/composition? Better yet, why not begin with the famous 1963 CCCC in Los Angeles or maybe with the Dartmouth Conference and write a history of composition studies from there?

My answer is that such cultural or disciplinary histories mislead everyone about the nature of classroom practice in the teaching of writing. Admittedly all composition teachers operate under the influence of Cicero, Quintilian, Augustine, Erasmus, Wilson, Ramus, Bacon, Blair, Vico, Priestly, Campbell, Whately, Bain, and a host of other figures in the history of rhetoric, but for the vast majority of composition teachers (more than 95 percent), these "fathers" of rhetoric remain at best shadowy, subliminal presences. They "exist" merely as unknown influences whose ideas appear on syllabi and in classroom pedagogy from the dimmest recesses of our discipline's history. Undeniably our more recent history, the one that begins somewhere in the 1960s, has a more direct influence. The move from "product" to "process" can be easily encapsulated in a "bad-way, good-way dichotomy." But even that history functions for most writing teachers as little more than a myth that goes something like this: "Back in the current-traditional days writing teachers tormented their students with excessive and useless emphasis on grammar, mechanics, and finished products. Now we are more enlightened, and we know that writing courses should build toward products through careful, recursive process pedagogy." In my opinion, any of these possible histories—whether beginning in ancient Greece, Enlightenment Scotland, contemporary America, or somewhere else—leads to a phylogeny of composition studies. Such phylogeny explains both the historical development of and the general nature of "the composition teacher." As anyone can see, however, American colleges are far, far removed from a situation in which a significant percentage of composition teachers can be expected (let alone required) to know such a phylogeny. Any such phylogeny remains accessible only to a few. For those few, history unquestionably informs pedagogy, always for the better. This book is not written for or about "the composition teacher"; rather, it is written for and about "a particular composition teacher." It is written for all those composition teachers who cannot realistically seek more than ontogeny. Phylogeny will have to wait for the minuscule percentage of composition teachers who become lifelong professionals.

The ontogeny of this particular composition teacher begins with Aristotle. That is why this book almost never strays from the site called "Aristotle" and the conversation called "rhetoric." Quite by accident, Aristotle's *Rhetoric* was the first text I read as a way of understanding how to teach writing. Since reading that text (or rather, since reading Lane Cooper's 1932 translation of that text), my notions of how to teach writing have operated in a constant relationship with Aristotle, a relationship sometimes dialectical and sometimes antagonistic, but usually merely dependent. Prior to reading the *Rhetoric*, I had done nothing more than sample a random variety of textbooks as I tried to adapt the New Criticism to the teaching of writing. Stephen North would probably call my situation in those days "pre-lore." I began in 1971 with Randall Decker's *Patterns of Exposition* and, in order, moved through Brooks and Warren's *Understanding Poetry*, Laurence Perrine's *Story and Structure*, James McCrimmon's *Writing with a Purpose*, and Sheridan Baker's *Practical Stylist*. Not until I met James Kinneavy, however, did it occur to me that I might try to work out a notion of pedagogy *before* I chose a textbook or developed a syllabus. After meeting Kinneavy, I turned to Aristotle; thus, Aristotle became my point of departure. Of course, I now realize that his *Rhetoric* and *Poetics* had been my point of departure all along; I just did not know it. Patterns books such as Decker's come right out of the Aristotelian topics; Brooks, Warren, and Perrine offer critical strategies that have developed over the years from the *Poetics*; and the McCrimmon and Baker of the early 1970s were little more than a truncated rhetoric that had, over the years, been reduced from Aristotle.

I do not wish to argue that everyone who teaches writing should make a study of Aristotle. Admittedly, I am enough of a historical determinist to believe that composition teachers who remain ignorant of Aristotle are probably ignorant of their conceptions of discourse, but that is merely an opinion bred of prejudice, not an opinion I would try to defend professionally. I do, however, want to argue throughout this book that all composition teachers are situated politically and socially, both as part of the institutions in which they teach and as beings with lived histories. This complicated, exceedingly local situation is more formative of, and more important to, composition teachers than to the teachers in any other discipline on campus, whatever "campus" may mean in the particular situation.

I think Aristotle offers as interesting and complex a situation as any from which to mount a critique of composition studies, but I cannot deny that I burrow so deeply within Aristotelianism because I find so much of myself there. On a daily basis I present myself to students as someone who writes well and can help them learn to write well; I spend time thinking programmatically so as to help my college meet the needs of a diverse student body; I meet with apprentice teachers and try to help them improve as teachers; and I attempt to make honest decisions about competence. These four composition-related actions seem natural and necessary to me. These four actions account for almost all of my working days and occupy most of my leisure hours. But I wish to resist the notion that I can "know" composition in a way that some TA right out of an M.A. program cannot, or that I can "know" writing in a way that some first-year student diagnosed (by *my* diagnostic procedures) as needing "remediation" cannot.

But if I succeed in such resistance, how am I to present myself as a "Professor of Composition Studies"? This book, which is nothing but an extended study of ontogenesis, attempts to answer that question. The answer comes in five stages. In chapter 1, I try to situate Aristotle's *Rhetoric* as a political document, something that we in composition studies rarely do. In chapter 2, I try to situate the *Rhetoric* in the Aristotelian system. In chapter 3, I offer my own working hypothesis about how professional discourse came to know itself through Aristotle's way of studying the world. In chapter 4, I study the operation of the *Rhetoric* inside itself. And in chapter 5, I explain why I have turned to Aristotle's notion of sophistry as a way of negating the authority of his system. In a larger and more important frame of reference, however, these five chapters attempt to articulate a methodology for ontogenesis. Of course any ontogenesis of "a particular composition teacher" will always have the self-reflexive, half-complete, (anti)intellectual limitations I described above. Such ontogenesis can, however, be done by anyone at any time. It entails nothing more than answering the following five sets of questions, which correspond to the five chapters described above: (1) What are the social and political implications of the sources of my pedagogy? Given my way of conceiving the classroom, what sort of person must I become to inhabit the position "teacher"? What sort of people must my students become to be recognizable to me as students? (2) Since the sources of my pedagogy are themselves situated, how are they situated? What are the assumptions about epistemology in the situation where my sources become effective? (3) To teach my course I must become a professional. Even if I diligently seek the voice of an "amateur," the moment my voice speaks as the "teacher," it becomes a professional voice. What, in terms of my own course, constitutes professional discourse? (4) As I review the sources of my pedagogy and of my professional voice, what can I know about the internal operation of those sources? Is there any difference between the way my sources tell students to write and the way the sources themselves are written? (5) Since I am always the novice, always the partially informed preprofessional, how can I respond to the sources of my pedagogy so that I am more than a tape recorder?

Naturally, such an ontogenesis will, in time, lead to phylogenesis. Although I do not expect to be alive when the majority of composition teachers will have learned their phylogenesis, I would not be at all surprised if such a day were to come late in the next century. In the meantime, I suspect ontogenesis, which is a formidable undertaking, is the best we can hope for.

This book concludes with a Michelangelo sculpture quite different from the captive Atlas shown above. The book ends with the figure of Night on the sarcophagus of Giuliano de' Medici's tomb (see Epilogue). Like the Atlas, this sculpture is caught forever escaping from stone. Unlike the Atlas, however, Night's situation is neither agonistic nor violent; indeed, from the front, Night's "partially complete" situation is not apparent at all. Rather than fighting to become herself, she reposes *as* herself. With this book, my struggle with Aristotle (as well as my struggle with Plato, which grew out of the struggle with Aristotle) is, I think, largely over. Increasingly I imagine myself in the repose of Night, not the agony of Atlas. As will become clear, however, my comfort raises an entirely new matter of concern. Even though my students can no longer see the raw stone from which I have been made, I know exactly what the concealed part of my professional self looks like, and at all moments I am aware of the process by which I came to seem so complete and at ease. I am convinced that this is the most important knowledge I can take with me into the classroom.

1

THE *RHETORIC* AND THE *POLITICS* OF SLAVERY

For James Chaney, Andrew Goodman,
and Michael Schwerner

Mississippi 1967

I have seen the truth. I have known some of the people who believe that the truth has set them free. Their discourse has a cool, clinically detached quality about it. Their discourse allows them to rise above life and understand it.

In March 1967, I was in the process of leaving both the place where I saw the truth and the truth that place told. I remember sitting late into a Saturday evening in an elegantly furnished living room near Silver City, Mississippi. I was a college junior home for spring break, and my Saturday ramblings around Humphries County had led me to a house I knew well where I was surrounded by friends I knew well. I had not yet thrown away the AuH_2O button that was my souvenir from the 1964 presidential campaign, nor had I met Al Lowenstein, whose visit to Mississippi the following year would draw me into Gene McCarthy's presidential campaign. My job in that campaign would be to work as a field organizer for a political movement referred to in those days as the "Mississippi Black Democratic party."[1]

I spent that Saturday evening listening to a set of arguments

10

that I knew to be wrong, but at the time I did not know how to contend with them. I listened with a mixed feeling of horror and regret: horror because I had read Ralph Ellison and listened to Martin Luther King; regret because I knew I would never again hear the evening's conversation expressed in its jocular, open, and natural manner. Aside from the pleasantries of arriving and departing, throughout the evening I remained silent, which is not my usual demeanor. Somewhere deep in my being I could sense that I was "at home" for the last time. The truth was slipping away from me, taking with it the safe home where I had grown up. The arguments raged well into Sunday morning, which would find everyone in the room at one of the five white-only churches (Baptist, Catholic, Episcopalian, Methodist, and Presbyterian) in Belzoni, Mississippi, the only town of any size in the county.

The conversation was about race. Those who participated argued vehemently over three different ways of justifying the American system of racial segregation. One group (I call them the "Noah group") based its argument for segregation on an interpretation of the events of Genesis 9, whose story goes like this: After the floodwaters recede, Noah celebrates too much, finally falling into a naked, drunken stupor. The youngest of his three sons, Ham, "the father of Canaan," dishonors Noah by looking on his nakedness and then describing it to Shem and Japheth, Noah's other sons. When Noah awakens and learns of Ham's disrespect, Noah condemns Ham with this curse:

Cursed be Canaan;
lowest of slaves shall he be to his brothers.
. . . .
Blessed by the Lord my God be
    Shem;
  and let Canaan be his slave.
May God make space for Japheth,
  and let him live in the tents of
    Shem;
and let Canaan be his slave.[2]

According to the Noah group, this passage means that the African, Asian, and Caucasian races were engendered by Noah's three sons and that the curse on Ham, the father of the Africans, is hereditary and eternal. Because of this curse, black servitude is both biblical and godly.

A second group (I call them the "Lilith group") justified racism through an interpolation of Genesis 2–6. In this interpolation, for which there is no canonized text, God ejects Adam and Eve from Eden for disobeying him. Soon thereafter, Adam copulates with a nonhuman female named Lilith (there was dispute among those arguing this position over whether Lilith was a fallen angel in female shape or a humanlike beast, some sort of female higher primate). From this copulation, whether demonic or bestial, springs a race of humanlike creatures who enjoy much the same physical and mental gifts as humans, but who have no souls. These soulless creatures become the progenitors of all black people, who, because of their soulless nature, are amoral and shiftless. They must be held in servitude to keep them under control, and since they have no after-life, their intrinsic value is not significantly different from that of other nonhuman, higher primates. Black servitude is, therefore, a natural and necessary human responsibility.

A third group (I call them the "oligarchs") responded to the first two groups with a pragmatic elitism. This group also buttressed its argument with Scripture, but it did so more out of convention than out of faith. At that time anyone living in the Mississippi Delta had to offer some sort of Scripture in order to be taken seriously as a social theorist. In the Old Testament, the oligarchs explained, the prophet Zephaniah writes "I will also leave in the midst of you a people humble and lowly" (3.12). In the New Testament Christ himself says, "you always have the poor with you" (Matthew 26.11). Those arguing this position contended that there have always been and will always be inequities in the way life is lived. Some people must be poor for others to be rich; some must work hard for others to have leisure. Some, through their suffering and deprivation, must constitute the foundation on which others can build the art, music, philosophy, and politics that life at its finest requires. This situation is unfortunate, but true. And this truth shows that black people in the modern world, whatever their ancestors may have been like, simply do not work as hard, think as deeply, understand as thoroughly as do white people. Of course, as the Bible makes clear, this leads to a double obligation: neither to abuse black people because of their inferiority nor to pretend that the inferiority does not exist.

No one changed positions during the evening. And to any African American living in the Mississippi Delta during those years, the prevailing position mattered little because all three led to the same thing: segregation, injustice, racism, suffering. As far as I know, all of the people present in that room are still living today. I doubt that their positions have changed much over the years, though perhaps I am wrong, for I have been in Humphries County only once since 1972, and I have not seen any of the people in that room in two decades. For many years, I viewed them as good and decent people, salt of the earth; for many more years I viewed them as demons incarnate, emblems not only of American racism but, more generally, of what I have always understood Conrad's Kurtz to mean when he whispers, "The horror! The horror!" Nowadays I have difficulty characterizing those people at all, except to say that it makes me exceedingly nervous to discuss them or to repeat what I heard them say as they reaffirmed the political and theological discourses of my childhood. I am, however, certain that the discourse they spoke with such clinical detachment that evening will haunt me for as long as I live.

It would be nice if we could dismiss this scene with an incredulous shake of the head, grateful that such habits of thinking and such patterns of living are behind us, confident that everyone now knows better. But any drive from Greenwood, Mississippi, through Tchula and over to Belzoni, or any drive through the neighborhoods between the University of Chicago and the Congress Parkway, or the neighborhoods around Yale University, or almost anywhere in the South Bronx (few readers of this book would be likely to *walk* in those neighborhoods), or any time spent on land managed by the Bureau of Indian Affairs, or any evening spent watching a film by Julie Dash or John Singleton or even Spike Lee demonstrates that those dark and dangerous conversations of the Mississippi Delta are very much with us today, with all of us.

This is, I recognize, an odd approach to Aristotle, especially from the perspective of composition studies. Perhaps I have no business inflicting the wounds of my own past on others, the vast majority of whom no doubt grew to adulthood in better places than I, hearing better arguments and traveling on less troubled roads. And in treating Aristotle and his *Rhetoric* in the way that I am about to do, I know that I stand wide open to the charge that I am finding my own past, my own family, social, and professional drama in a place where I alone can see it. But my motive in this book is to

foreground the professional discourse in which teachers of writing
are situated. I do not think we pay enough attention either to the
dynamics or to the assumptions of that discourse. Nor do I think
we pay enough attention to the way professional discourse both
enables and blinds those who speak and write it in the innocence
of academic safety. For well or ill, Aristotle is where I begin. All of
us, and especially those of us in composition studies, are situated
in Aristotelianism; we teach the voice of professional discourse that
Aristotelianism creates.

Athens 325 B.C.

Rhetoric is my destination, but I cannot go there directly because Aristotle's system makes the art of rhetoric a subsidiary within
the art of politics, which Aristotle names the "master art." He makes
the hierarchy clear in both the *Nicomachean Ethics* and the *Rhetoric*.
Political science, he explains in the *Ethics*,*

> ordains which of the sciences are to exist in states, and what
> branches of knowledge the different classes of the citizens are to
> learn, and up to what point; and we observe that even the most
> highly esteemed of the faculties, such as strategy, domestic econ-
> omy, rhetoric, are subordinate to the political science. (1094^{b}1–5)

He repeats this hierarchy in the *Rhetoric* (1359^{b}2–19) where he
defines rhetoric as less rigorously intellectual and less trustworthy
than political science, of which rhetoric is a kind of dependent
offshoot (1356^{a}25).[3]
Now I surely understand how to make the argument that right-
thinking, fair-minded people in the modern world can extract Aristotelian rhetoric from the Aristotelian system. By doing so we can read
the *Rhetoric* without reading the *Politics*. Those of us in composition
studies who read the history of rhetoric usually protect the *Rhetoric*
this way. We find the proofs, the canons, the commonplaces, indeed
the whole Aristotelian system of taxonomizing discourse too useful
and too historically important to jettison.[4] We teach it and employ

---

*Unless otherwise indicated in parentheses, all quotations from Aristotle
are taken from the respective edition of the Loeb Classical Library, Harvard
University Press. In all cases, I refer to the Aristotelian canon using numbers
keyed to Immanuel Bekker's 1831 editions of the Greek text of Aristotle.

it as neutrally and innocently as the New Critics ever taught those other Aristotelian terms—*plot, character, theme,* and *metaphor.* We know, however, that neither poetry nor rhetoric is innocent, and we know that no set of terms can become neutral tools that generate innocent analysis and explanation. I fear that we sometimes forget the degree to which the teaching of writing is and must be a political undertaking.

Aristotle did not forget. His rhetoric is, from beginning to end, part of his politics, and a subsidiary, dependent part at that. I want to argue that when we see discourse as consisting of invention, arrangement, style, memory, and delivery; when we teach the ethical, pathetic, and logical appeals; when we divide argument into induction and deduction; when we urge the virtue of the plain, middle style; when we organize our courses around such apparently innocent topics as analogy, definition, description, cause-effect, comparison-contrast, and example; when we teach the pro and contra process of public debate; when we allow ourselves to think even for a moment about a paper's "style" as opposed to its "content"; when we assume any of these perspectives on discourse, we look through Aristotle's eyes. Those eyes saw a terrible reality. I know. I have seen some of it myself.

Of course the term *rhetoric* has taken on such warm and cuddly connotations in the postmodern era, and we feel so good about having recognized the rhetoricity of nearly everything that we tend to forget the politics and world view in which rhetoric is and always has been embedded. It seems that half of all university press books in the humanities and social sciences now have the word "rhetoric" somewhere in the title, most members of CCCC (myself included) claim to be "rhet/comp" specialists, and Stanley Fish can attack elitism by writing, "there is always just beneath the surface of the antirhetorical stance a powerful and corrosive elitism" (473). Fish's sentence sounds so good to those of us in composition studies that we forget to interrogate the rhetorical stance itself. We play the roles of Robin Hood and Little John in the Disney animation. Like Little John, we can ask, "Are we good guys or bad guys?" Like Little John's, our question is utterly innocent, entirely "rhetorical."

Slavery does not appear often in the *Rhetoric.* When it does, the offhanded, desultory way in which Aristotle presents it shows that the social theories in the *Rhetoric* are of a piece with those in the *Politics.* In contrasting anger with mildness, Aristotle explains that we easily forgive those who admit their offenses and reconfirm their subordination to us. Evidence of this, he explains,

> may be seen in the punishment of slaves; for we punish more severely those who contradict us and deny their offence, but cease to be angry with those who admit that they are justly punished. . . . Men are also mild towards those who humble themselves before them and do not contradict them, for [those who submit] seem to recognize that they are inferior. . . . Even the behaviour of dogs proves that anger ceases towards those who humble themselves. (1380ª3–20)

In explaining the superfluousness of long introductions, Aristotle gives slaves a character identical to that of Scarlett O'Hara's slave, Prissy, in *Gone with the Wind*. Long introductions are okay, Aristotle explains, when the speaker has a bad case. If the case is bad, "it is better to lay stress upon anything rather than the case itself. That is why slaves never answer questions directly but go all round them, and indulge in preambles" (1415ᵇ10–15).

Aristotle did not need to spend much time on slavery in the *Rhetoric* because he had justified it in detail in the *Politics*, the master art in which his rhetoric is a subsidiary.[5] Throwaways like the two above glow at their full intensity only when one reads them in the light of the *Politics*, where Aristotle begins by explaining that he will follow his "regular method of investigation" (1252ª19). This method requires that he analyze the composite whole "down to its uncompounded elements." Political science turns out to consist of two elements. Element one is the "union of female and male"; element two, "the union of the natural ruler and natural subject."

The master term that plays throughout the first section of the *Politics* is the Greek noun φύσις. As one might expect, this term is difficult to render in English, but generally it carries the following three notions: (1) the essential, structural nature of a thing, (2) the teleological whole toward which a thing inevitably develops, (3) the genetic, predetermining origin of a thing. Most translators use the word "nature" as the English equivalent of φύσις, but it is important to remember that Aristotle used φύσις in a much more determined and determining way than we now use "nature." When Aristotle describes the φύσις of a thing, he means the essential being that the thing should have, must have, and will have.

Of the "natural" union between ruler and ruled, Aristotle says, "one who can foresee with his mind is naturally ruler and naturally master, and one who can do these things with his body is subject and naturally a slave; so that master and slave have the same interest" (1252ª30–35). The one who is a natural ruler "must have his tools, and of tools some are lifeless and others living. . . . a slave is a live article of property" (1253ᵇ27–32). Aristotle leaves no doubt about the absoluteness of the slave's nature: "whereas the master is merely the slave's master and does not belong to the slave, the slave is not merely the slave of the master but wholly belongs to the master" (1254ª11–14). To make the master-slave relationship clear, Aristotle compares it to the relations between genders, between humans and animals, between body and soul, and between intelligence and appetite:

the soul rules the body with the sway of a master, the intelligence the appetites with constitutional or royal rule; and in these examples it is manifest that it is natural and expedient for the body to be governed by the soul and for the emotional part to be governed by the intellect, the part possessing reason, whereas for the two parties to be on equal footing or in the contrary positions is harmful in all cases. Again, the same holds good between man and the other animals: tame animals are superior in their nature to wild animals, yet for all the former it is advantageous to be ruled by man, since this gives them security. Also, as between the sexes, the male is by nature superior and the female inferior, the male ruler and the female subject. And the same must also necessarily apply in the case of mankind generally; . . . [some men] are by nature slaves, for whom to be governed by this kind of authority is advantageous, inasmuch as it is advantageous to the subject things already mentioned. For he is by nature a slave who is capable of belonging to another (and that is why he does so belong). (1254ᵇ5–24)

Aristotle endlessly reiterates this sort of social theory in the *Politics*. "The usefulness of slaves," he continues, "diverges little from that of animals." He finds it "manifest . . . that there are cases of people of whom some are freemen and the others slaves by nature." Lest anyone wonder about race or geography, Aristotle makes clear that the one who by nature is a slave is a slave everywhere, for "the principles of natural slavery" make clear that "there exist certain persons who are essentially slaves everywhere and certain others who are so nowhere" (1254ᵇ25–1255ᵃ35).

And by now, of course, it is clear why we read the *Rhetoric* alone, pretending that it can be extracted from the political and social theories in which Aristotle embedded it. How in the world would anyone ever justify taking seriously a theory of communication that had any sort of relationship at all with such notions as Aristotle's? Once one begins to look at the world through his eyes, things "make sense" in a terrifying way. For example, since nature has made the souls of freemen and slaves so different, "The intention of nature . . . is to make the bodies also of freemen and of slaves different— the latter strong for necessary service, the former erect and unserviceable for such occupations, but serviceable for a life of citizenship." One would expect, Aristotle repeats a few pages later, that nature would set a clear physical mark on those intended to be slaves.

Does nature do this? Well, no. "As a matter of fact," Aristotle admits with not a hint of sheepishness or embarrassment, "often the very opposite comes about—slaves have the bodies of freemen and freemen the souls only." In other words, nature intends to put slaves in slaves' bodies and freemen in freemen's bodies, but nature "is unable to bring it about." After admitting the difficulties of interpretation implied by this little failing on nature's part, Aristotle blithely concludes, "It is manifest therefore that there are cases of people of whom some are freemen and the others slaves by nature, and for these slavery is an institution both expedient and just" (1254ᵇ27–1255ᵃ2; 1255a39–1255ᵇ4).

How does that make sense to anybody? Given nature's brilliant success in the creation of souls, or individual φύσεις, how can nature have failed so miserably in getting these souls appropriately embodied? Would such an outrageous lack of fit not cause the prudent to pause for a moment and rethink their prior categories? After all, the souls of freemen, as Aristotle openly admits, actually wind up in the bodies of slaves, and vice versa. In working through all this, Aristotle even admits that "beauty of soul is not so easy to see" as is beauty of body (1355ᵃ1). Does this give him pause? Not a whit. Indeed it seems to let him see the truth of his notion more clearly.

To Aristotle, slavery and all the concomitant vestiges of a hierarchical society simply *are*. The notion of natural slavery is deeply embedded in Aristotelian thought. In the *Categories*, for example, he uses "master-slave" as a way to demonstrate the concept "relationship." "All relatives," he explains, "have their correlatives. 'Slave' means the slave of a master, and 'master,' in turn, implies slave" (6ᵇ29–31). The essential quality of the slave *as a slave* is so important, Aristotle continues, that if "slave" is defined "in relation to 'man' or to 'biped' or what not, instead of its being defined (as it should be) by reference to 'master,' then no correlation appears, for the reference is really inaccurate." "Suppose we remove," Aristotle muses, all the "irrelevant attributes" from the master, "such as his being 'two-footed,' 'receptive of knowledge' or 'human,' and leave but his being 'a master,' then 'slave' will be still the correlative, 'slave' *meaning slave of a master*" (7ᵃ28–7ᵇ1).[6]

Anyone can readily see the many ways to ignore or obscure Aristotle's social theory, beginning with the patronizing claim that slavery was part of the ancient world and thus we have no right to condemn Aristotle for living and thinking as all others of his age did. A. H. M. Jones estimates that there were 20,000 slaves in Athens (*Athenian* 78–79); Chester Starr (*Birth* 38) estimates 30,000; M. I. Finley (*Ancient Slavery* 80) doubles that estimate to 60,000; G. E. M. de St. Croix (112–269) and S. Laufer (5–13) each raise the figure as high as 80,000; A. W. Gomme pushes it up to 160,000 (20–26); and Athenaeus, who is the only surviving ancient source, estimates a whopping 400,000.[7] Of course, the number of slaves at any given time between 480 and 322 depended on the relative wealth and success of Athens at the moment, and the figure was probably lower in the fourth century than in the fifth. Nevertheless, whether the figure was 20,000, 400,000, or somewhere in between, there were *a lot* of slaves in Athens. R. K. Sinclair's estimate that slaves constituted slightly more than one-third of the people living in Athens throughout the fifth and fourth centuries is probably accurate (192–202).

Unquestionably, Aristotle himself owned numerous slaves. Anyone can read his will and see that at his death he owned well over twenty slaves, and probably many more than that. He grew up in an affluent family, the son of a king's personal physician; slave ownership would almost certainly have been a structural part of his life from birth. And justifications of slavery do appear elsewhere in Athenian literature. Euripides (*Iphigenia* 1400) implies the propriety of Greeks' subjugating and owning barbarians, Plato (*Republic* 470ᶜ–

471ᵃ) and Isocrates (*Panegyricus* 3, 184 and *Panathenaicus* 163) both argue that non-Greeks can be enslaved, or even exterminated, and so on. According to Peter Green (59), a kind of structural racism so pervaded Greek intellectual life that the use of slaves was almost compulsory. A. Jones ("Economic" 32) explains that slavery was an established institution protected in an ideological way by the Athenians' longstanding, unquestioned belief in the sanctity of private property. Oswyn Murray ("Life" 223) suggests that slavery was about as widespread in fourth-century Athens as automobile ownership is in Europe today and that it attracted about the same degree of attention. After describing the hideous conditions at the Laurium silver mines, which were worked largely by slaves, many of them children, Murray goes on to lament, "It is indeed an appalling indictment of Athenian indifference that Nicias, whose money was made from child labor of this sort, could widely be regarded as the most moral and religious man of his generation" ("Life" 224). The "Background Book" on Athenian culture, given to all students who learn Greek using the system developed by Britain's Joint Association of Classical Teachers (JACT), contends that the Athenian way of life depended on slavery (P. Jones 179–87). Sinclair points out that "a master who killed a slave seems to have been required to do no more than submit to the ritual act of purification" (28). Donald Kagan (*Great* 221) and David Ross (4) both explain that Aristotle's racism and his endorsement of slavery fit nicely with the opinions of other Athenian aristocrats. And anyone who reads Greek history discovers endless battles that led to the enslavement of entire city-states. In 335, for example, about the time Aristotle returned to Athens for his most productive years as a writer and teacher, his Macedonian countryman and friend Parmenio destroyed the town of Grynium and sold its inhabitants into slavery. In that same year, Aristotle's most famous student, Alexander, did basically the same thing to Thebes. The act of reducing a city to rubble and selling its inhabitants into slavery was so common that the Greeks gave the practice a name ἀνδραποδισμός.[8] So why is it fair to hold Aristotle to a standard both higher than and unknown to his own time?

There are two equally important reasons. First, if we are not careful, we run the risk of absolving Aristotle on the grounds of absolute innocence by making a statement such as this: "no one, in the ancient world, as far as we know, advocated the abolition of slavery" (Mulgan 40–44).[9] This way, we skip Book I of the *Politics* and we have political science; we skip the defense of slavery in the *Economics* and we have economics; we go directly to *Ethics, Metaphysics,* and *Analytics* where we get philosophy; we take physical science from *Physics, On the Heavens,* and *Meteorology;* biological science from the various works on animals and plants; psychology from works having to do with the human psyche; and from *Rhetoric, Sophistical Refutations,* and *Topics,* we get communications theory. From *Categories* we learn how to create taxonomy, from *Poetics* and *On Interpretation* we develop critical theory, from *The Constitution of Athens* we learn how to carry out and present research in history and social science.[10] In other words, we build the West. Our problem, of course, is that we must live in what we build.

It may be true that no surviving ancient manuscript includes a carefully reasoned argument for abolishing slavery, but that does not let Aristotle off the hook. A century before Aristotle wrote the *Rhetoric,* the sophist Antiphon wrote a treatise entitled *On Truth* in which he laid the theoretical foundation for abolition. "We revere and venerate" those born of a great house, he writes, but

> those who are born of a humble house we neither revere nor venerate. On this point we are barbarized in our behavior to one another. Our natural endowment is the same for us all, on all points, whether we are Greeks or barbarians. We may observe the characteristics of any of the powers which by nature are necessary to all men. . . . None of us is set apart either as a Greek or as a barbarian. We can all breathe air through our mouth and nostrils. (Barker 98)

Eli Sagan (80) shows at length that this argument by Antiphon could appear only in a society where the notions of individual rights and "equity" were well established. Indeed, several of the sophists, according to the JACT authors, "held that slavery was contrary to nature and, because it was based on force, morally wrong." This explains why Aristotle "spends the opening chapters of his *Politics* trying, not very successfully, to refute those unorthodox sophists and prove that slavery was natural" (P. Jones 185–86).

The most damning evidence, however, comes not from the scraps that remain of the sophists but from Aristotle himself. In his own text he makes absolutely clear that arguments for abolition were in circulation around Athens. Simply to excuse his defense of slavery based on an argument that abolition was unknown to him and unthinkable by him will not do. Abolition was, as his own text shows, quite well known to him, and he thought through it as carefully as any bigot ever has. Although it may be true, to return to Murray's analogy, that giving up his slaves would have been as unusual, inconvenient, and unpleasant for Aristotle as giving up our private automobiles would be for us, it is also true that we know very well just how wasteful and destructive our automobiles are, and we can expect no forgiveness from future generations if, through our insistence on private, personal automobiles, we make life on our planet hellish for our descendants. We know exactly what we are doing. And so did Aristotle. He tells us in his own words.

When he takes up the master-slave relationship, he sets out to see it fully, both as a theoretically grounded social institution and as a practical way of living. Some people, he admits, "maintain that for one man to be another man's master is contrary to nature, because it is only convention that makes the one a slave and the other a freeman and there is no difference between them by nature, and that therefore it is unjust, for it is based on force" (1253^{b}15–23). He lets the question drop for a few pages, but then he returns to it, making clear that he understands with excruciating clarity the arguments against slavery:

> we must next consider whether or not anyone exists who is by nature of [the character of a slave], and whether it is advantageous and just for anyone to be a slave, or whether on the contrary all slavery is against nature. And it is not difficult either to discern the answer by theory or to learn it empirically. Authority and subordination are conditions not only inevitable but also expedient; in some cases things are marked out from the moment of birth to rule or to be ruled.

He goes on like this for several more sentences, concluding finally that all of nature depends on hierarchies in which the few rule and the majority are ruled. In all things "there is always found a ruling and a subject factor, and this characteristic of living things is present in them as an outcome of the whole of nature, since even in things that do not partake of life there is a ruling principle, as in the case of a musical scale" (1254^{a}17–34).

Though it seems closed here, the argument does not end. Aristotle returns to the matter of slavery yet again, this time showing even more clearly both the care with which someone in Athens had made the case for abolition and the care with which Aristotle had formulated his defense of slavery. Having concluded that slavery is "an institution both expedient and just," Aristotle turns again to the abolitionists, admitting that they do have one good argument (1255ᵃ3–1255ᵇ15). The words "slave" and "slavery" are rather ambiguous, he admits, because they apply both to those who are slaves by nature and to those who are slaves by accident of military conquest. Both the logic and the Greek at this point in his text are hard to follow, but Aristotle seems to deal with this ambiguity in two ways. First, excellence, or virtue (the Greek noun is ἀρετή), when it has sufficient resources, has great power, and indeed this sort of ἀρετή carries with it enough moral strength and superiority to justify its use of force. This argument is more complicated than Callicles' bald claim that "might makes right" in *Gorgias*. Aristotelian ἀρετή privileges moral excellence first, and this moral excellence attracts might naturally. Right is not made by might; rather, such right, such ἀρετή, by the nature of its own virtue attracts might. Therefore, a military force superior in ἀρετή has a certain moral justification for enslaving people who have lost a war because the ἀρετή of a superior, conquering force makes the conquerors categorically better than the conquered.

Second, without really sorting out the difficulties raised by the notion of ἀρετή and its militarily embodied moral power, Aristotle goes on to admit that those enslaved in an unjust war or those enslaved who do not have the nature of slaves should not suffer slavery. Otherwise, "we shall have the result that persons reputed of the highest nobility are slaves and the descendants of slaves if they happen to be taken prisoners of war and sold."[11] Aristotle elides all this with a just-among-the-boys shrug by saying that no right-thinking person would accuse him of arguing that Greeks deserve to be slaves; anyone but a sophist should understand automatically that only the barbarians deserve slavery, those who are clearly recognized by all people in all places as naturally slaves. In light of the sophists' arguments, then, Aristotle allows for two classes of slaves: those who are slaves by nature, and hence deserve to be slaves, and those who are slaves by the misfortune of evil chance. Those in the latter category deserve to be set free. Thus the abolitionists do have a case in those instances where warfare has brought a naturally free people into slavery. They do not, however, have a case when it comes to the genuine, natural slave. This sort of slave, Aristotle finally closes the matter,

> is a part of the master—he is, as it were, a part of the [master's] body, alive but yet separated from it; hence there is a certain community of interest and friendship between slave and master in cases when they have been qualified by nature for those positions, although when they do not hold them in that way but by law and by constraint of force the opposite is the case.[12]

Now this sounds for all the world like the arguments I heard that Saturday night in Silver City, Mississippi. True, the theology has changed, but the end result is the same: one group of people, usually a race identifiable by language or complexion, has a natural right and a moral obligation to subjugate another. Jessica Benjamin has explained in detail the drive for dominance and control that characterizes the modes of discourse Aristotle left for us. Absoluteness, she writes, "the sense of being one ('my identity is entirely independent and consistent') and alone ('There is nothing outside of me that I do not control') is the basis for domination—and the master-slave relationship" (33). Working from Benjamin's ideas in his Freudian reading of ancient Athens, Sagan describes this drive as the ever-vigilant, frightened control attempted by the tyrant (154). And this brings me to the second reason why we cannot ignore Aristotle's social theories. The rage to categorize, taxonomize, arrange in hierarchies, and define teleological destiny too easily spills over into life. The role in discourse offered by Aristotle is that of a separate, perceiving intellect ($\nu o\hat{\nu}\varsigma$) capable of disinterested, objective analysis. In no way is this intellect implicated or imbricated in what it "knows."[13] This separation of 'being' into its constituent elements allows the three proofs to exist in a hierarchy, beginning with logos, moving to ethos, and reaching bottom with pathos. It allows the proofs to be the soul and body of discourse, with style and delivery as the body's adornment. It allows an "unsituated" intellect to use analogy, cause-effect, deduction, induction, description, and other such "rhetorical" strategies to control and present an argument. It allows the right-thinking person always to recognize the true side of opposing arguments. This cool, professional voice allowed Aristotle to disembody himself and see life through the eyes of a disinterested professional; alas, it also blinded him to the human existence of all those around him whose lives were all too *un*professional.

Aristotle, for example, seems to have held a position similar to the second position (the Lilith position) I described when I began, the one in which black people are the soulless offspring of a union between Adam and some nonhuman or demonic female. This is surely the most virulently racist of all possible positions because it holds that some people, whether they are black or barbarian, are naturally inferior to others and that these inferior people draw their very identity from that inferiority. There is, at least to me, a terrible "logic" (or λόγος) at work here. In this λόγος a natural slave is one who belongs to someone else because of the inherent, self-evident capability of so belonging. And if such normal categories as physical appearance do not reveal the natural slave's true nature, then nature merely failed in its intention to make the distinction plain to all. The slave, of course, "naturally" remains a slave; no thought is given to the possibilities that "nature" might be wrong, or that the interpretation given to the results of "nature's" attempt might be wrong, or even that the very notion "nature" might be an utter fabrication rather than some absolute teleological destiny.

Slavery, sexism, and racism made perfect sense to Aristotle, even though he clearly knew persuasive and cogent arguments against them all. As a very young man writing on rhetoric in the now-lost *Protrepticus*, he already thought of people as occupying different ontological states. Iamblichus quotes him as writing:

> in my opinion we do not need the same kind of philosophic knowledge or wisdom as regards plain ordinary life that we need for living the perfect (philosophic) life. The majority of men may wholly be excused and justified for doing this—for being satisfied with that sort of knowledge which is sufficient to lead a normal, average life. These people, to be sure, wish for a higher form of happiness, but on the whole they are content if they can simply stay alive.[14]

As a mature and somewhat more cynical scholar, Aristotle repeats this notion in the *Politics* (1280ª31–1280ᵇ40), where he explains that the state (πόλις) depends on the social clubbing of clans who intermarry and share the same cultural assumptions. Otherwise, "a collection of slaves or of lower animals would be a state, but as it is, it is not a state, because slaves and animals have no share in well-being or in purposive life." The state exists because it is enabled by "brotherhoods and clubs for sacrificial rites and social recreations" coupled with patriarchically controlled intermarriage among the elite and the agnatic transmission of property.

Composition Studies 1993

Just as they did to Aristotle, segregation and racism make perfect sense today all over the world. One can read about them on any day in any newspaper. Not a day goes by without someone on the planet killing someone else—or, more likely, several people—for racist reasons. There is, I fear, a risk that the place from which we speak carries with it a notion of "we," a notion of "they," and a notion of the "unspeakable ones." Before Burkean consubstantiality has the opportunity to develop, before Rogerian argument finds the time to begin, the community coalesces through its differences from and its inability to imagine the perspective of the "other." Only after this process of coalescing is complete does consubstantiality become a driving force of rhetoric, only then does anyone imagine seeing an argument through the perspective of an opponent. Unfortunately, to occupy the speaking position, "opponent," one must already occupy a place within the community.

In Aristotle's system, soul is privileged over body, intelligence over emotion, humans over animals, men over women, and freemen over slaves. Is it possible for the field of composition studies to extract the first three hierarchies—the ones privileging soul, intelligence, and human—while leaving aside the other two hierarchies—the ones privileging male and freeman? What, in other words, is the φύσις, the nature of the composition teacher and the composition student? If each has a telos, a shape and function that it must inhabit, what is the shape? What the function?

In most universities, students are "placed" in writing courses, whether basic, general, advanced, honors, specialized, or whatever; thus, they are doubly located. First, they are located in the American system of education, with all the social and economic implications such location implies—from the privilege of the Ivy League and its imitators to the "practicality" of the two-year college and the for-profit, job-training institute. Almost without exception each student's "location" implies preparation for a place in the economic system. Only an infinitesimally small percentage of students, even of those in the most elite colleges, regard a degree as anything other than preparation for some form of "employability." Within this larger context, location has ontological implications for each individual. Those placed in basic courses—especially if the basic course is located in a public institution with "low" or "open" admissions standards—have already received a mark of identification. They are "at the bottom of the American educational hierarchy" because they *belong* there, and they belong there because they *are* there. As Glynda Hull, Mike Rose, Losey Fraser, and Marisa Castellano have shown with such force, race and class prejudice can create a social position that the "remedial student" cannot stop filling so that the place remains occupied. Those basic students fare best who, in the words of Aristotle, "do not contradict us and deny their offense." These good ones "cease to be angry" and "admit the justness of their situation." In short, those "who humble themselves" and "recognize that they are inferior" are most likely to curry the favor of the teacher, the one located in such a position as to understand and remedy the students' "natural" deficiencies—so far, of course, as such deficiencies can be remedied.

I am describing, of course, only one "take" on the composition teacher's situation, but it is extremely important for those of us who train teachers and work with teaching assistants to recognize the dynamics of this situation. Much too often composition classes, taught by those who are far from ready to do the work, take on nightmarishly Aristotelian features. Because the teachers are so completely unprepared for what they find in the classroom, they retreat immediately into an imagined position of linguistic, aesthetic, and hence moral superiority. Their students become barbarians while they themselves become, or at least attempt to become, tyrants. The communal offices inhabited by composition faculty foster this sort of oligarchic, virtuous-among-the-barbarians thinking. None of us can help laughing at paragraphs like the following, written by a first-year composition student at a public, regional, midwestern university in 1992:

What is suicide? When one thinks of suicide, different images begin racing through one's mind. One definition that denotes suicide is "one who takes or tries to take one's own life" (*Webster's New World Dictionary* 736). How does one define *teenage*? Is a teenager someone who thinks as would a young adult of these ages? *The Doubleday Dictionary* defines *teenage* as "of, being in, or related to the years from thirteen to nineteen inclusive" (756). Men and woman are physically different, although when it comes to mental and emotional competence they are much alike. A *male* is classified as "designating or of the sex that fertilizes the ovum" (364). Meanwhile, a *female* is classified as "designating or of the sex that bears offspring" (225). As I mentioned before, I am concerned with the questions "why" and "what if." In *Webster's New World Dictionary why* is defined as "for what reason, cause, or purpose" (683). *What if* is defined as "what do you think" (680). All of these definitions in one way or another are related to teenage suicide.

And we believe our laughter is an innocent, necessary, sanity-inducing defense mechanism—defense against the barbarians, of course. All composition teachers feel an ownership of the above text that is far superior to that of the student who wrote it. We can understand the teleological wholeness toward which the text is destined and know exactly what needs to be done to get it there. The text itself reconfirms the naturalness of our rulership over the student.

Those of us in positions to appoint, train, supervise, and later "place" writing teachers must, in my opinion, answer the same question I am asking Aristotle, who, great as he was, could see no reason to abolish slavery; the categories within which he thought would not allow him to hear the arguments of the sophists. In this he was all too lamentably human, for few people can imagine abolishing what they consider natural or undertake thinking outside their own categories of knowability.

What are the practices and procedures that we cannot conceive of abolishing because they are natural? Is it possible that our ways of placing and evaluating are embedded in a kind of politics and that they imply a social order? By extracting Aristotle's *Rhetoric* from his *Politics*, as we so commonly do, do we run the risk of imagining that we can extract our own pedagogy in a similar way?

The Venue of the True Intellect

All of us in composition studies who hold tenure have participated in the early, halting attempts to professionalize what we now think of as "our discipline." We have pushed hard to have our research accepted so that we can be accorded tenure, promotion, and status based on our particular kind of "research." In the last five years, the "research professor" in composition studies has become an actuality in more than a dozen universities. Some of us have watched with pride as our Ph.D. students were wooed by major universities with (for beginning assistant professors of English) large salaries, light teaching loads, and considerable support for research. While the national prejudice against those who teach writing has remained predominant, it is no longer monolithic.

Because of the history of composition studies, however, including its integral involvement with open admissions colleges, basic studies, general education, and social transformation, the professionalization of the discipline in so traditional a way is more than a little troublesome. Although one can find the pure social elitist inscribed most clearly in Plato, the academic elitist, the publishing professional "philosopher" whose work need have no particular relevance to classroom practice, appears first in Aristotle's *Metaphysics* and *Nicomachean Ethics*. The nature of this professional intellectual bears close scrutiny, especially now that those of us in composition studies may soon have the opportunity to inhabit the position.

Aristotle opens his *Metaphysics* (981^b14–982^b28) by describing the pure philosopher. Such a person, from primitive times onward, according to Aristotle, has always been not only "wiser" than but also categorically "superior" to other people.[15] Such superior people cannot, however, emerge into history until society learns to set apart a special, leisured class, a class for whom "practically all the necessities of life were already supplied." The first such class, Aristotle continues, was the Egyptian "priestly class," which developed mathematics. This "superior man" in the "priestly class" must be absolutely "independent," one who is freed from any obligation to provide "the necessities of life," one "who exists for himself and not for another." Such a wise person naturally occupies a commanding place, "for the wise man should give orders, not receive them; nor should he obey others, but the less wise should obey him" (982^a18-20). This superior person knows things in their abstract, universal, foundational way, the way in which they can be known truly; this person need not, and usually does not, know particular things. The wise person "can comprehend difficult things, such as are not easy for human comprehension. . . . he is more accurately informed and better able to expound causes." What this superior person knows is desirable for itself; it is not "desirable for its results." Indeed, what the superior person knows *must be* speculative and *cannot be* productive. The superior person's inquiry must lead to knowledge for its own sake, not to knowledge that is useful or that generates some specific set of results. That the most noble science "is not a productive science is clear," Aristotle explains, for the great thinkers always pursue "science for the sake of knowledge, and not for any practical utility."

Aristotle takes up this "superior being" again at the end of the *Ethics* ($1177^a13–1181^b24$). The highest possible activity available for humans, he explains, is pure theorizing that leads to "pleasures of marvelous purity and permanence." This theorizing sort of life allows one to extract oneself from the vicissitudes of life thereby entering a realm of absolute self-sufficiency. "While it is true," Aristotle admits,

> that the wise man equally with the just man and the rest requires the necessaries of life, yet, these being adequately supplied, whereas the just man needs other persons towards whom or with whose aid he may act justly, and so likewise do the temperate man and the brave man and the others, the wise man on the contrary can also contemplate by himself, and the more so the wiser he is; no doubt he will study better with the aid of fellow-workers, but still he is the most self-sufficient of men.

Pure theorizing, Aristotle continues, is "the only activity that is loved for its own sake: it produces no result beyond the actual act of contemplation." Most importantly, theorizing depends on unlimited, unencumbered leisure. Such leisure is essential because theorizing has no product and leads to no practically useful end. Political and military lives lead to public honor, but because the general and the politician are unleisured and because each seeks specific, realizable goals, both are inferior to the intellectual because intellectual life is leisured, freed from any practical goal, and utterly self-sufficient. So noble is the theoretical life that Aristotle compares it to the divine: "If then the intellect is something divine in comparison with man, so is the life of the intellect divine in comparison with human life." Compared with the life of theorizing, "the life of moral virtue . . . is happy only in a secondary degree. For the moral activities are purely human." Moral activities have a situated, temporal, social quality about them, "whereas the happiness that belongs to the intellect is separate."

Indeed, the life of theory is so pure that it requires very few external goods. Oh sure, the intellectual must have a wife to run the household, a fair amount of inherited land to free him from the grubbiness and inferiority of commerce or industry, and some slaves to provide the "external goods" necessary "to carry on . . . life as a human being." Of course, the wife and the slaves must forego any opportunity for the speculative, theoretical, most excellent kind of life, but because they received their "natures" from god, they must live accordingly. The superior person capable of, and willing to undertake, the theoretical life is "the man most beloved of the gods." Doubtless that is why the gods created women and slaves to serve him.[16] And Aristotle will have none of the bleeding-heart liberalism that one so often finds among composition studies people. "If discourses on ethics were sufficient in themselves to make men virtuous," he writes, " 'large fees and many' (as Theognis says) 'would they win.' " But such is not the case. While the life of theory may "have power to stimulate and encourage generous youths, and, given an inborn nobility of character and a genuine love of what is noble, can make them susceptible to the influence of virtue, yet they are powerless to stimulate the mass of mankind to moral nobility." In the Aristotelian institution of higher education, the professor's most important task is to ensure high admissions standards. Students who do not have the proper inborn qualities and the requisite prior education must never cross the threshold. Since most people do not and cannot hope to qualify, Aristotle admits that "we shall need laws to regulate the discipline of adults as well, and in fact the whole life of the people generally; for the many are more amenable to compulsion and punishment than to reason and to moral ideals."

The Aristotelian system, of which the *Rhetoric* is a fully functional and necessary part, offers a textbook example of the danger inherent in the notion "higher education." One simply cannot think of oneself as superior to others without at the same time thinking of those others as inferior and—at least in some small way—less truly realized and less truly real than oneself. If all people are capable of nobility of character, Aristotle poses an entirely rhetorical question, "How could it be proper for the one to rule and the other to be ruled unconditionally?" Well, comes the easy and already decided answer, the ruler and the ruled, while each capable of

virtue, have different kinds of virtue (different ἀρετή). How do we
know that different people are capable of different sorts of virtue?
Easy, we look at the soul, which Aristotle has already described for
us as hierarchically arranged, and presto (εὐθύς) we remember that
"the soul by nature contains a part that rules and a part that is ruled,
to which we assign different virtues, that is, the virtue of the rational
and that of the irrational." With that metaphysics in place, we can
now think of the family, where we find "by nature various classes
of rulers and ruled." Of course in the family the ruling one—the
father—always rules, but he rules different sorts of souls differently
and for different reasons:

> For the free rules the slave, the male the female, and the man
> the child in a different way. And all possess the various parts of
> the soul, but possess them in different ways; for the slave has not
> got the deliberative part at all, and the female has it, but without
> full authority, while the child has it, but in an undeveloped form.
> Hence the ruler must possess intellectual virtue in completeness
> . . . while each of the other parties must have that share of this
> virtue which is appropriate to them. $(1259^b20–1260^a18)^{17}$

The professional discourse generated for us by Aristotle allows its
speaker to inhabit a position of "intellectual virtue in completeness."
The power and the attraction of that speaking position are as difficult
to demystify as they are to resist. After all, the discourse allows one
to seem to strip off the metaphysics of the Western patriarchy while
inhabiting the virtuous and disinterested position from which that
metaphysics speaks.

The Dis-Easy, Particular Situation of the Composition Teacher

Now that we in composition studies have begun to escape the
scorn of the academy, we occupy an increasingly legitimate place
in an institution thought up by Plato and perfected by Aristotle.
The highest goal of the faculty in such an institution is leisure time,
theoretical activity. The sort of discourse prized by such an institution is the disinterested, unsituated discourse of knowledge and
power. Most often such discourse appears in the world as if it had
been written by no one, as if it were merely the medium through

which the pure knowledge resulting from pure speculation presents itself. Such discourse almost never reveals how the writer came to "know" what the discourse "reveals," or how the discourse of knowledge itself works.

Composition studies as I envision it will always have an uneasy *situation* in the university because it never aims higher than the practical and productive;[18] its theories can never exist for their own pure sake. Everything we do in some way connects to the daily, messy, applied, and practical tasks (1) of helping students learn how to write and (2) of showing students who do not wish to write the degree to which they marginalize themselves in the (written) discourses of the West. Unsituating either the students' essays or our own "theorizing" about those essays makes both their writing and our scholarship into leisure-time, theoretical activities, activities that reinscribe the social hierarchy of Aristotelianism with every stroke of the pen or keyboard. While we can make ourselves "complete" in the Aristotelian model by unsituating ourselves and turning composition studies into philosophy or social science, we will remain "complete" only so long as we remain outside the classroom. Teaching is not the price a composition studies person pays to do research; research is the price a composition studies person pays for getting to teach.

If composition studies continues to develop into a "true" discipline, the time will come early in the next century when composition studies majors, or perhaps writing majors, will appear in every college. Before this occurs, we must remember both our recent history and our ancient metaphysics. Our recent history is, for me at least, foreboding. In the 1880s the modern literatures, enabled by the founding of the MLA in 1883, began to seize control of college curricula. By the end of World War I, classical studies departments, which had dominated throughout the nineteenth century, were completely marginalized. As English departments led the way in this power shift, they carefully situated themselves so as to appear just as elitist, just as Aristotelian as the classics had been. English departments made themselves elitist by degrading the teaching of rhetoric and composition. A century ago, the teaching of writing in English departments became the "other" through whose exclusion the study of literature could coalesce and know itself as being elevated and refined. I would urge all who consider themselves "rhet/comp" specialists to read the issues of *PMLA* published in the 1880s. Each early issue shows how the MLA degraded rhetoric and composition so as to claim that the study of literature equaled in rigor and quality the study of classical texts.[19] The standard move—the litany, one might say—of every early *PMLA* author was to separate the study of literature from the teaching of rhetoric and composition.

Our ancient metaphysics is rather more obscure than our recent history, which, given my love for the obscure, probably explains my interest in, and antipathy for, Plato and Aristotle. The notions about discourse that have informed the West for 2,500 years grow out of a politics and a social theory that all of us in composition studies (dare one say all "right-thinking" people?) abhor. I do not intend to argue that we are trapped either in Aristotelianism or in the West, nor do I think we can or should try to abandon or destroy them. I do, however, think we must articulate as clearly as possible the ways in which our history situates our pedagogy. I truly believe that composition studies cannot do its job without behaving so as to deserve the contempt of Aristotle as well as that of his teacher and of all those who accept aristocratic notions in which a "superior man" can extract himself from the vicissitudes of ongoing, lived experience and thus be freed to seek pure knowledge for its own pure sake, knowledge that presents itself through the disembodied voice of professional discourse as if no lived history at all stands behind it. Even though we live more than twenty-three centuries after Aristotle, we live in a metaphysics that one finds written out first in the Academy and the Lyceum. Even now, after all these years, we are not far beyond that metaphysics. I know firsthand what it is like to grow up in, and have to struggle against, Aristotelian social theories. Aristotle unsituated knowledge, dehumanized it. He made it into something that transcends any particular situation. Only in the knowing of particular things, however, can a composition teacher "know" anything at all inside the classroom. The teaching of writing cannot, in my opinion, ever be unsituated—unless, that is, those who teach writing decide to live in Aristotle's world.

2

METAPHYSICS AND THE DEMONSTRATION OF RHETORIC

For Mina Shaughnessy

Coming into the (Rhet/Comp) Country

As anyone who keeps up with "composition studies" surely knows, if that phrase names anything at all, it names a problem. Nearly everyone who joined CCCC and accepted the label "composition specialist" before 1980 assumed a professional role that his or her professors considered infra dig. In those not-so-long-ago days the teaching of writing was almost universally regarded as mindless and tedious—the sort of grunt work one escapes as quickly as possible.

When Joel Conarroe became executive director of MLA in fall 1978, I was on staff as the resident, retrained "composition person"; he was fresh from a stint as chair of the English department at Penn. At a staff meeting soon after he arrived, he said, quite without malice and with no expectation of being contradicted, that research in the teaching of writing was impossible. I disagreed, expressing myself with the overzealous vigor characteristic of those who are insecure, threatened, and new at their work. A brief but heated argument ensued. In fact, at least in the context of the MLA of the 1970s, he was right. Few MLA members at that time would have regarded the work being published in composition studies as research. I was well aware that no one on the MLA's Executive Council taught, or would have considered teaching, a composition course, and both Mr. Conarroe and I knew that I had been invited to teach the new advanced composition course at NYU, where Mr. Conarroe had taken his Ph.D., only because it was an upper-level course that a graduate student could not teach.

Because of the low status of composition in the seventies when I was a graduate student and an assistant professor, I have often wondered why it attracts me with such power. From the beginning of my graduate-school days I was more interested in how one teaches composition than in any other aspect of an English department's mission. The English department where I took my Ph.D. offered no courses in rhetoric or in the teaching of writing. In 1975, the year I finished my dissertation, the department created a one-hour, noncredit "workshop" course, but I can still hear the muffled sneers some of the faculty members whispered when the course was announced. In those years, and for another decade afterward, anyone with a Ph.D. in English could seek a position as a specialist in the teaching of writing. No particular coursework and certainly no particular type of dissertation was necessary. Claiming rhet/comp was, I suspect, an unavoidable, undeniable act of self-deprecation.

I do not believe that any of us who "made the jump" expected to be important scholars or even thought of composition studies as a field in which one could become an "important scholar." At most, we wanted to learn to be better teachers. We saw so many students whose lives were straightened by their poor language skills, so many whose imaginations were unused because of their ignorance of rhetoric that we wanted to know how they could learn to help themselves. In those days, neither CCCC nor the MLA's Division on the Teaching of Writing (which did not even exist until 1976) offered members the opportunity of enhancing scholarly credentials; indeed, most people, like Mr. Conarroe, still considered "scholarly credentials" and "the teaching of writing" to be contradictory notions. I remember CCCC in the early seventies as a place where people who wanted to be better teachers could exchange ideas and offer each other support. Before 1980 *very* few people in composition studies—none that I know of—saw the field as a place where one could "build a career" or stake out scholarly and theoretical turf. Getting on the program at CCCC required little more than willingness. For most of us, nothing that we could have done at CCCC would have been regarded by our professors or our senior colleagues as scholarship.

I suppose my own attraction to composition studies has to do with its shade-tree mechanic image, its second-class status, its troubled and perilous entry into the world of intellectual respectability. My attraction to a specialization that exists largely in the United States, that most professional academics still regard as schoolwork, and that my European friends find totally mystifying is part of who I am. It would be both foolish and self-defeating to try to pretend that I am like my colleagues in "normal" fields of study. I am, however, much smitten by a love for academic respectability. Unquestionably, this is the reason I turned to the history of rhetoric as a way of creating a place for myself within composition studies. I do not, of course, claim to be a rhetorician, nor do I intend to try to make myself into one. There are real rhetoricians in the world, and most of them would see through me anyhow. I suppose the same tic, or lack of confidence, or cantankerousness, or lack of intellectual rigor, or whatever it was that prevented me from pursuing the work my Ph.D. trained me for (that is, the study of Anglo-American literary history) prevents me from becoming a genuine rhetorician. I now know that I am and always will be a "composition studies" person. I am used to the fact that no one outside the CCCC membership knows what I mean by the phrase, that most of the CCCC membership would, given a chance, dispute what I *should* mean by the phrase, and that throughout my entire professional career I will have to live with the fact that I cannot in any meaningful way tell "people at parties" what I do. Admittedly I am a little jealous of my colleagues who can answer "I teach Shakespeare" or "I do combinatorics in the math department." Such answers have an elegant, simple cleanness about them, and what I do is so amorphous, so messy, so inseparable from pedagogy, so inextricably linked with administration and institutional politics.

Like most composition studies people of my generation, I came to rhetoric through the back door. I had just completed my Ph.D. and taken a job at Baylor University in Waco, Texas. This put me near enough to Austin to drive down occasionally, hang around with Jim Kinneavy and Neal Nakadate, and then go home and read the books and articles that Jim and Neal seemed to think were important.

Given Jim's orientation, it was inevitable that classical rhetoric would come up and that I would feel compelled to learn something about it. By the time I read Aristotle, I had been teaching college-level composition for five years, and I held an appointment as an assistant professor in a good university. On my résumé I claimed a dual specialization: seventeenth-century British literature and rhetoric/ composition. Until I began my meetings with Kinneavy in the spring of 1976, no one had ever suggested that I should read Aristotle or any other rhetorician. Teaching composition in utter ignorance both of the history of rhetoric and of research in the teaching of writing was just fine.

Two qualifications had secured the job for me at Baylor, which in those days was still owned outright by the Texas Southern Baptist Convention. First, I had grown up a Southern Baptist and held a B.A. from a Southern Baptist college; second, I was truly eager to teach composition—and teach a great deal of it. My training in British literature and my dissertation on an obscure seventeenth-century mock epic poem named *Hudibras* were necessary but insignificant. According to the MLA, in 1975 when I was on the job market several thousand Ph.D.'s in British literature were competing for a few hundred jobs. Besides, Baylor already had several senior professors in the seventeenth century who could offer more than enough period courses. Seventeenth-century literature was tagged onto my specialization because no one in 1975 would have taken seriously a job candidate in English with no literary specialization.

During my time at Baylor, I taught only freshman and sophomore courses, I was the only Ph.D. on the faculty who carried such a load, and I was the only one whose office was in Carroll Library, the "other" English department building, the one that housed (except for me) only M.A.'s, only women, and only those who were by department policy prevented from teaching upper-division (i.e, serious literature) courses. In my first year at Baylor, I taught three sections of composition plus a survey of British literature each semester. I did not feel exploited in any way. I loved the teaching and the students, and a four-four workload with three composition sections per term seemed quite fair to me. In a fifty-hour week I could, I felt, do a good job of helping seventy-five young people learn to write, and I knew enough about the British literary canon to offer lectures in an extra course on the side. I had no inclination at all to try to publish. And even if I had wanted to publish, I had no idea about how to do it or what I might try to say. Certainly I knew that few in the world would care to read my interpretation of *Hudibras*.

During my stay at Baylor, I read widely under Kinneavy's generous and gracious guidance, including the back issues of *College English* and *CCC* as well as occasional essays in *Quarterly Journal of Speech* and *Rhetoric and Philosophy*. Perhaps because Jim was the only "expert" I had access to, I tended to be less interested in the work of Emig and Shaughnessy and more interested in the history of rhetoric as a way to formulate the teaching of writing. I do not, of course, intend to downplay the power of *The Composing Process of Twelfth Graders*, which was the most liberating and informative book on teaching I have ever read. And, like so many others, I was thrilled and inspired by Mina Shaughnessy's famous papers at MLA during the mid-seventies. Mina offered the sort of gentle and wonderful evangelism that I needed to hear. Though I was already converted when I heard her speak the first time, the experience of seeing this elegant, soft-spoken woman captivate an MLA audience while explaining how to "dive into" the teaching of basic writing crystallized in my imagination the professional identity I sought. But throughout these years, it was the notion "rhetoric" that intrigued me. The more I learned about its problematic, less-than-noble birth, the more comfortable I felt relaxing into its inferior, democratic, demagogic, manipulative, and occasional world.[1] I knew, of course, that speech departments had studied the history of rhetoric for decades, but I felt as if I were rediscovering a great and powerful tradition that the world had forgotten. Certainly my colleagues in English knew nothing of it.

At the beginning, given my lifelong schooling in New Criticism, I expected "rhetoric" to remain still while I caught up with it, to be an entity with a clearly defined being and an understandable history, something one could know and teach. In 1976, even though *Grammatology* was nine years old and had been available in English for three years, I had never heard of Derrida, deconstruction, poststructuralism, or (to say the truth) even structuralism. Before reading Aristotle, I read Golden, Bergquist, and Coleman's introduction to him in their newly published *Rhetoric of Western Thought*. With their introduction and my theoretical orientation, I truly expected Aristotle to give me a "scientific," reliable articulation of rhetoric, and I had no doubt at all about the claim that the *Rhetoric* is "the most important single work on persuasion ever written" (Golden et al. 30).

Well, I did not find what I expected. Over the years, however, I have learned to like what I found, though I like it in a way that I suspect Aristotle would disapprove. What I found is the first full articulation of the metaphysics that degrades rhetoric. By 360 B.C. when Aristotle probably began his first lectures on rhetoric, Plato had finished *Phaedrus* and presented his final notions about rhetoric. As I have argued at length elsewhere,[2] I believe that Plato's *Phaedrus* essentially turns rhetoric into philosophy, thereby preventing it from offering a pedagogy that can inform any sort of classroom practice. Aristotle's response to his teacher does "save" rhetoric by showing how rhetoric can lead to pedagogy, but this salvation, in my opinion, effectively dooms rhetoric, both in the ancient Athenian philosophical academies and in the modern university. As I read through Aristotle, first the *Rhetoric*, then many of his other texts, I learned a great deal about why my students often resist the sliding, iffy, messy world of rhetoric, and why my colleagues doubt whether there is a place for it in their universities. Thus my readings of rhetoric and the *Rhetoric* are very much situated in my own lived experience—the experience of someone who came to rhetoric late, who learned Greek late, and who found his own intellectual situation inscribed two and one-half millennia ago by Aristotle.

Aristotle's Anti-Strophe

As everyone knows, the two most famous sentences in the *Rhetoric* appear at the beginnings of the first two chapters: "Rhetoric is a counterpart of Dialectic," Aristotle begins his first chapter, for both rhetoric and dialectic "have to do with matters that are in a manner within the cognizance of all men and not confined to any special science" (1354^a1–3). Rhetoric, he takes up the definition again as he begins his second chapter, "may be defined as the faculty of discovering the possible means of persuasion in reference to any subject whatever" (1355^b25). From these two statements one can derive all the power and explore all the problems of both rhetoric and the *Rhetoric*. The power is obvious. Ignorance of the term *dialetic* does not prevent one from understanding that rhetoric is universal and necessary, nor does such ignorance prevent one from employing rhetoric's profoundly enlightening methods of discovery and presentation. In 1976 I wanted very much to learn the methods as a way of mastering and teaching the power. But the problems that I could see, even without reading through the scholarly apparatus, troubled me a lot. I wanted to extract the power, leaving the problems behind. I no longer wish to do that. Now I want to foreground the problems with as much patience and detail as possible so that I never forget the way the power is situated.

The word "counterpart" ("Rhetoric is the *counterpart* of dialectic") is one of the oldest, most worn paths into the *Rhetoric*. No single term in the text has been more thoroughly discussed. The first entry under "counterpart" in the *OED* describes the word as legal jargon, which seems appropriate, since rhetoric "began" in the law courts of Syracuse. This first entry makes clear that a counterpart "is not considered the principal part or original." The *OED*'s second and third entries—perhaps trying to remedy with quantity what they lack in priority—define "counterpart" as "A duplicate, or exact copy," or if not that, at least a "thing so answering to another as to appear a duplicate or exact copy." Entry four offers the definition that we most often use to explain the word "counterpart" as it appears in the *Rhetoric*: "One of two parts which fit and complement each other; a person or thing forming a natural complement to another." Entry five, which turns to music, reintroduces the uncertainty of the first three entries by defining a counterpointed melody as being either against or in accompaniment with another melody. All told, the English word "counterpart" has musical, legal, and philosophical uses; it means both a less principal, less original part and a natural complement; both an exact duplicate and the *appearance* of an exact duplicate; both harmony and dissonance.[3]

Turning to the Greek word ἀντίστροφος does little to clarify the relationship between rhetoric and dialectic. Rhetoricians usually mention the counterpointed, or antistrophic, relationship between the two as if the statement "Rhetoric is the antistrophe of dialectic" had a univocal clarity about it. Certainly most of us in composition studies pass through Aristotle's first sentence and into "rhetoric proper" as if ἀντίστροφος were a doorway and not a problem. Actually engaging the words "counterpoint" and ἀντίστροφος would be nightmarishly complicated because such engagement demands not only an articulation of the terms themselves but also a definition of dialectic, for dialectic *is* the "thing" to which the words, "counter-

point" and ἀντίστροφος relate rhetoric. In other words, asking what
an antistrophic relationship *is* opens one aporia while asking what
dialectic *is* opens another. The notes offered by Edward Cope and
William Grimaldi as well as an extraordinary essay by Lawrence
Green open the way into each aporia.

   Green shows in detail that ἀντίστροφος was a problem from
the beginning. The speculation begins with Alexander of Aphrodisias
a few decades after Aristotle's death and continues until today. All
of the possible interpretations, Green argues, had been articulated
by the Renaissance; "subsequent scholarship has done little more
than choose sides." Green takes good-humored pleasure in quoting
a claim made by John Rainolds in the sixteenth-century that "There
are as many interpretations of this little word as there are interpreters" (5–6). When interpreters try to agree, they fail. Worse yet,
similar explanations "mask real differences in understanding, and
conversely, seeming differences in explanation obscure areas of critical agreement" (10–15).

   The oldest and most common way of trying to deal with the
ἀντίστροφος problem is to argue that it links rhetoric with dialectic
at the level of theory while leaving the two separate in practice. As
Alexander of Aphrodisias makes clear, "the resemblances between
rhetoric and dialectic are all on a theoretical level, while the differences are all on the level of practical application" (Green 11). Grimaldi, surely this century's most comprehensive student of Aristotle's *Rhetoric*, falls generally in the Alexandrine camp, suggesting
that "analogue" or "correlative" might be more appropriate than
"counterpart." Grimaldi does, however, add an overlay to the Alexandrine position when he claims that Aristotle uses ἀντίστροφος as
a reply to Plato's use of the term in *Gorgias*. This allows Aristotle
to link rhetoric with dialectic and thus save rhetoric from Platonic
condemnation. George Kennedy, surely the most comprehensive
living student of the *Rhetoric*, sees ἀντίστροφος as making rhetoric
and dialectic "parallel movements, virtually identical in content."
Both rhetoric and dialectic, he continues, deal with "common subjects," and neither "falls within any distinct science" (*Classical* 65).[4]

   Grimaldi's notion that Aristotle uses ἀντίστροφος both to describe the relationship between rhetoric and dialectic and to rehabilitate rhetoric from Platonic condemnation has fairly wide contemporary support. Jacqueline de Romilly repeats Grimaldi almost exactly
by translating ἀντίστροφος as meaning "parallel and correlative"

and claiming that Aristotle's use of that particular term, which is so prominent in *Gorgias*, makes for "a complete reversal of Plato's criticism" (*Magic* 48, 61–62). Kathleen Welch adjusts de Romilly's reading slightly, agreeing that the term rehabilitates rhetoric but also claiming that it cordons rhetoric off from dialectic, giving it a separate and secure identity (17–18).[5]

Of course there are many other contemporary ways of phrasing the relationship. Larry Arnhart, echoing Grimaldi by arguing that "counterpoint" implies similarity in forms of reasoning, claims that rhetoric is not like sophistry; rather, it is like dialectic because "it is a rational art that involves a form of reasoning similar to that of dialectic" (13). Christopher Johnstone sees the counterpoint as occurring between kinds of truth with dialectic discovering "general philosophical truths, truths about the universal first principles of philosophy," and rhetoric discovering "what is true about the realm of the probable and contingent, particular truths about correctness in practice" (5). Other contemporary explications, however, are not so friendly. Theresa Crem, for example, argues that ἀντίστροφος implies a clear hierarchy that degrades rhetoric because "the antistrophe is always consequent on the strophe" (58).[6] Sally Raphael contends that Aristotle was himself so confused about the relationship between rhetoric and dialectic that no useful explication of ἀντίστροφος is possible. Jonathan Barnes comes to the same conclusion as Raphael but for different reasons. Whereas Raphael sees the *Rhetoric* as internally inconsistent, Barnes sees it as a failed attempt to cobble together a new art by extracting various components of already existing arts. The result, Barnes contends, is a confusing mess best left alone. All this disagreement over the term does not, however, prevent Thomas Cole from using "counterpart" in his 1991 book in a quite straightforward, plain-meaning sort of way (10), nor does it prevent Green from ending his splendid essay on ἀντίστροφος with the bizarre request that we "take Aristotle at his word" because he "meant just what he said" (27), as if the hundreds of scholars over the millennia did not all believe themselves to be doing just that.

We have, to this point, looked at only the first four words of the text. Ἀντίστροφος, the fourth word and the first modifier in the text, is only the beginning of the problems, for as the text goes on, Aristotle makes other kinds of comparisons between rhetoric and dialectic, as well as between rhetoric and things other than dialectic. As with nearly everything else about the *Rhetoric*, rhetoricians have disputed these sliding definitions ever since Aristotle died. In what modern editors now present as the "second chapter" of the *Rhetoric* (1356ᵃ20–33), Aristotle changes the language with which he relates rhetoric to dialectic. Rather than as a counterpart, he describes rhetoric as a "branch" of both dialectic and political science using the Greek word παραφυές, which implies offshoot, a clearly subordinate role in that both dialectic and political science are "main plants" of which rhetoric is a dependent branch.[7] In this analogy, either dialectic or political science can live without rhetoric, but rhetoric, as a dependent branch, cannot live without its parent plant(s) through whose roots and foliage it draws life. The problem with the metaphor is obvious. One can imagine rhetoric as a dependent branch of either dialectic or political science, but the image of one branch (rhetoric) being attached to two different parent plants (both dialectic and political science) is a botanical impossibility that calls to mind a "Far Side" cartoon. Συμβαίνω, which is the verb in this passage, states the relationships between rhetoric and dialectic and between rhetoric and political science. John Henry Freese and Rhys Roberts translate συμβαίνω as "appears" ("it appears that Rhetoric is as it were an offshoot of Dialectic"); Lane Cooper translates συμβαίνω as "follows" ("it follows that rhetoric is a kind of offshoot of dialectic); Kennedy translates it as "result" ("The result is that rhetoric is a certain kind of offshoot"). One might more nearly capture the Greek by violating elegant English with a translation like this: "Rhetoric comes to terms with or receives support by being joined with both dialectic and the ethical part of political science as a kind or type of dependent offshoot."[8]**

This mixed metaphor is only the beginning of the problems, for Aristotle goes on to say that rhetoric, rather than behaving like a *branch* of political science, sometimes slips into the garb of political science, masquerading as the thing itself.[9] After this slight digression on rhetoric's ability to pretend to be its parent, Aristotle ends this second definition by returning rhetoric to its initial position, as some sort of relationship with dialectic, but this time Aristotle uses

---

**I will use one asterisk to indicate that my translation is slightly out of keeping with standard translations and two asterisks to indicate that my translation is dramatically out of keeping with standard translations. A single asterisk usually indicates that I have changed a word. Two asterisks mean that I have offered more of a "transterpretation" than a translation.

different terms to describe the relationship. Rather than ἀντίστροφος or παραφυές, Aristotle uses μόριον, which clearly means inferior part of a superior whole (Hugh Lawson-Tancred translates μόριον as "fragment"), and ὁμοίωμα, which can mean anything from likeness or resemblance to counterfeit. With this gradual sliding from the word ἀντίστροφος, which can mean anything from convertible equal to dependent response, through words like παραφυές and μόριον, which clearly mean dependent offshoot, to a word like ὁμοίωμα, which probably means little more than "has something to do with" and could actually imply false imitation of, it is easy to see how Crem might come to the conclusion that Aristotle himself was too confused about the relationship between rhetoric and dialectic for anyone in the twentieth century to articulate a meaningful definition. But Crem is in a clear minority. Kennedy says that the latter terms "are not significantly inconsistent with" ἀντίστροφος (*Classical* 65), and Green passes over the second set of terms, choosing instead to concentrate on the difficulties associated with ἀντίστροφος (7).

In chapter 4 (1359^b2–19) Aristotle makes his third try at a true definition of rhetoric. "What we have said before is true," he picks up the argument from chapter 2. "Rhetoric is composed of analytical science and of that branch of political science which is concerned with Ethics, and . . . it resembles partly Dialectic and partly sophistical arguments." This recapitulation makes some changes in the previous formulation, repeats some old information, and introduces some new information. Both the main verb and the main comparison change. The verb changes from συμβαίνω (stands with and draws assistance from) to σύγκειμαι, a passive verb with the meaning "to be composed, compounded, concocted, or contrived from." The thing with which rhetoric is compared also changes—from dialectic to analytical science. Whereas the metaphor in the second formulation has rhetoric as a dependent branch or offshoot of dialectic and political science, the metaphor in this third definition describes rhetoric as a compound, consisting of analytical science and political science. Aristotle does not, however, give up the old comparison entirely, for he goes on to say that rhetoric bears a general similarity to dialectic. Although he no longer calls rhetoric a counterpart, branch, or part of dialectic, he does repeat that rhetoric and dialectic resemble each other. The information that appears here for the first time is that rhetoric also resembles sophistical arguments.

Needless to say, the new information in this third definition makes the ontology of rhetoric more complicated than ever. The changed verb and the changed subject complements make rhetoric a blend of analytical science and political science. As long as it was a dependent offshoot of dialectic and political science, one could, with a little creative imagining (the sort required to imagine the "tangled boughs of Heaven and Ocean" in Shelley's "Ode to the West Wind") conjure up an image of rhetoric. But analytical science (ἀναλυτικῆς ἐπιστήμης) introduces the notion of epistemology from the *Analytics*, and, as I try to show below, epistemology, or true science that can demonstrate true knowledge, is the one thing absolutely excluded from Aristotelian rhetoric.[10] At this point in the third try at a definition then, rhetoric is "composed of" an intellectual activity (epistemology) from which it is excluded and an intellectual activity (political science) of which it is a subordinate part. More problematically, as I will try to show below, analytical science and political science do not occupy the same rank in Aristotle's intellectual and moral hierarchies; thus, rhetoric is a blend of different and exclusive layers of the same system. In addition, it resembles dialectic (of which it is a counterpart or a dependent part or just an undifferentiated part) and sophistical argument, which, as Aristotle has already made clear at the end of chapter one, differs fundamentally from dialectic. "What makes a sophist," he explains there, "is not the faculty, but the moral purpose" (1355^{b}17–21). Admittedly this particular passage relating rhetoric, sophistry, and dialectic is notoriously difficult to translate, but Freese's gloss (which closely parallels Grimaldi's) comes closest to the sort of distinction Aristotle seems to be making. "The essence of sophistry," Freese comments,

> consists in the moral purpose, the deliberate use of fallacious arguments. In Dialectic, the dialectician has the power or faculty of making use of them when he pleases; when he does so deliberately he is called a sophist. In Rhetoric, this distinction does not exist; he who uses sound arguments as well as he who uses false ones, are both known as rhetoricians.

In other words, the dialectician who uses false arguments ceases at that moment to be a dialectician and becomes a sophist; the rhetorician who does so, on the other hand, remains a rhetorician.

Moral purpose in this conception of intellectual inquiry becomes the absolute divide between dialectic and sophistry. When one crosses that divide one changes essence, much the same way the goblets and faces transmogrify into each other in the famous Escher print. Rhetoric, in contrast, is the messy, ill-defined place where dialectic and sophistry can work on the same site at the same time, the place where intellectual activities and moral purposes that mutually exclude each other can cohabit.[11] In the starkest possible language, it seems clear that while dialectic includes sophistry in that it has the capability of recognizing sophistry, dialectic does not have the luxury of using sophistry. Rhetoric, on the other hand, is amoral. The use of sophistry poses no threat whatsoever to the rhetorician's status *as* rhetorician.

By now it is surely clear to anyone why nearly everyone stops with the conundrum ἀντίστροφος. Just sorting out the difficulties with that simple comparison has proven practically impossible. If one adds the other stages into the bargain, any sort of linear, straightforward notion of what rhetoric is and is not becomes utterly hopeless. Those who try to interrelate all three definitions will never begin to approach arguments about the ontology of rhetoric because they will have to spend all their time trying to sort through what does and does not count as part of the definition. At the risk of tedium, I will summarize the shifting relationships that, according to Aristotle, rhetoric has with dialectic: counterpart, dependent part, smaller part, entity standing with so as to be assisted by, entity generally similar to in a partial sort of way. And this does not even begin to deal with rhetoric's relationships with political science (in which it is a subordinate art, from which it is compounded, and whose place it can take by presenting itself *as* political science), with epistemology (for which in the Aristotelian system it is a sort of antimatter), and with sophistry (with which it shares a lack of moral purpose, an absence that should exclude it from dialectic altogether). Rhetoric, in other words, is surely the place in the Aristotelian system where the law of noncontradiction is suspended.[12]

Just before Aristotle gives the third definition of rhetoric, in a shrugging, off-the-cuff sort of way, he makes clear that he recognizes his definitions of rhetoric are, by his normal standards, a little sloppy. "There is no need at present," he explains, "to endeavor to enumerate with scrupulous exactness or to classify those subjects which men are wont to discuss, or to define them as far as possible with strict accuracy, since this is not the function of the rhetorical art but of one that is more intelligent and exact" (1359^b2–5). The language conforms nicely with what one would expect from a distinguished philosopher lecturing in the afternoon to a popular audience. For example, try to imagine this scene. It is a Wednesday afternoon late in August. In Charlottesville, Virginia, and Irvine, California, Jacques Derrida and Richard Rorty are conducting last-minute workshops intended to prepare new teaching assistants to begin their composition classes the next morning.[13] Try to imagine the demeanor and focus of each workshop. (Yes, I'm smiling too.) In fact, Aristotle was not only sloppy about his definition of rhetoric, he knew he was sloppy and said so. But given the way he situated rhetoric in his metaphysics, this sliding, half-baked, oddly hybrid notion of rhetoric was inevitable.

The most common way of dealing with the complexities of Aristotle's definitions is to argue that the different definitions were written at different times, some perhaps early in the Academy period, others twenty years later during the Lyceum period. And there are all sorts of possibilities in between. The text of the *Rhetoric* that we now have, in other words, represents various drafts written at widely different periods and reflecting radically different notions of rhetoric. Some of the extant text may be nothing more than compilations from students' lecture notes. Because the early editors of Aristotle's manuscripts could not bear to give up any of the text he might have written, they put in everything they had, even though Aristotle clearly changed his mind, as most people would over a forty-year period.

Be that as it may, "rhetoric" as it emerges from the *Rhetoric* is a mess. Brilliant and wonderful, but a mess nevertheless. And to this point, we have looked at only half of the mess created in the first clause, for we have explored only one of the aporias—the meaning of the word ἀντίστροφος. The noun on the other side of the word is "dialectic." If rhetoric is the counterpart of dialectic (or even a subordinate part, or just generally similar to dialectic), what is dialectic? This leads out into the Aristotelian system as a whole, and it shows the place that rhetoric has always occupied in the West. It is a place I am not only comfortable in but have come to like. Perhaps my affinity can be attributed to the fact that I am not a rhetorician. But then neither was Aristotle.[14]

Aristotle When He Was a Mere TA

While it is true that he taught rhetoric long before he taught dialectic and epistemology, Aristotle never thought of himself as a rhetorician. Reading through Anton-Hermann Chroust, Friedrich Solmsen, and Ingemar Düring as they discuss Aristotle's student days at Plato's Academy, one cannot help being struck by the degree to which Aristotle's first teaching assignment resembles that of the contemporary TA in an American college English department. Throughout the 360s, a fierce rivalry raged between Isocrates' school and Plato's Academy. The Isocrateans saw the Platonists as hopelessly idealistic elitists who had no clue about how life was lived in the real world. The Platonists, on the other hand, saw the Isocrateans as amoral, unethical panderers to emotion and prejudice. About 360 when he was in his mid-twenties, Aristotle published a book on rhetoric entitled *Gryllus* in which he bitterly denounced Isocrates and his school. Soon thereafter, Plato allowed Aristotle to begin offering lectures on rhetoric at the Academy (Chroust 1.102–16 and 2.29–42; see also Vickers 18–19 and Ross 2–3). Of course, everyone knows that Plato's Academy was devoted to philosophy, not rhetoric, at least not the sort of rhetoric that might lead one to give a speech intended in any way to placate or cater to democratic opinions. Although *Phaedrus* does outline a Platonic notion of rhetoric, this rhetoric is clearly dependent on and subordinate to philosophy.[15] No one came to the Academy to study rhetoric, particularly if they meant by that the techniques of becoming a powerful, persuasive speaker in the Assembly. All extant evidence suggests that Aristotle's *Gryllus* was heavily influenced by Plato's *Gorgias* and *Phaedrus*. And the picture, for me at least, is clear. Aristotle was at the Academy to study philosophy. He offered an independent set of lectures in rhetoric in much the same way that the contemporary graduate student in an English department offers classes in composition while pursuing advanced training in literary studies.

Throughout his career Aristotle treated rhetoric much as the contemporary literature professor treats composition. As a graduate student Aristotle taught rhetoric while studying subjects that he found both more rigorous and more important, and when he returned to Athens in the 330s as an established professor, he offered lectures on rhetoric in the afternoons "when less intellectually demanding topics were treated" (Vickers 19). One can almost hear the derisive comments that the inner circle (at both the Academy when Aristotle was an advanced student and at the Lyceum when he was the distinguished professor) made about the weak-minded students who came late in the day to follow the lectures on rhetoric after the rigorous, serious morning's work had exhausted the real scholars. "Rhetoric was hardly a major interest with Aristotle," Kennedy says. "He seems to have taught it as a kind of extracurricular subject in the afternoon" (61–62; see also Quintilian 3.1.14).[16] Just as most contemporary professors of literature wish to keep composition in their departments simply because composition carries with it so much money and so many students, Aristotle, according to Lawson-Tancred, "cultivated an interest in rhetoric to counterbalance the effectiveness of rhetoric as a form of tertiary education as established by his rival Isocrates" (Introduction 7).

I believe that this extracurricular, less-than-philosophy, less intellectually demanding conception of rhetoric determined the location that Aristotle gave rhetoric in his system, and I think it laid out the theoretical matrix in which Western metaphysics would always degrade communication so as to elevate what it communicates. Oriented by his conception of intellectual endeavor, Aristotle had no choice but to think of rhetoric as a degraded, intellectually impoverished sort of undertaking. Of course the number of rhetoricians who will rush to argue with me about this is legion. Both Eugene Ryan and Grimaldi have published extended studies of Aristotelian rhetoric arguing that it is whole, complete, consistent, noble, moral, good, and generally above reproach. To that litany Johnstone adds community building, courageous, and humbling (in the good sense of being humble about one's ideas). "Rhetoric, as the counterpart of dialectic," Johnstone concludes, "functions to promote a dialogical exchange of moral perspectives, and thus to establish a common moral perspective upon which cooperative behavior can be based. The moral truths thus discovered and clarified become a basis upon which genuine community can be founded" (16–17). Both Brian Vickers and Eugene Garver see Aristotelian rhetoric as on par with his philosophy, though each chooses a different definition from the *Rhetoric* on which to build his argument. Working from the "counterpart" definition, Vickers places rhetoric on the same level as dialectic (though he admits that both are beneath demonstration). Far from opposing rhetoric to philosophy, he says, Aristotle connects it "closely to dialectic, and is at some pains to integrate it into the whole circle of human sciences" (160–62). While admitting that the *Rhetoric* is an anomaly in Aristotle's corpus, Garver argues that by "looking at the *Rhetoric* through speech act theory glasses," and departing from the second definition (the branch-part-similar definition), one can read it as being "of a piece with Aristotle's other works" and "by modern standards, as a work of philosophy" ("Work" 1–20).

Undeniably, one can read the *Rhetoric* Garver's way, as the shelves of every library show. The only constraint I would like to place on those who do is that they have no professional stake in the outcome. In other words, it would make me more comfortable if those who locate Aristotelian rhetoric at any but the most debased place in Aristotle's system had no professional stake in continuing the study of the history of rhetoric. But perhaps this desire merely reveals me as the sophistical skeptic that I am, the degraded sort of self-seeking relativist Aristotle describes when he says that most people find it hard "to believe that a man deliberately does anything except what pays him" (*Rhetoric* 1417ª35 Roberts).

Although I believe that I could formulate and defend the thesis that Aristotle does not degrade rhetoric, I also believe that arguing the other side is much, much easier. "That which is true and better is naturally always easier to prove and more likely to persuade," Aristotle claims (*Rhetoric* 1355ª37–38), and it seems clear to me that only those with a personal interest in rehabilitating rhetoric could see Aristotle's treatment of it as anything but degrading.

I agree with Grimaldi (*Studies* 7–18), Andrea Lunsford and Lisa Ede ("Classical"), and the host of other scholars who claim that it is impossible to read the *Rhetoric* without some notion of how it fits into the Aristotelian system as expressed in the *Organon*, the *Metaphysics*, the *Ethics*, and the *Politics*.[17] These ten theoretical works, as Kinneavy observes, clearly differentiate "rhetoric from science, from dialectic, from poetry, and from sophistic. Each of these has its own heuristic, its own organizational techniques, and its own style" ("Grimaldi" 197).[18] The problem is not that Aristotle's canon presents a system of intellectual inquiry or that he divides this system into different undertakings of different kinds. The problem is that the Aristotelian system, in saving rhetoric from Plato's utter condemnation, saved rhetoric in a way that would obviate it in the modern world. No less distinguished a classicist than Julia Annas, writing in no less distinguished a publication than *The Oxford History of the Classical World* (edited by three of Britain's most distinguished classicists, John Boardman, Jasper Griffin, and Oswyn Murray) can with astonishing self-confidence praise Aristotle while dismissing rhetoric utterly. Aristotle's "real breakthrough," she explains, is marked by the *Prior Analytics*, the first work of formal logic, where by the use of schematic letters he first isolates the notion of logical form and systematically classifies the forms of valid argument. Having made it possible for the first time to distinguish the soundness of an argument from its power to persuade, Aristotle also, in the *Rhetoric*, performs the complementary task of classifying the various sources of persuasion in argument. To sort out so rigorously and definitively the various aspects of the "art of argument" from its muddled state in the fifth century, and even in Plato, was an amazing achievement, displaying both the powers of Aristotle's intellect and his concern not to lose any aspect of the subject he is analysing. The logical and rhetorical works remained more prominent in estimations of Aristotle until the twentieth century; new developments in logic have shown the limitations of Aristotelian logic rather strikingly, and rhetoric is no longer a serious study. 249–50

The calm, disinterested way with which Annas dismisses rhetoric almost takes one's breath away.[19] And this paragraph was written in 1986! Has Annas never heard of Kenneth Burke, Chaim Perelman, or I. A. Richards? Does she not know that much of poststructural analysis operates under the name rhetoric? What, one wonders with naive curiosity, might she say about the "discipline" of composition studies, if she ever heard of it? Compared with the (in her opinion) now defunct rhetoric, composition studies is both ill formed and fly-by-night.

While I do not know Professor Annas and, to say the truth, have never read any of her work other than this essay (in a book that no doubt she and her colleagues regard as hopelessly elementary and general, the sort of thing written for the "polite" reader who needs to be informed for purposes of social chitchat), I suspect she is doing no more than articulating the opinion shared by nearly everyone who is not a Western academic specializing in critical theory or rhetoric. Aristotle's system could not help leading to such a public opinion. People who use the term *rhetoric* outside literature and speech departments use it to mean either "unscrupulous and dishonest manipulation of an audience" or "language divorced from any intent to mean." Nearly every human being living on the planet thinks of rhetoric as one of those two things, or perhaps both together. Although it certainly is not fair to blame Aristotle alone for this, it is also pointless to pretend that his metaphysical system, which has been so influential in creating what the West construes as "thinking," could lead to any other popular conception. One could, in fact, make a fairly good case that Ramus's division of rhetoric in the sixteenth century, as well as the attacks on rhetoric by Hobbes, Spratt, and Locke in the seventeenth century, Kant's attempt to obliterate rhetoric in the eighteenth century, and Croce's contempt for rhetoric at the turn of the twentieth century are all already inscribed in Aristotle. When Aristotle "saved" rhetoric by dividing it into a "thought element" versus everything else, and when he rehabilitated rhetoric by giving it a place at the very bottom of his system, he virtually guaranteed that an increasingly scientific world, a world controlled by professional discourse, would wish to rid itself of anything "merely rhetorical."[20] Even those who spend the major part of their professional careers working on the *Rhetoric* are likely to accept Aristotle's notion of its worth. Lawson-Tancred, for example, begins the preface to his 1991 translation by classifying the *Rhetoric* as "less than central" to Aristotle's "whole corpus," and describing it as the origin of "the middle-brow culture of antiquity" (xi).

The Demonstration of Demonstration

Aristotle organizes human inquiry and communication in a variety of ways, and rhetoric appears and plays a role in all the schemes he concocts. In one of his schemes, the one that I believe to be his most basic and pervasive, Aristotle ranks intellectual endeavors according to their foundations and their methods. First, Aristotle argues that intellectual inquiry can be neither more reliable nor more productive than the premises from which it departs; second, he argues that no inquiry can be more effective than the methods of reasoning that it follows. Who could argue with these two basic criteria? Without questioning a discourse about the assumptions from which it departs and the methods of argument by which it makes its case, how would a professional of any sort proceed? These are, after all, the criteria of thinking.

In working my way through the Aristotelian system—from demonstration to dialectic to rhetoric—I intend to be as detailed as I can (even at the risk of tedium) because I wish to offer an interpretation different from the one offered by Martha Nussbaum. Although Nussbaum and I agree that the Aristotelian system at its foundation stands on an individual's intuitive interpretation of appearances, we disagree about the effect of this foundation. As Nussbaum reads Aristotle, the Aristotelian system responds "defiantly" to Plato, substituting the contingent and constructed interpretation of daily experience for abstract and immutable Forms. Nussbaum even goes so far as to imply that Aristotle's system attempts "to rehabilitate the discredited measure or standard of tragic and Protagorean anthropocentrism" (242). According to Nussbaum, the intuitive interpretation of appearances is not a natural phenomenon; rather, it is learned as part of the *paideia*. Anyone who asks for a demonstration of a demonstrative premiss does so "out of *apaideusia*," or, as Nussbaum quotes M. F. Burnyeat, out of improper "intellectual habituation" (251–53).

In opposition to Plato, Nussbaum concludes,

Aristotle has defended the view that the internal truth, truth *in* the appearances, is all we have to deal with; anything that purports to be more is actually less, or nothing. The standpoint of perfection which purports to survey all lives neutrally and coolly from a viewpoint outside any particular life stands accused already of failure of reference: for in removing itself from all worldly experience it appears to remove itself at the same time from the bases of discourse about the world. Our question about the good life must, like any question whatever, be asked and answered within the appearances.

This leads Nussbaum to the opinion that no difference exists between dialectic and demonstration and that Aristotle is essentially contemporary because he argues that the basis of any argument is and must be socially constructed. And this is where, in my opinion, Nussbaum goes wrong. As I try to show below, when Aristotle gets to the foundation of his system, he admits that it stands on a kind of noetic intuition, and he also admits that this noetic intuition is "socially constructed" in the Greek world. Thus it is undeniable that Aristotle constructs his system on the appearances. But as a true racist must, Aristotle also believes that the system constructed on his noetic intuition is the *right* system. In other words, when the noetic intuition is situated in the psyche of the right man living in the right country descended from the right race, the foundation it offers to discourse really is indemonstrable. In no way is it conventional; nor can it be wrong.

Aristotle makes this clear in *Metaphysics* (1009ª6–24), in which he explains carefully that he does not accept any sort of Protagorean view of the world. From Protagoras, Aristotle writes, comes the theory that the same phenomenon can be simultaneously true and false. "If all opinions and appearances are true," Aristotle responds to this Protagorean relativism, "everything must be at once true and false; for many people form judgments which are opposite to those of others." Such logic as this, Aristotle throws up his hands in despair, would lead to a world in which everyone would be right all of the time.

So, how does the philosopher proceed when the philosopher encounters someone who responds out of *apaideusia* and asks that the demonstrative premise be proved? Well, first the philosopher tries persuasion. If that does not work, the philosopher uses whatever form of violence the situation requires to bring the unlearned questioner into line, or at least into silence. The Greek noun βίας, is accusative plural. The pluralness implies that "violences" of different kinds are all acceptable. In singular form, βία comes into English as bodily strength, force, power, or might; an act of violence; and the compulsion to do something against one's will. Any combination of these behaviors is acceptable for the philosopher when confronted by a questioner who wants to delve into the origin of an indemonstrable premise.

I would not, however, wish to make an accusation such as this against Aristotle, nor would I wish to differ with so brilliant a classicist as Nussbaum, without "showing" (in good apodeictic fashion!) in careful detail how I arrived at my opinion (even though my opinion is "nothing but" sophistry). Such a "demonstration" "naturally" (as Aristotle would say) begins with the term ἀπόδειξις itself.[21] What Aristotle calls ἀπόδειξις[22] and we usually translate as "demonstration," is, according to Aristotle, the soundest, most reliable mode of inquiry and communication. A "premiss will be demonstrative," he explains at the beginning of *Prior Analytics* "if it is true and based upon fundamental postulates" (24ª31). "Reasoning is *demonstration*," he repeats at the beginning of *Topics*, "when it proceeds from premises which are true and primary or of such a kind that we have derived our original knowledge of them through premises which are primary and true" (100ª25–30). The starting point for a demonstration he says again in *Posterior Analytics* must be "primary," a premise "which has no other premiss prior to it" (72^a7–11). Since the object of demonstration is "truth," he continues later, "we must base our investigation on the actual facts" (81^b23–4). For demonstration to begin, he explains in *Metaphysics*, "in every case the first principles of things must necessarily be true above everything else" (993^b29). In sum, demonstration begins from the base of absolute knowledge. From that base it follows an irrefutable pattern of reasoning to a new, indisputable conclusion, a conclusion that has been derived "from premisses which are true, primary, immediate, better known than, prior to, and causative of the conclusion" (*Posterior Analytics* 71^b20–23; see also 72^a26–35). Aristotle calls the route to this conclusion a συλλογισμός; we call it everything from reasoning and deduction to logic and (in an act of Anglicization) just plain syllogism.[23] "A syllogism," Aristotle explains,

> is a form of words in which, when certain assumptions are made, something other than what has been assumed necessarily follows from the fact that the assumptions are such. By "from the fact that they are such" I mean that it is because of them that the conclusion follows; and by this I mean that there is no need of any further term to render the conclusion necessary.
>
> I call a syllogism perfect if it requires nothing, apart from what is comprised in it, to make the necessary conclusion apparent. (*Prior Analytics* 24^b18–25)

The demonstrative premise coupled with a syllogism "produces scientific knowledge," a type of knowledge so secure and well constructed that it "enables us to know by the mere fact that we grasp it" (*Posterior Analytics* 71^b17–19).[24] The syllogism takes its starkest form in the old cliché "All men are mortal. Socrates is a man. Socrates is mortal." The major premise is considered indemonstrable and absolute. Men *are* mortal. Beings who are not mortal are also not men—no further argument allowed. The minor premise is considered irrefutable because Socrates was indeed a man. No serious person would argue that Socrates was something other than a man. The conclusion is then unassailable. Only a fool, an ignoramus, or a sophist would undertake to refute any of the three statements. The result of demonstration is absolute, immutable, eternal, self-consistent, self-contained knowledge: "one who has absolute knowledge should be unshakable in his belief" (*Posterior Analytics* 72^{b}4); "If a thing has been proved, it cannot be otherwise" (74^{b}14–15); "if the premisses of the syllogism are universal, the conclusion of a demonstration of this kind—demonstration in the strict sense—must be eternal" (75^{b}21–24); "every truth must be in all respects self-consistent" (*Prior Analytics* 47^{a}9); "a syllogism [is] perfect if it requires nothing, apart from what is comprised in it, to make the necessary conclusion apparent" (25^{b}23–24).[25]

Although I am oversimplifying in that I do not intend to discuss the various kinds of syllogisms,[26] I do not consider the oversimplification important because Aristotle does indeed set up a metaphysics in which absolute and pure reasoning can be conducted from unassailable premises to irrefutable conclusions. The response to such a demonstration is silence because the demonstration itself, if done properly and based on proper assumptions, leaves nothing to say.

Now this metaphysics has a double effect on the teaching of writing. First, even though only the most hidebound and narrow-minded pure scientists believe in the sort of demonstrative, cumulative knowledge Aristotelian ἀπόδειξις demands, the myth of such knowledge pervades American colleges.[27] Testing procedures that depend on correctly worked problems, final grades that depend on correctly run lab experiments, weekly tests that depend on single-answer questions, and all the other measuring devices that imply "right-wrong" answers merely reinforce the myth. As a result, composition classes, because they are so utterly not demonstrative, are by their very nature degraded. They neither depend on any sort of testable, reliable formula, nor do they generate measurable knowledge. Indeed, by the standards of demonstration, they do not generate knowledge at all. At best, they help students learn how to communicate preexisting knowledge.

Second, the myth of demonstrative knowledge hovers over the mess of the composition classroom. And this effect is worse than the first because students, especially those who are not doing so well as they would like, long for the absolute procedures of demonstration. "Tell me how to learn the indemonstrables," they plead, "and then show me the formula for building a syllogism. Tell me what you want and I'll do it." But neither composition nor its ancestor, rhetoric, can do this. Each is an alien in the academy. Worse yet, many students believe themselves to be operating demonstratively. They bring *apparent* "syllogisms" such as these to class with them:

1. Murder is wrong. Abortion is murder. Abortion is wrong.

2. All nations have the inherent right to territorial sovereignty. Kuwait is a nation. No nation has the right to invade and usurp Kuwait.

3. America is a Christian nation. Atheists, Jews, Muslims, and other such infidels are not Christian. There is no place in America for such people.

4. Advanced industrial capitalism (à la Fukuyama and Reagan) is the culmination of human history. Marxism (monarchy, feudalism, aristocracy, theocracy, Islam, etc.) are not capitalism. Such noncapitalistic forms of government are perverted, evil, or both.

In students' own private intellectual lives and in the communities from which they come, these major premises are indeed indemonstrables, and they have become indemonstrables in exactly the way Aristotle describes. When these students confront a writing class that takes its direction from rhetoric, they feel an awkward and terrifying downward tug. They feel themselves being dragged down from the clear purity of fundamental premise-based demonstration into the relativistic, transient, and occasional world of rhetoric. Sometimes students resist by opting out of the class through what I have called antiwriting, sometimes by formally withdrawing from the course, or by actively challenging both the goal of the course and the competence of its instructor. Students who enter the course firmly grounded in a foundationalist metaphysics must mount some form of resistance or engage in a long, agonizing process of giving up their foundationalist principles. Their resistance is, therefore, both understandable and predictable. What we usually do not recognize, however, is that the rhetorical world we offer them carries with it the trappings of a classical, theological metaphysics. Rhetoric knows itself through its oppositions with demonstration and dialectic. The air of the academy tells students that rhetoric exists and always has existed through its uncertainty and inferiority. Students know full well that they can ascend from our classes at least into dialectic and probably into what will present itself to them as demonstration. The resulting tension is palpable in almost every composition classroom.

'Απόδειξις, as the paradigmatic method of intellectual inquiry, structures and orients the Aristotelian field and allots rhetoric its space in that field, just as the legacy of ἀπόδειξις—the notion of pure, cumulative science—structures and orients the modern university and allots the teaching of writing its space in *that* field. Ἀπόδειξις always begins with absolute truth, then follows perfect reasoning (or syllogism), and concludes in irrefutable conclusion. "The most exact sciences," Aristotle explains again and again, "are those which are most concerned with the first principles"; once we understand the "primary cause" of a thing, we can claim to know the essence of the thing itself" (*Metaphysics* 982ª26, 983ª25–26).[28] There are, however, times when we cannot begin from the kind of indemonstrable, absolute premise of ἀπόδειξις. Aristotle certainly knew this, and he accounted for it in his system. When such premises are unavailable, the nature of our inquiry changes, and Aristotle articulates the nature of this change frequently. Reasoning that cannot proceed from true and primary premises cannot be demonstrative. The next best point of departure, when absolute premises are unavailable, is "generally accepted opinions." Premises are "true and primary," Aristotle explains,

> which command belief through themselves and not through anything else; for regarding the first principles of science it is unnecessary to ask any further question as to "why," but each principle should of itself command belief. Generally accepted opinions, on the other hand, are those which commend themselves to all or to the majority or to the wise—that is, to all of the wise or to the majority or to the most famous and distinguished of them. (*Topics* 100ᵇ18–23)

"A premiss is one or the other part of a proposition," Aristotle repeats. "If dialectical, it assumes either part indifferently; if demonstrative, it definitely assumes that one part is true" (*Posterior Analytics* 72ª9–11).

Dialectic as the Happy and Necessary Loss of Foundation

The nature of the shift from demonstration to dialectic can hardly be overemphasized. The former must begin in the self-presence of truth and end in the silence of irrefutability; the latter, on the other hand, begins with "universally accepted opinion." And

already Pandora's box is open, for Aristotle formulates and reformu-
lates the foundation of dialectic throughout the *Topics*; he repeats
the formula so often that it begins to sound like a mantra.[29] Dialectic
begins at one of five levels: (1) with universally accepted opinions
that everyone recognizes, (2) with opinions that the majority accept,
(3) with opinions that the wise accept, (4) with opinions that the
majority of the wise accept, (5) with opinions that the "most famous
and distinguished" of the wise accept.[30] One need not be a leveling
democrat to see the problems with such a sharply constricted franchise as Aristotle gradually narrows it from general democracy to
limited aristocracy. Even Aristotle would have admitted that a category of human beings called "the most famous and distinguished of
the wise" is a fairly impressionistic, iffy group. Though he certainly
would have included himself in the group, there are hints throughout
his canon and his biography that he would not have included Plato,
and it seems clear that such sophists as Isocrates and such demagogues as Demosthenes would have been well beyond the pale.

Although it is true that the dialectician uses the syllogism (see
Prior Analytics 24^{a}23–^{b}16 and *Topics* 104^{a}8), the point of departure
makes all the difference. There is a clearly delineated hierarchy.
At the most basic level, the difference exists between truth and
plausibility: "if we are arguing with a view to plausibility," if, that
is, we are arguing "only dialectically" (μόνον διαλεκτικῶς, the "only"
is significant), "clearly we need only consider whether the conclusion
proceeds from premises which are as widely as possible accepted."
If, in contrast, "our object is truth, we must base our investigation
on the actual facts" (*Posterior Analytics* 81^{b}18–24). "When our object
is truth," Aristotle explains in *Prior Analytics*, we work "from terms
which are arranged to express a true relation"; when "we require
dialectical syllogisms," we work "from plausible premises" (46^{a}7–
10). By no means does Aristotle suggest that dialectical inquiry is
unworthy; quite the contrary, he argues that it is necessary. At the
same time, however, he makes quite clear that it is less noble than
demonstration simply because opinion is less noble, less desirable,
less permanent than truth. Dialectical opinion (δόξα) is qualified;
demonstrative knowledge (ἐπιστήμη) is unqualified: "We consider
that we have unqualified knowledge of anything . . . when we believe that we know (i) that the cause from which the fact results is
the cause of that fact, and (ii) that the fact cannot be otherwise"
(*Posterior Analytics* 71^{b}9). Although one may develop a syllogism

without the sure premise of demonstration, one cannot thereby produce demonstration. With a dialectical, opinion-based premise, the conditions for knowledge simply are not present: "Syllogism indeed will be possible without these conditions, but not demonstration; for the result will not be knowledge" ($71^{b}21$–25).

There is a second difference between demonstration and dialectic. Whereas demonstration includes several kinds of sciences, sciences that can be ranked according to their priority and importance, dialectic includes no such categories. In *Posterior Analytics* ($87^{a}30$–$^{b}4$) Aristotle explains that one science can be more precise than another and prior to it. Arithmetic, for example, is more precise than, and prior to, both harmonics and geometry. And he makes essentially the same point twice in *Metaphysics*, where he argues that "the most exact of the sciences are those which are most concerned with the first principles; for those which are based on fewer principles are more exact than those which include additional principles; *e.g.*, arithmetic is more exact than geometry" ($982^{a}26$–28). The two highest pure sciences are physics and mathematics, but there is an overarching science that precedes and enables even the purest of the pure sciences. Aristotle names this the science of Being *qua* Being, or theology. The philosopher who undertakes this study does two things: first, this Supreme Scientist determines the absolute premises of the highest, most all-encompassing science; second this "student of the whole of reality" must "investigate also the principles of syllogistic reasoning" ($1005^{a}19$–$^{b}17$ and $1026^{a}7$–32).

Any true science must develop its own premises and methods; otherwise it cannot build a knowledge base or a set of procedures that are teachable, learnable, and productive.[31] Dialectic can never do this because it operates in the temporal, mutable arena of opinion. The scientist, Aristotle explains, "must deal with propositions from the point of view of truth, but for purposes of dialectic, with a view to opinion" (*Topics* $105^{b}30$–31). Equally as compromising, the dialectician, unlike the scientist, must consider how the interlocutor will respond; thus, the opinion-based response of the opponent colors the progress of an inquiry (*Topics* $155^{a}2$–22). "Dialectic," Aristotle explains, "treats as an exercise what philosophy tries to understand" (*Metaphysics* $1004^{b}26$).

Dialectic, as the scientific method based on accepted opinion, occupies the space in the Aristotelian field nearest demonstration, preempting any other pretenders to scientific thought. In its own way, dialectic is as important as demonstration. Just as demonstration is useful in the study of the immutable, dialectic is useful in the study of the mutable. Since everyone agrees with Aristotle that human matters are variable and that human situations do not often admit of absolute points of departure, some way of studying and deciding about the uncertain and the unstable must be found. This way, when properly done by the intellectually gifted who are well trained, is dialectic. In both the ancient Athenian Academy and the modern university, the dialectical method has been adopted by what the French call the "human sciences" and what we in America tend to call the humanities. If the pure sciences operate in a discourse arena much like demonstration, the humanities operate in a discourse arena much like dialectic. Historians and literary critics, for example, rarely pretend to depart from absolute premises or to approach the silence of absolute knowledge, but they do pretend to a rigor equal to that in the sciences. Humanities students must learn to "demonstrate" in acceptable discourse what they think and why they think it, and they must learn how to anticipate and respond to the objections of others on similar dialectical quests.

Indeed, the humanities often claim a kind of moral high ground in that they claim to teach "critical thinking." Critical thinking allows the humanist to critique the results of pure science, determining—or at least demanding the opportunity to determine—how the pure knowledge of science ought to be used in the day-to-day world. Aristotle allots to dialectic a function quite similar to that of critical thinking in the modern university. Through dialectic, he explains, the Supreme Scientist can study the relative claims of the various individual sciences operating within demonstration. Because dialectic can float above any sort of particular premise and because it has "true reasoning," it

> is useful in connexion with the ultimate bases of each science; for it is impossible to discuss them at all on the basis of the principles peculiar to the science in question, since the principles are primary in relation to everything else, and it is necessary to deal with them through the generally accepted opinions on each point. This process belongs peculiarly, or most appropriately to dialectic; for, being of the nature of an investigation, it lies along the path to the principles of all methods of inquiry. (*Topics* 101^{a}37–^{b}4)

Aristotelian dialectic, therefore, serves the same group of thinkers as demonstration; the only real difference between the two is the point of departure. Once the inquiry has begun, dialectic demands the same intellectual rigor as demonstration. Indeed, at the level of the study of Being *qua* Being, dialectic plays a role in demonstration as the Supreme Scientist works toward absolute knowledge of absolute things.

Rhetoric as the Fall into Stupidity

When one descends to rhetoric, however, a second major category shift occurs. Not only does one give up the absolute premises of demonstration, but one also gives up the careful and rigorous syllogistic method, replacing it with enthymeme. The debate about what an enthymeme is has raged for millennia, and I do try to work through a little of this debate in chapter 4 below. Of this one claim, however, I am certain: whatever an enthymeme may be, it *is not* a syllogism. For "enthymeme" to be meaningful, there must be some difference between it and syllogism, else there would be no need at all for the word "enthymeme." More importantly, without the shift from syllogism to enthymeme, no such thing as rhetoric would exist in Aristotelianism because syllogism conducted on the basis of general opinion is dialectic.[32] Aristotle makes the hierarchy clear in both of the *Analytics*. "We must now observe that not only dialectical and demonstrative syllogisms are effected by means of the figures already described," he explains near the end of *Prior Analytics*, "but also rhetorical syllogisms and in general every kind of mental conviction, whatever form it may take" ($68^b10–14$). At the beginning of *Posterior Analytics* he explains again that rhetorical arguments operate in the same way as demonstrative and dialectical arguments, except that they use enthymeme and example instead of induction and syllogism. And at the beginning of the *Rhetoric*, Aristotle explains that "when, certain things being posited, something different results by reason of them . . . such a conclusion in Dialectic is called a syllogism, in rhetoric an enthymeme" ($1356^b12–18$).[33]

There is a reason for this change, and Aristotle makes it unmistakably clear repeatedly in the *Rhetoric*. The difference, as James Berlin has rightly pointed out, is audience (12). The only reason anyone would ever abandon dialectic and turn to rhetoric is that the intended audience is incapable of the detail and rigor of dialectic.

"The function of rhetoric," Aristotle explains quite clearly, "is to deal with things about which we deliberate, but for which we have no systematic rules; and in the presence of such hearers as are unable to take a general view of many stages, or to follow a lengthy chain of argument." The presumed audience for rhetoric, he says a few lines later, "is supposed to be a simple person" (1357^a1–12).[34] The reason the rhetorician can resort successfully to maxims (which neither the demonstrator nor the dialectician could ever do) is the clownish, coarse, vulgar ($\phi o \rho \tau \iota \kappa \acute{o} \varsigma$) nature of a rhetorical audience (1395^b1). Unlike dialectic, in which the discussants can and should work through to their conclusions with as much care and detail as possible, in rhetoric, "it is impossible to ask a number of questions, owing to the hearer's weakness. Wherefore also we should compress our enthymemes as much as possible" (1419^a14–19). The audience for rhetoric is so intellectually straightened that even if we have demonstrative knowledge available, our audience will not be able to comprehend it. "In dealing with certain persons," Aristotle explains, "even if we possessed the most accurate scientific knowledge, we should not find it easy to persuade them by the employment of such knowledge. For scientific discourse is concerned with instruction, but in the case of such persons instruction is impossible; our proofs and arguments must rest on generally accepted principles, as we said in the *Topics*, when speaking of converse with the multitude" (1355^a21–29). The most damning indictment of rhetoric comes when Aristotle takes up the enthymeme near the end of Book II of the *Rhetoric*. He begins by repeating his explanation that an enthymeme is "a kind of syllogism"; then he continues the explanation by showing that a rhetorical argument cannot extend too far back toward original premises, "nor should it include all the steps of the argument." Indeed, the reason why "the ignorant" are often more persuasive in rhetorical settings than the educated is that they know better than to engage in the sort of inquiry characterized by dialectic (1395^b21–31).[35]

   If one juxtaposes the goals of demonstration, dialectic, and rhetoric, the descent is clear. Demonstration must lead to $\grave{\alpha}\lambda\acute{\eta}\theta\varepsilon\iota\alpha$. Liddell and Scott render this term in English as "truth as opposed to a lie" and "reality as opposed to appearance." Demonstration has a divine quality about it in that it puts a matter outside human hands, outside the reach of opinion or persuasion. Its lure is profound, especially in the classroom where the attraction of truth,

correctness, ironclad learnability, and certainty beckon with such
power. Dialectic leads only to δόξα, which Liddell and Scott render
as "a notion, true or false," an expectation, a mere opinion or conjecture, an imagination, a supposition, or even a fancy. The shift is
dramatic and clear. Demonstrative knowledge is the sort that physics, mathematics, and the pure sciences have always sought. The
truth of the inquiry lies in the thing being studied, not in the person
studying it.[36] Any hypothesis can be proved true or false—absolutely,
if the research is available. With dialectic, the location of truth moves
from the object studied to the person making the study, focusing
attention, in Grimaldi's words, on "an area of reality which is at a level
definitely below Plato's world of forms and Aristotle's metaphysics"
(*Studies* 22–23; see also Garver 385, Halloran "Tradition" 234–36,
Ross 49, and Short 272–73). The dialectician moves toward opinion,
knowing all along that absolute opinion is self-contradictory, but
nevertheless being as careful as possible to construct and defend
true and reliable opinion. The location of dialectic is both the curse
and the blessing of the traditional humanities: the curse because
the humanities can never compete with the pure sciences in the
creation of "knowledge"; the blessing because the humanities retain
the role of critical, evaluative thinking that can at least claim the
right to judge the absolute results of science.

Rhetoric can never offer more than πίστις, and another, equally
important metaphysical downshift occurs. Πίστις comes into English, according to Liddell and Scott, as faith, persuasion, good faith,
trustworthiness, faithfulness, honesty, confidence, the sort of proof
used by an orator, and trust in others. Thus with the move to
rhetoric, the location of truth changes once again, this time to the
perceived believability of the speaker. In demonstration, truth exists
absolutely in the thing being studied. In dialectic, truth exists within
the rigor of the argument itself. In rhetoric, truth exists in the
strategies necessary to persuade a simple audience.[37]

Both Thomas Cole and Edward Schiappa have argued recently
that Plato and Aristotle created the term *rhetoric* as a backward and
backhanded way of degrading their opponents, from Isocrates back
to Protagoras. "Whenever the conclusions to which philosophy leads
must be made acceptable to those whose philosophical attainments
are one-sided or imperfect or nonexistent," Cole explains, "or when
true opinion is sought as a goal rather than the *logos* that is able to
give account of itself, or when the likeness of truth is to be presented

as a substitute for truth itself, rhetoric is necessary—so necessary that, had it not existed already, Plato and Aristotle would surely have had to invent it," which, Cole goes on to say in the next paragraph, "they effectively did" (28).[38] By the time Aristotle left Athens in 323, Schiappa continues the argument, he had completed the conceptual and terminological separation of philosophy and rhetoric ("Neo-Sophistic" 197–98).[39]

Such a separation necessarily, in my opinion, degrades rhetoric. Each time Aristotle sets up a hierarchical system, he puts rhetoric at the bottom, where none but the weak-minded and poorly trained ever venture. Those who are eager to argue that Aristotle conceives rhetoric as necessary should remember that he also considered slavery necessary. In the *Metaphysics* and the *Ethics*, as he presents his notions of epistemology and ontology, Aristotle erects the ἐπιστήμη on the tired and degraded exclusion of rhetoric. Within the Aristotelian system, rhetoric serves the necessary function of being the thing excluded so that knowledge can know itself by having something to be better than and different from.

In Book II of the *Metaphysics* as Aristotle puts together the moves that will finally enthrone philosophy as the supreme human endeavor, he separates knowledge (ἐπιστήμη) into two kinds, theoretic and practical: "philosophy is rightly called a knowledge of Truth. The object of theoretic knowledge is truth, while that of practical knowledge is action; for even when they are investigating *how* a thing is so, practical men study not the eternal principle but the relative and immediate application" (993^{b}20–24).[40] In Book VI, Aristotle changes the word being defined from "knowledge" (ἐπιστήμη) to "thought" or "intellectual activity" (διάνοια), which he expands slightly by dividing it into three types: theoretical, practical, and productive. Of course his hierarchy is obvious. Theoretical science is the most noble and desirable because it deals with causes and principles (1025^{b}4–11; see also 983^{a}25, 994^{b}29–31, and *Physics* 194^{b}19). And theology, the study of Being *qua* Being, is the Supreme Science: "The speculative sciences . . . are to be preferred to the other sciences, and 'theology' to the other speculative sciences" (1026^{a}22).

Aristotle complicates this grid in the *Ethics* (1138^{b}18–1139^{b}13), when he turns to psychology to try to locate the place where demonstration, dialectic, and rhetoric occur. He begins by dividing the soul into its rational and irrational halves, and then he divides the rational half into two halves, "one whereby we contemplate those things whose first principles are invariable, and one whereby we contemplate those things which admit of variation." Aristotle names the first the "Scientific Faculty" (ἐπιστημονικόν), the second the "Calculative Faculty" (λογιστικόν). In chapter 3, Aristotle takes up the five ways in which the rational soul operates:[41] art (τέχνη), science (ἐπιστήμη), prudence (φρόνησις), wisdom (σοφία), and intelligence (νοῦς). These five "operations" relate to each other in complicated, interdependent ways, and nothing I can say about them would be free from dispute.[42] It is, however, fair (and not very controversial) to argue that Aristotle goes on to repeat the tripartite division he makes in the *Metaphysics* by again dividing intellectual inquiry into the scientific, the productive, and the practical. As one would expect, the most elevated of the modes of inquiry is science, which studies eternal objects through demonstrative reasoning leading to certain conclusions. Beneath science come the actions of the practical and productive intellects. These two actions are different and somewhat antithetical, with neither being part of the other. As their names imply, one focuses on the product, the other on the process of doing. The productive intellect, according to Aristotle, is art, and "art is the same thing as a rational quality, concerned with making, that reasons truly." The practical intellect (φρόνησις), on the other hand,

> is not the same as Science. Nor can it be the same as Art. It is not Science, because matters of conduct admit of variation; and not Art, because doing and making are generically different. . . . It remains therefore that it is a truth-attaining rational quality, concerned with action in relation to things that are good and bad for human beings. (1140^a24-^b5)

In distinguishing art from prudence, Aristotle offers a splendid example: we can speak of excellence in art but not of excellence in prudence. The self-evident reason is that one can be an artist without being an especially good artist, but one cannot be prudent without being good at prudence for a person poor in prudence is ipso facto not prudent.[43]

Geography and the "Invention" of Knowledge

All this description of the landscape of the soul is remarkable indeed. It is so clear, so persuasive, and, after all these centuries, so completely habituated that we tend to forget that soul, or ψυχή, is metaphoric all the way down. Sorting through the word "ψυχή," the closest one ever gets to a concrete signified is "breath," and the ways in which Aristotle uses the word "ψυχή" never penetrate that far into the term's etymological history. Aristotle uses the word to mean "soul," "spirit," or (in Hegelian terms) "pure self-presence." In Aristotelianism ψυχή functions as the place of adjudication in which pure, self-present intellect (the νοῦς) comes to know itself and to make its decisions. But Aristotle gives this metaphor a physical ontology. It has halves, which in turn themselves have halves. And once this ontology appears on the horizon the West has a vocabulary of inclusion and exclusion. The irrational "half" of the soul is always already excluded. Once anything can be branded irrational, unreasonable, or emotional, already it has been ruled out of bounds. And of course we all know that rhetoric can do its dirty work by appealing to the irrational half of the soul. If the audience consists of low quality, poorly educated people, the speaker can win the day by showing the irrational half of the soul how to override the rational half.

In the other half of the soul, the admissible and good half, the *rational* half (τῆς φυχῆς, τό τε λόγον), there is a yet another hierarchy. In this good half, the theoretical, speculative, and scientific reign supreme; the prudential comes in second; and the practical trails along as a poor, but occasionally necessary, third. The parallel between the landscape of Aristotle's soul and the landscape of his society (which I discussed in the preceding chapter) is unmistakable. Society, as Aristotle sees it, divides neatly into Greek and barbarian, with the slavish barbarian functioning as the excludable anarchy through which Greek order and goodness define and know themselves; in like manner, the soul divides neatly into the irrational and the rational, with the irrational serving as the excludable psychic phenomenon through which the rational defines and knows itself. Inside the safety of the Greek home, one finds the male master who thinks, the female subordinate who arranges and through whose body the heirs pass, and the slave who carries out the thought of the master; inside the safety of the rational mind one finds the speculative, theoretical, and scientific through which one "knows," the prudential through which one lives, and the practical through which one does.

But how, finally, does someone come to "know" all this "knowledge"? How do these theories and geographies come to have such trueness about them? How do we "know" the "knowledge" of theoretical physics? How do we "know" to rank it so far above "mere persuasion"? How do we know with such precise clarity that we have rational and irrational parts and that the rational should always dominate and control the irrational? In the most precise question of Aristotelianism, "Where do the indemonstrable premisses of theoretic knowledge come from?" After all, everything depends on (and from) them. The indemonstrables do not come from prudence, wisdom, or art:

> the first principles from which scientific truths are derived cannot themselves be reached by Science; nor yet are they apprehended by Art, nor by Prudence. To be matter of Scientific Knowledge a truth must be demonstrated by deduction from other truths; while Art and Prudence are concerned only with things that admit of variation. Nor is Wisdom the knowledge of first principles either: for the philosopher has to arrive at some things by demonstration. (1140ᵇ33–1141ᵃ3)

First principles, Aristotle explains, "must be apprehended by Intelligence," the pure, noetic νοῦς itself (1141ᵃ8). Throughout his system, Aristotle is careful to reiterate that one knows something better and more truly if one knows it from premisses that "are themselves uncaused." First principles, in other words, are "those facts which cannot be proved" (*Posterior Analytics* 76ᵃ21–32). "The knowledge of immediate premisses," he states repeatedly, "is not by demonstration. "It is evident that this must be so; for if it is necessary to know the prior premisses from which the demonstration proceeds, and if the regress ends with the immediate premisses, the latter must be indemonstrable." There is, he insists, "a definite first principle of knowledge" (72ᵇ19–27). Not until the very last chapter of *Posterior Analytics* (99ᵇ15–100ᵇ17), however, after he has explained both demonstration and syllogism, does he explain where the first principles come from. To anyone situated in the textual theories of poststructuralism and reading Aristotle for the first time, the origin of the absolute (and absolutely hallowed) first principles comes as a rather amusing confirmation of antifoundationalism. We have, Aristotle explains, a certain faculty (τινα δύναμιν) that he calls "sense perception" (αἴσθησις). When this sense perception is coupled with memory (μνήμη), as it is in humans, it gives rise to experience (ἐμπειρία). Experience, Aristotle continues, "is the universal when established as a whole in the soul—the One that corresponds to the Many, the unity that is identically present in them all." This universal, unifying, all-present experience "provides the starting-point of art and science: art in the world of process and science in the world of facts" (100ᵃ6–9). Having made his generalization, Aristotle offers an analogy to explain how sense perception aided by memory generates experience, which in turn leads to indemonstrable first principles. "When a retreat has occurred in battle," he explains,

> if one man halts so does another, and then another, until the original position is restored. The soul is so constituted that it is capable of the same sort of process. . . . As soon as one individual percept has "come to a halt" in the soul, this is the first beginning of the presence there of a universal. . . . Then other "halts" occur among these universals, until the indivisible genera or <ultimate> universals are established. (100ᵃ12–ᵇ2)

In other words, a process of naturally sophisticated induction establishes the first principles in an entirely unconscious and self-evident way. Or, said more crudely, we know the first principles because we know them—end of case. "No other kind of knowledge," Aristotle concludes the book, "except intuition is more accurate than scientific knowledge." The most secure things we know are indemonstrable, and we know these indemonstrables intuitively.

If this construction of the foundation of knowledge were not so crucial in the construction of the West, Aristotle's closing defense of (male!) intuition and the concomitant reification of demonstration would be comic. "First principles are more knowable than demonstrations," Aristotle assumes,

> and all scientific knowledge involves reason. It follows that there can be no scientific knowledge of the first principles; and since nothing can be more infallible than scientific knowledge except intuition, it must be intuition that apprehends the first principles. (100ᵇ5–17)

The assumptions that operate throughout this construction of metaphysics are breathtaking. Scientific, absolute knowledge must exist,

Aristotle assumes. But he can see both that such knowledge depends on its premises and that these premises cannot themselves be available to science if science is to avoid an infinite regress. His way of dealing with this intractable problem is to allow the νοῦς, the simple self-presence of truth itself to coalesce in experience as the absolute foundation of knowledge. And to make his metaphor clear, he uses the analogy of a military encounter!

Deep inside the νοῦς lives the entity that Aristotle finally names both "prime mover" and "God" (*Metaphysics* 1072ᵃ19–1073ᵃ13). The intuition allowed by such divine intellect, as Ross explains, "is as it were in direct contact with its object; it is not then knowing one thing by means of another as middle term." The character of pure mind, Ross continues,

> is to have no character of its own but to be characterised entirely by what at the moment it knows; if it had a character of its own, that would interfere with the perfect reproduction of the object in the knowing mind. . . . Thus in knowledge mind and its object have an identical character, and to know an object is to know one's mind as it is in knowing the object. (182)[44]

With the νοῦς firmly in control and freed from any need to found itself, the metaphysics of the West simply appear, shining forth in the absoluteness of their self-authorization like Athena springing fully developed from Zeus's forehead.[45] And immediately words like "knowledge," "wisdom," "intelligence," "prudence," and, yes, even "rhetoric" take on lives of their own. No longer are these terms linguistic constructs, "mere metaphors"; rather, they are discrete, measurable, haveable entities. Wisdom (σοφία) can become "the most perfect of the modes of knowledge," and the wise can not only "know the conclusions that follow from [their] first principles," but they can also "have a true conception of those principles themselves." Enabled by intelligence (the νοῦς, the innate ability to "know"), science can consummate itself in "knowledge of the most exalted objects" (*Ethics* 1141ᵃ16–23), and "education" can appear in the West, not as training or indoctrination but as the certain, unimpeachable process of learning to think. Having established the law of noncontradiction in which "it is impossible for the same attribute at once to belong and not to belong to the same thing and in the same relation" (*Metaphysics* 1005ᵇ19–20), Aristotle can define education as the state of knowing which questions to ask and which questions not to ask. "Some, indeed, demand," he says with impatient exasperation

> to have the law [of noncontradiction] proved, but this is because they lack education; for it shows lack of education not to know of what we should require proof, and of what we should not. For it is quite impossible that everything should have proof; the process would go on to infinity, so that even so there would be no proof. ($1006^a7–10$)

With scientific demonstration enthroned, prudence and all the things it enables, as well as art and all the things it enables, become less elevated, less noble, less important. And rhetoric? Well, rhetoric remains as the leftover, the art not founded on self-present knowledge, the procedure not capable of fully disclosing the process of an argument, the discourse that one speaks to the mob, the subject one turns over to graduate students, the subject one teaches to the weak-minded, the subject that stands in perpetual need of remediation, of being fixed or tidied up a bit. Education, Aristotle explains in the *Ethics*, enables the West to remain sure of its hierarchies,

> for it is the mark of an educated mind to expect that amount of exactness in each kind which the nature of the particular subject admits. It is equally unreasonable to accept merely probable conclusions from a mathematician and to demand strict demonstration from a rhetorician.* ($1094^b23–27$)

Prudence and art control the daily aspects of living life in the Aristotelian system. They have no access to "general principles," nor can they presume to tell the "truth" in any but a provisional way. And rhetoric, as I have tried to show above, is the lowest of these degraded forms. It stands as a sort of impossible hybrid in that prudence, to which rhetoric must appeal, and art, through which rhetoric must operate, are opposites. "Correctness," Aristotle says, "cannot be said of knowledge" (1142^b10). Calling knowledge correct would be like calling prudence prudent. Knowledge ($ἐπιστήμη$) is in and of itself correct; if the thing known is not correct then what is known is not knowledge. In the realm of prudence or dialectic, of course, there is a kind of truth; one might call it "correctness in thinking." In rhetoric, the best one can hope for is a similarity to correctness in thinking. Knowledge is out of the question.

Rhetoric as Aristotle saves it for us becomes a sort of self-eradicating violation of the law against self-contradiction. It depends on demonstration and dialectic as a way of knowing itself, but it can neither generate knowledge nor fully justify opinion. It is an art, but it must appeal to the prudential faculty, which is absolutely separated from art. It can be conceived and understood only by a academician, but it can be used only with an audience incapable of understanding how the academician conceived and understood it. In sum, Aristotelian rhetoric creates the possibility of an intellectual world much like the one inhabited by contemporary composition studies. All the metaphysics are in place.

In one gesture, rhetoric is saved from the sophists, domesticated by the academics, and made into a kind of remedial course. One teaches it to poor students late in the afternoon. The good students exempt the course entirely, or if they like to slum, they hang around for the easy afternoon lectures, smiling archly among themselves about the clods who have to take rhetoric. In another gesture, however, a professional discourse having nothing to do with those late afternoon remedial lectures appears on the scene. In this second gesture, "true" rhetoricians reveal themselves. These true rhetoricians, like Aristotle, have all the intellectual capacities and all the education necessary for dialectic and demonstration. With such minds and such training, they can forever debate the exact ontology of rhetoric, and, of course, they can conduct their debate in a discourse and a metaphysics that carefully guard the sanctity of science, philosophy, and dialectic through the exclusion and degradation of rhetoric. That is to say they present themselves to the world as the demonstrators of rhetoric, not as rhetoricians. Rhetoric itself ends up so stripped of anything intellectually pretentious, so available to almost everyone, that almost anyone can teach it. Who would be the wiser? Who would care? Above all, who would be situated in such a way as to say, "No! What you're teaching isn't rhetoric."

Living in the (Rhet/Comp) Country

A few years ago I attended a session at CCCC that focused on "the canon" in composition studies. The session was part of a larger project under the direction of Pat Bizzell and Bruce Herzberg to assemble and publish an anthology that would serve for composition studies the way anthologies of literary criticism serve courses in the history of criticism or anthologies of women writers serve introductory courses in women's studies. When the anthology appeared, it turned out to be an anthology of rhetorical theory in which the notion "composition studies" plays only the obscurest of roles. The pre-twentieth-century authors that Bizzell and Herzberg chose constitute an anthology that one would expect to find in a history of rhetoric course taught in most undergraduate speech departments. The authors Bizzell and Herzberg chose to represent the twentieth century (Bakhtin, Derrida, Kristeva, etc.) are the gurus of postmodern antifoundationalism. Without a doubt these famous twentieth-century philosophers and theorists are important intellectuals, and they surely influence composition studies, but not one of them would be likely to know what the phrase "composition studies" means, nor would any of them have the slightest idea what "discipline" she or he is contributing to by being anthologized this way. "When we began working on this anthology," Bizzell and Herzberg write in their preface (in a sentence that, to me at least, sounds like an apology), "we envisioned a collection of works on composition theory," beginning with "important works of premodern rhetoric" and then focusing on "very recent work in the field of composition studies" (v). What they produced was a radically expanded gathering from premodern rhetoric coupled with a brief anthology of recent critical theory.

I do not intend to criticize Bizzell and Herzberg. Had I been charged with assembling an anthology to serve as the history of composition studies, I could have done no better than they did. If there are seminal texts in composition studies, none of them was written by a "composition studies person," and no one knows with any certainty what the seminal texts are. It is surely true that each composition teacher in his or her intellectual autobiography brings to the classroom an "anthology" different from all other composition teachers. It is also true that no one can with any certainty claim superiority for one "anthology" over any other and that nearly everyone in the academy would regard this sort of chaotic anarchy as unprofessional or preparadigmatic or irresponsible or all three. How insecure should this state of affairs make us? How insecure should we feel because we cannot imagine the questions that would lead us to a quest for a respectable and stable anthology?

Not very, in my opinion. After all, composition studies entered the university through the back door, and it continues to be an uncertain thing, staffed largely by those with no training in, or commitment to, the field. For me, at least, this anarchic amorphousness is the field's greatest attraction. The worst thing that could happen would be for someone to "discipline" it, give it a reading list, articulate a set of methods, develop a curriculum.

I like reading against Aristotle, showing how ridiculous it is to base anything (whether rhetoric, the university, or the West) on something called the νοῦς. If we are to be antifoundationalist, let's be antifoundationalist all the way down, which means that we must recognize the situations of the students in our classes and of the teachers who teach those classes. Writing courses then must grow into and out of those situations.

By making rhetoric a "thing," by making it an object of study, Aristotle brought it under the sway of demonstration. As a result, professional rhetoricians have been debating the ontology of rhetoric ever since. We can do the same with composition studies, but if we do, if we try to make it possible for someone to be "an important scholar in composition studies," we are likely to give up the transformative power that brought most of us into the teaching of writing. And what will we gain? We will gain the grudging approval of those who already "know" that what we do is inferior, truthless, and weak-minded.

Yes, there is an element of smugness in this peroration. Indeed I do think I "know" something that my professors did not "know" and that most of my colleagues do not "know." I have a hunch, however, that Aristotle "knew." That is why he was so eager to save rhetoric in such a way as to tame it. Had it been left to the sophists, who knows how knowledge (not to mention society) might have been transformed?

3

ARISTOTLE'S BEARD, OR S(H)AVING THE FACE OF PROFESSIONAL DISCOURSE

For Lysias

Populist Work in the Fugitives' Lair

Vanderbilt's Ph.D. program in English is a little unusual. We admit an average of six new students each year and award an average of four Ph.D.'s; though we do award an M.A. at the end of the first year, we do not have an M.A. program as such because we admit students only to the Ph.D. program. At any given time, we have about twenty-six active graduate students. With a faculty of thirty-one, the program is small enough for the faculty to know each graduate student well at the end of five years. As the only rhet/comp person in the department, I work closely with our graduate students throughout their stay in the department and especially during the three middle years when they are teaching (first-year students do not teach and most fifth-year students receive dissertation fellowships). Though almost all of our students seek careers as professors of literature, I consider myself obligated to ensure that they know something about the history of rhetoric and a good bit about contemporary composition theory, and I have designed our three-year teaching internship program to meet that obligation. We have an active computer-supported composition program, one that is, I believe, at the center of contemporary process ideology, with all its contradictions and uncertainties. Obviously I am proud both of my department and of our writing program, which I administer; however, as the nation, and my region in particular, have drifted rightward over the last few years, I have begun to worry a bit.

The best teacher in our current fifth-year class telephoned me last week, in part to seek moral support but primarily to complain. He had just received word that a recent campus interview, the only campus interview he received this year, did not lead to a job because his ideas about teaching, especially those about teaching writing, had left his prospective colleagues aghast. He believes he had the job and then lost it because of the way he described his most recent writing course, a course I had helped design. The core of the course consisted of a portfolio of five essays. Four of those essays had been rewritten and two of those four had been rewritten twice. Before each of the six rewrites, he had critiqued the students' essays, as had a small student group. For the two essays rewritten twice, he had provided considerable feedback, and he had assigned each student to a writing support group in which collaboration was an ongoing activity. He had allocated considerable class time for collaboration workshops, both in the classroom and in a computer lab, and had encouraged students to find their own "writing space," to feel free to work alone, in a group, or with him. The demeanor of each individual class had not been entirely predictable as students dealt with different kinds of problems and successes in different kinds of ways.

Before the term began, he had chosen the readings for the first seven weeks, but readings for the second seven weeks had grown out of the students' essays. By midterm the students had written enough to know where their term-long interests lay, and since our composition classes are limited to fifteen students, all the students in his class knew enough about the work being done by their peers for the class to spend the last meeting before spring break negotiating its own reading agenda for the meetings after break. He spent part of his break assembling and copying a packet of reading for the second seven weeks. In addition to regular class meetings, he had conducted weekly conferences. The final grade, which was the only grade assigned all semester, was based on the portfolio, with particular attention paid to the two essays that had received the most work.

The faculty at the university where he interviewed—a private, southern university with a good academic reputation but with a strong conservative tradition and with roots deep in one of the most conservative of the fundamentalist denominations—had responded to his pedagogy with horror. They accused him of not knowing what he was doing, of turning his class over to the students, and of cowardice for his unwillingness to give regular grades. They also argued that in fact he had no grounds on which to assign grades because, by the end of the term, the portfolios had been influenced by so many people—he being one—that it would be impossible to assess the true writing ability of each student.

This young man, a splendid teacher and truly fine person, first encountered all of this "unusual" pedagogy in my seminar and through the workshops I require of teaching interns. He will be unemployed next year, and he is heartsick, truly worried that he has learned "all the wrong things."

I know exactly what would have secured that job for him. If he truly wanted to teach in that university with those colleagues (and in his situation I would have wanted the job just as much as he did), he should have described a course in which students read texts from the standard canon, with one black writer and one woman writer sandwiched in. The students should have written three, one-time-only essays on which they received final grades and one "research" paper, written entirely out of class with very little assistance other than the assigned topic. He should have required daily quizzes on the reading as well as midterm and final exams. He should have described himself as a well-trained humanist who knows what students should read and how they should be evaluated for their comments on that reading. He should, in short, have described the freshman writing course that I took in the fall of 1964 at a small Southern Baptist liberal arts college in Mississippi. If he had, he would be employed now.

The course this young man described was designed to engage his students as human beings in the process of constructing themselves and their world. The one his interviewers expected would have introduced students to the world of professional humanism. There is a difference. Let me explain it by juxtaposing two student essays from the 1985 Bedford Prizes (Sommers and McQuade 128–

32 and 180–87). The first is by Kelly Mays, a first-year student at Emory University, who, at the time of writing the essay, was an English major intending to pursue a Ph.D. in English. The second is by Earnestine Johnson, a first-year student at George Mason University, who, at the time of writing, was a sociology major intending a career as a social worker. Each essay is, in my opinion, superior work for any first-year writing class.

An Analysis of Images and Structure Within Andrew Marvell's "On a Drop of Dew"
Kelly J. Mays

Within "On a Drop of Dew," Andrew Marvell uses a single comparison to examine the nature of the soul and the possibility of its salvation. Marvell uses a drop of dew and the natural cycle of which it is a part to illustrate the nature of the soul and its relation both to the heaven which creates it as well as to the earthly body in which it lives. His vision of the soul is one of a pure and complete entity which embodies, at birth, the Heaven which created it. Yet, as a drop of dew is threatened with contamination from its contact with the earth, so, he implies, is the soul threatened by the potentially corruptible elements of an earthly form. He ends by suggesting that salvation comes not only from the natural state of the soul, which tends toward the goodness of its creator, but also from the active grace of God and, perhaps from the actions of man himself. Marvell expresses this idea through this overriding comparison with the dew in addition to other underlying images and finally through the structure of the poem itself.

The poem is based on the metaphysical comparison of a drop of dew to the soul. Marvell begins this image by describing the inherent innocence, youth, and purity of the newly created drop through such references as "orient dew," which suggests its innocence of thought, and "little globe," which, as a diminutive phrase, again emphasizes the dew's childlike state. These descriptions not only vividly portray the natural state of the soul, which is inherently connected to God's goodness, but also set up the contrast between this state and the earthly. This contrast is furthered by the darker, more active descriptions of the earth implied by "blowing roses," "purple flow'rs," and the soul's subsequent, "trembling," and "restless" and "unsecure" "roll[ing]." By achieving such a great contrast Marvell points up the fear of the dew or soul for its own contamination. The image of the drop continues within the second verse paragraph as it is "exhal[ed]" back to its birthplace and so provides the transition within the poem to a more direct comparison between it and the soul. This transition is aided also by the connection between the images of the human flower to the images of the actual flowers in the beginning. The dew image again returns within the last section in active references to manna, and within the first three phrases which connect the characteristics of the soul to those of the dew. That is, "loose" and "easy" refer back to "restless" and "unsecure," "girt" to "round in itself incloses," and finally "moving but on a point below" to "scarce touching where it lies," so that with this last paragraph Marvell rounds off the comparison between the soul and the dew strengthening both images with the support of the other. This support relies not only on the actively described characteristics but also on the natural cycle of which the dew is known to be a part. By using the cyclical falling-evaporating of the moisture, he emphasizes the transitory and similarly cyclical nature of the soul's states.

In addition, this idea of a perpetuated cycle connects with a second prevalent image of the poem, which is the circular or round ideal. Marvell presents images of the circular through-out his poem. From the beginning he uses such words as "round," "incloses," "globe," "sphere," "circling," "wound," and "girt," which emphasize this image of roundness. He ties this image, both through implication and active association within the poem, to the heavenly, especially its virtues of purity, eternity, wholeness, and harmony. This idea connects not only with the underlying cycles within the poem but also with the images of the drop, the world and the soul. As a circle or globe, all of these are connected, able to face every way and yet to turn away and so connect both the purity of heaven with the earth, goodness with sin, and disdain with love. Further, this image of the sphere refers not only to the general heav-enly sphere but ties in more specifically with the sun at its center.

The sun becomes almost an embodiment or symbol for

God's power within the poem. Marvell achieves this powerful image through both the implied power of the sun within the water cycle but also through its active presentation within the action of the poem itself. The first time it is mentioned explicitly it is presented as the powerful body which "pit[ies]" the "pain" of the drop/soul and "exhal[es]" it back to the sky. Thus it is presented in a Godlike way through its mercy and its ability to bring the drop/soul back to its original state of grace. This idea seems to connect the sun to the "sphere" (line 14) of the dew's actual origin. Further, the sun becomes an active participant again within the last paragraph in Marvell's reference to Manna as well as in his ending, which emphasizes the power of the "almighty sun" to dissolve the body and reclaim the soul. This image is also supported within the poem by the references of "shed" (radiate), "shines with a mournful light," "that ray, " and "eternal day."

Many other images also lend richness to the poem. The drop of dew is in some ways compared to a tear since it is "shed" and "shines . . . like its own tear." But it also seems to be compared to a drop of blood in the same references to "shed" and the later phrase "congealed." In these two comparisons, then, Marvell ties the poem to the biblical not only through reference to manna but in this allusion to the blood and tears of Christ. Through these images of active grace and Christ's suffering, in conjunction with the strong and active portrayal of the "almighty sun," Marvell seems to suggest the action of grace within the idea of salvation. To this idea, however, he seems to add the suggestion that there is some action necessary on man's part. This idea seems to come through his reference to the drop's "pain," its action of "shun[ning]" and "moving," as well as the idea of "climbing" inherent in the word "ascend." In addition, there may be some connection within the idea of "piety" in the root of "pity."

Connecting images of warmth and light, cold and darkness also play a major role within the poem. Largely, they serve to emphasize the contrast between heaven and earth, good and evil, and yet their ultimate connection. To this end the author uses such phrases as "orient" (shining), "clear region," "shines," "its own light," "warm sun," "bright above," and "white" to refer to the heavenly nature of the soul/drop. These images of light and warmth emphasize the purity of heaven, its goodness and its compassion, and by implication the holy light, the good. Contrasting these images are the dark, colder ones of the earth. These images are found not only in the flower descriptions but also in the phrases "dark beneath" and "congealed and chilled." These images again emphasize the contrast between the qualities of heaven/earth, soul/body through their active portrayal within the poem and through traditional connections between light and dark with goodness and evil. These images also, however, point to the ultimate connection of these forces. Marvell achieves this connection through yet another cycle, that of night-day (where the sun is again the chief power), and through the circular image of the world, which may both reflect and accept light just as the soul connects both good and evil.

Through these images, Marvell has moved the reader from a basic description of a dewdrop, to an active comparison between it and the soul, and finally, to his conclusion of both the comparison and of his vision of the soul. The structure clearly follows and aids the movement of Marvell's ideas by its three verse-paragraph form. Within these paragraphs too, Marvell's structuring mirrors and supports his ideas. As the drop of dew exists in a "restless," "unsecure," and "trembling" state, so the poem begins with an erratic meter and rhyme scheme. As the drop becomes "inclosed" and assumes its "coy figure," so does the poem tighten in form. Within lines 27–32, Marvell increases the regularity of the length and meter of his lines as well as the rhyme scheme so that they, too, move toward harmony and balance with the soul's movement. This regularly [sic] also emphasizes the culmination of his active comparison, which occurs within this section. In the third verse paragraph, the same rhyme scheme is retained so that regularity is still apparent, but Marvell uses too, the somewhat loose, flowing and yet highly regulated iambic lines to emphasize the contrasting description of the soul as being "loose" yet "girt." At the last, the poem again seems to largely lose its regularity perhaps reflecting the dissolution of the soul; yet, there are also many heavy stresses, caesuras, and strong couplet rhyme, which emphasize the summation of his poem, the power of the almighty and the salvation of the soul itself.

Through the strong, basic image of the dew, underlying images of the sun, the cycles of water and light, the suffering of Christ, and the eternal circle, in addition to the structure of the poem, Andrew Marvell creates a complex vision of the soul. Through the opposing and yet connecting nature of his images and structures, he creates the portrait of a soul which is similarly divided and whole. He stresses, especially with contrasting imagery, the inherent goodness of the soul and suggests this inherent connection with the good, Heaven, as the essential element in its salvation. He also, however, hints at the importance of God's active grace and the soul's own attempts (at reconnecting with its good) in the process of salvation. Thus Marvell ends by creating a hopeful vision of life, which is by nature transient and yet eventually connected to the pure and whole of God by its fall from, and eventual return to, grace.

Thank You Miss Alice Walker
Earnestine Johnson

I was required to read the book, *The Color Purple*, by my English course professor. I enjoy reading and therefore I did not mind the assignment. I read the first page and closed the book. I was ashamed of the ignorant definitions given to the parts of the body. I was embarrassed by the explicitness of the sex act. I opened and closed the book many times before I could go beyond the first page. But I did read beyond the first page. I understood the lack of communication between Celie and her mother. Celie was fourteen years old and did not understand or appear to know the functions of her body.

A few days after starting to read this book, I was listening to a news report and heard, ". . . ten-year old mother and baby both doing fine. The young girl and her family did not know she was pregnant until she was ready to give birth, after complaining of severe stomach pains." The newscaster went on to say the authorities were questioning two male acquaintances of the family. Celie's circumstance, like that of the child-mother's, is ageless. Miss Walker, you brought the situation out into the open, awakening my senses. I did not want to see it, read it, feel it, or be a part of it. This was no longer "just a reading assignment." I was enthralled. I had to read on. How else would you shock me, embarrass me, and shame me?

My class is comprised of a mixture of nationalities, but only four of us are black and female. I, embarrassingly, thought of all of them reading the lines of shame and ignorance of my people. I listened as one male classmate disassociated himself from the males in the story. I wondered if it was because the characters were black, or was he so naive that he believed such things did not happen? As a contemporary black female, I have buried the Celies of my past. Then why, Miss Walker, do you awaken those emotions? What do you expect to accomplish by telling me how it was, or is? Why, of all the subjects to write about, do you choose one which hurts me so deeply? I am furious with you.

I knew a lot of Celies in my teenage years. I met a few Sofias. I heard about one or two Shug Averys too. I left them behind along with the old neighborhood. Those encounters were during an impoverished and ignorant period of growth. I chose to forget them. I have grown and expanded from the narrowness of my childhood and developed through the heritage passed on to me. I have also risen through the classes of the ruling society. I speak like them, dress like them, yet I know that I am but a shadow of them.

Miss Walker, I was compelled to go on with the reading of *The Color Purple*. It was the language usage you gave your characters that held my interest this time. My mind's voice spoke the words by Celie so clearly that I could hear Mrs. Brown, from my youth, "Baby, run across to the store. . . ." Sofia became Mama Liz, big boned, dark complected, mammoth breasted, and as stubborn as the day was long, but oh what a heart. She was full of compassion and empathy for all who encountered her. It's the wonderful memories like those that made the reading of your book painful. Celie and Sofia's language was so familiar to me that in spite of the pain, I settled into the good memories the dialogues conjured up. I was also interested in what Nettie had to say, but Nettie's dialogue had connotations of my own language, educated and refined. I heard it every day. It catalyzed no images. But the other characters' dialect brought memories of faces and voices that had long ceased to exist. Those faces had diminished to

just a flicker until your book revived them. Those good memories came with the people you portrayed, along with their
examples of survival. Some of the people I knew were very
much like Shug Avery and many were like Sofia.

Your message was subtle, Miss Walker. Now after the
shame, anger, and memories, I continued to read to the end
of the story. Your characters came full circle. They survived.
They matured and became wiser from their experiences. You
showed me how they accomplished that. Sofia's way was that
of self-reliance and stubbornness. She was not just physically
strong, but she had a strong nature as well. She was also patient
and long suffering. I cannot say that Sofia's way was successful
because she lost so much. She lost her husband and children
to another woman. She lost her freedom to the ruling society,
first jail and then to the mayor's family. Shug Avery was independent and worldly. She learned to stroke the egos of the
people she could not easily maneuver. Shug was a free spirit,
her own person. Celie developed and escaped to a future of
her own making by learning another method of survival than
the one she lived. Celie took a portion of Sofia's stubbornness
and self-reliance and mixed that with a little of Shug's independence and literally walked with a survival plan of her own.

I have read your message Miss Walker, and anguished
through the learning of it. This teaching of survival will not
soon be forgotten because it was too painful an experience to
relearn. It is for the lesson learned that I thank you.

Who's the Fugitive? What's to Flee?

These two essays, even though each was written about a literary
text, differ strikingly. Mays's essay shows absolute confidence in the
security of its situation. Marvel's poem and the English literary
tradition in which it exists need no justification, nor does the act of
explication, which is so utterly possible and desirable that no one
would think of explaining its necessity. Mays's subject embodies its
own self-evident worth; her audience's vital interest in the subject
defies questioning. Her essay speaks with the serenely impersonal
and scientific voice of New Criticism. Completely at ease speaking
with this voice, her essay assumes that the reader has highly sophisticated intellectual and discursive skills; thus, the essay makes no

apparent overtures of invitation to the reader, whose knowledge of
the poem is assumed to be minute. Clearly Mays is sharpening her
skills so that she can herself participate in the ongoing discussion of
Anglo-American canonized literature as her professor (Jerome Beaty)
already does with considerable success. The movement from image
to symbol to structure to theme is, for a first-year student, remarkable. Mays writes like a skilled craftswoman, utterly unconscious of
her technical vocabulary and of the cultural and aesthetic preconceptions that valorize that vocabulary, allowing it to operate with such
innocence, such seeming neutrality.

    Johnson's essay, in contrast, is a struggle from beginning to
end. The first sentence makes clear that she feels herself utterly
unsituated. As a result, she begins by forcing a situation into existence. She addresses her unknown and anonymous reader directly,
explaining why she is writing the essay. Once she has forced a
situation between herself and her reader, she does what the situation
requires; she explains her own reading process, and she explains
the process *as her own*. In the middle of paragraph 2, however,
after a brief anecdote relating Walker's novel to the events recounted
on a local newscast, she shifts her audience in a wrenching, radical
way by addressing Alice Walker directly. After this abrupt change,
her audience shifts back and forth between the anonymous reader
(whom she addresses in paragraphs 3 and 4) and Alice Walker (whom
she addresses in paragraphs 5, 6, and 7). At the point of discussing
Walker's novel in detail, Johnson obviously begins to feel uncomfortable with her anonymous reader, who might never have read have
read *The Color Purple*; as a result, when she needs to presume
knowledge about the novel, she broadens her situation so that she
can address Walker herself. By the end of her essay, Johnson stands
in front of the general audience, but while standing there, she allows
her gaze—in the manner of a character from *Our Town*—to move
back and forth between this general audience and the imaginary
Alice Walker.

    Mays, a fully and unconsciously situated New Critic, would
never begin by explaining that her teacher made her read a poem,
that she had resisted doing the reading, and that her essay had been
written as nothing more than a required classroom exercise. For
Mays, that would be like a new assistant professor's sending an essay
off to *PMLA* that begins,

Having been lucky enough to land a tenure-track job in this dreadful job market, now I've got to get this essay on Marvell published in a first-rate journal or I'll get fired. The reason I'm writing on Marvell is that I wrote my dissertation on him, and it's easier to recycle some of that than to try to come up with something from scratch. With three new course preparations this term, I'm swamped right now.

I wrote my dissertation on Marvell because I made my highest seminar grades in the Renaissance, but I didn't have time to do a dissertation on one of the biggies like Milton or Shakespeare because my assistantship lasted only four years. Anyway, here's what I think no one has yet thought of to say about Marvell. If you don't like this, I'll be more than happy to write what you do like, if you'll just tell me what it is that you like. (I hope you like Marvell. I don't really have time to start over with somebody new, but I can use any methodology you prefer.) I really need to get something in *PMLA* before my tenure review comes up in three years. I think a *PMLA* article would pretty well do the trick.

Mays, like any new assistant professor of literature, knows intuitively that interpretations of canonized literature must never in any way foreground the real reason why they were written (e.g., to get a grade, to get tenure, to get a raise or promotion, to buttress a political position, to refute an enemy or support a friend, etc.). Instead, such interpretations must always take the tone of newly developed, necessary, important, and vitally interesting information. The lived experience of the writer is wholly inappropriate. Johnson, on the other hand, makes no attempt to conceal her lived experience. Since she begins in a completely unsituated way—writing in an unfamiliar form for an uncertain audience on an anguish-ridden, humiliating subject—she does the best she can to bring shape to her situation. For Mays to begin this way would cheapen and debase the high-culture art whose operation she has set out to explicate. Marvell's poem, in the world of Mays's essay, exists absolutely and observably as a set of interrelated, describable features. The essay offers no hint at all about Mays's reading process. Indeed, the most salient feature of Mays's essay is that its own argument, having been constructed through many close rereadings, utterly obliterates any suggestion that the argument *was* constructed or that it could have been constructed differently using different "evidence" from the poem or even that it was constructed through several line-by-line searches, some of which did not reveal what Mays expected, some of which yielded things she knew immediately that she did not want. Her essay, in short, articulates the operation and meaning of Marvell's poem in much the same way that a physicist might write a prose description of the surface tension and molecular structure of a drop of dew. Unlike Johnson's essay, which draws its power from the way Johnson relates her own life situation to the experiences of the characters in Walker's novel, Mays's essay draws its strength from the smoothly elided way in which she excises both herself and Marvell from the essay, leaving the essay as an impersonal explication of an art object that is entirely separable from the lived experience of its author.

Mays and Johnson, in my opinion, embody the extremes of the writing situation. At one extreme, the writer exists in a clearly defined field whose rules and procedures must never appear in the writer's consciousness. At the other extreme, the writer is utterly unsituated and must struggle fiercely to force some sort of situation into existence, often having to shift the situation around as her needs change. Every writer stands somewhere on the spectrum between Mays and Johnson. Mays offers a thoroughly professional response to Marvell; Johnson, in contrast, offers an openly human response to Walker. All writing situations, I believe, begin in the human. With years of codification, however, professional discourses emerge. Most faculty, especially humanities faculty, have no idea at all about how to deal with human situations or with the all too human discourses they engender, but they know very well both how to write professionally and how to recognize those students who have managed to learn their professional discourse. This explains why most faculty prefer not to teach composition. The vast majority of students in composition courses must, like Earnestine Johnson, write as *human* beings; few have learned how to write as *professional* beings. One's tolerance for the human is probably the litmus test for a lifelong career in composition. Most faculty, as David Russell has shown, have no clue about how to teach their own professional discourse. Understandably they try to avoid the problem of teaching their own discourse by limiting their pedagogy to majors and graduate students, who have already begun to write as professionals. So powerful is the attraction of professional discourse, so plain does it appear to most professionals that almost to a person they expect composition teachers to teach one big, generalizable academicspeak. Of course, faculty are never satisfied with the composition program because no such thing as "general academicspeak" exists and therefore composition teachers cannot teach it.

Professional discourse offers the only secure sanctuary in which a teacher can operate. As long as a teacher speaks with a professional voice and teaches that voice to students, the teacher's life remains out of bounds because the teacher's ongoing process of self-construction (together with the unavoidable, unending, uncontrollable, and often maddening process of self-deconstruction) seems complete. The finished, cool, and manipulative sound of the teacher's professional discourse creates a magic spell in the classroom; indeed, to a large degree the teacher, exercising the power of professional discourse, becomes an integrated, completed being at the expense of the incoherent, voiceless, and ignorant students who have no (or at best limited) access to the professional voice. It matters not whether the teacher is going through a divorce, failing as a parent, struggling financially, worrying about academic and scholarly accomplishments, suffering over sexual identity, frightened about the environment, scared by political upheavals, or whatever other life crises may be happening.

Once the first word of human discourse gets spoken, however, all of the teacher's real life comes right into the classroom, and the students are free to treat the teacher as a human being just like themselves. The teacher's very process of self-situation becomes an issue as *the teacher's situation*, and the haphazard way the teacher finally came to inhabit this situation, becomes one of the discussable matters in the class. Behaving professionally prevents all this and carefully situates the students as initiates in a code of demonstration, a code that does its work and reveals its information quite apart from any human intervention, quite apart from anyone's life.

Like any binary opposition, of course, this opposition between professional and human discourses begs to be deconstructed. As usual, such deconstruction threatens only the privileged, professional voice. Because human discourse is always already discounted as being nothing more than the unprofessional musings of a human being, human discourse has little to lose if an analyst shows its dependency on professional discourse. Professional discourse, in contrast, has a great deal to lose. Because the purpose of professional discourse is to escape the human, professional discourse suffers immeasurably when an analyst reveals its dependency *on* the human. More importantly, professional discourse risks being discovered not as an opposition with human discourse but rather as the distorted voice *of* human discourse. No professional wants to be found guilty of offering a merely human opinion. Every human being already has an opinion; the professional needs to offer something considerably more than mere opinion. As a result, one of the roles of research in composition, even though it may be a minor role, is to show how the professional being is nothing more than a human being speaking some sort of historically constructed code. Such professional codes, and the professional beings who are allowed to exist and to speak through them, generate discourses that seem to escape the human in order to speak with the disembodied, disinterested, professional voice of scientific demonstration. Aristotle invented that voice. So that we who teach writing are never deceived when we hear it, let me offer a brief introduction to the anatomy and physiology of its original speaker, who turns out to have been a very "typical," *human* being. He had a larynx much like anyone else's, and he, like us, occasionally suffered from laryngitis. There are times when his voice, in spite of its profound power, is wrong. There are times, indeed, when his voice may not have been his at all. Indeed, it seems that the binary opposition between human discourse and professional discourse is not an opposition at all. The relationship is less opposition than ventriloquism. What one needs here is not deconstruction so much as history.

Aristotle: The First Process Writer

Aristotle's texts themselves embody just the sort of *human* situation I am describing. "Their repetitions and slight divergences of view" exist, as David Ross puts it, because Aristotle "did not deal with a subject once and for all, but returned to it again and again." Such recursiveness, coupled with "unskillful editorship has often preserved, through unwillingness to sacrifice anything that the master had written, double or triple versions of his thought on the same question" (17). The *Rhetoric*, appropriately enough, is the best example of what Ross describes.[1] George Kennedy says that the *Rhetoric*, like Aristotle's other treatises, is a "developing work," and he asks that we read the text accordingly.[2]

For Aristotle, rhetoric was a sort of intellectual strange attractor. He never quite got straight either what role he wanted it to play or how much importance he wanted to give it, yet he could never rid himself of it as a subject of interest. As a result, when one reads his *Rhetoric* one occupies moments of intellectual clarity, but as one moves from one moment to another the differing moments sometimes complement, sometimes conflict with, and sometimes negate each other. In spite of their shifting, incompatible nature, however, Aristotle could never bear to give up any of these moments, and neither could his editors, who wanted to keep everything, even if it had already been said, even, in fact, if it had been contradicted. In Book I, for example, it is easy to agree with Aristotle's attacks on, and contempt for, the demagoguery of an emotional appeal. It is, however, equally easy in Book II and Book III to learn a great deal about how to *make* an emotional appeal.

Attempts at establishing *the* text of the *Rhetoric*, or at least of determining which parts were written when, as Edward Cope said so trenchantly over a century ago, throw a mixture of "light" and "obscurity" on the text and are always "unsatisfactory." No matter how careful the textual bibliographer may be, Cope concludes, "no certainty is attainable; and we have to content ourselves with sufficiently vague and indefinite conjectures as to the time and mode of the composition of the work" (*Introduction* 37–45). Is there any way, for example, to know whether Aristotle says Isocrates was experienced or inexperienced in the law courts (1368^a20)? How can we hope to make comfortable and satisfactory sense of the less-to-greater argument at the end of Book II (1397^b15–20). Are we in fact justified in adding the iota to Socrates' name (1399^b9) even though every extant manuscript omits it? Did Aristotle merely have a slip of the pen? Questions of this sort are endless.

Very likely, different parts of the extant text of the *Rhetoric* were written in three different decades. "Awareness of this extended genesis," Brian Vickers explains, "is essential for the understanding of a text that otherwise seems in places self-contradictory." At any particular place in the text, the reader feels secure, but the security is always transitory because each moment of clarity is succeeded by a different moment, perhaps written at a time twenty years distant from the previous moment. This collection of moments, a collection spread out over most of Aristotle's adult life, gives the text, in Vickers's words, a "composite" feel, making "it impossible to form a clear view of Aristotle's final thoughts on the subject" (18). And when one adds in the intertextual way in which Aristotle wrote, referring again and again to other texts as a way of leaving the current text elliptical, the feeling of compositness grows even more pronounced.

Kennedy is more sanguine than Vickers. In the appendixes to his new translation he concludes with considerable confidence that "Aristotle left the treatise in substantially the form in which we have it and that it represents his thinking at one point in time, that it was read as a unity by students from ancient to modern times without serious difficulties, and that what is important is not how it evolved but how it can be understood as a theory of rhetoric." Achieving this comfort zone of understanding, however, as Kennedy goes on to admit, because of the hasty, haphazard feel of the *Rhetoric*, "does require the conscientious reader to exercise considerable ingenuity in interpreting some passages to mean something different from what they literally say."[3] Kennedy certainly knows all of the reasons for arguing that the *Rhetoric* is nothing but a hopeless mess. In *Classical Rhetoric*, for example, he admits that the structure of Book II after chapter 17 "is confusing," and he guesses "that the material stretching from Book I, chapter 3, through Book II, chapter 17, represents an insertion into an earlier stage of the text." This insertion, Kennedy continues, came "at a time when Aristotle became convinced that an art of rhetoric limited to the matter of rational proof" neither described the art he knew nor met the requirements of philosophical rhetoric laid down by Plato. Kennedy's catalog of the problems in Book II shows that he has tried to foreground all the reasons for concluding that the *Rhetoric* is a hopeless mess (76). Through his ingenious ability to interpret passages differently from what they literally say, however, Kennedy can admit that "Aristotle was not able to resist bringing into the discussion most of the material of which he was aware, even at the expense of his original definition" (72) while at the same time concluding that the *Rhetoric* holds together as a whole and intelligible work.

In other words, as Vickers teaches us, the *Rhetoric* "seems" self-contradictory only so long as one does not recognize that its parts were written in three different decades, or, failing that, as Kennedy teaches us, it seems incoherent only as long as one lacks sufficient ingenuity to discover how passages mean something other than what they "literally say."

Cope, Vickers, and Kennedy, eminent scholars and rhetoricians all, write as professionals, in the disinterested, demonstrative discourse of the academic humanities. They inherited that voice from Aristotle, and they have the luxury of speaking through it as if they themselves have never struggled as human beings, as if this detached professional discourse is the most natural thing in the world. Aristotle, of course, had no choice but to write as a human being trying to make sense out of life in troubled and frightening times. What we have from him is the record of a text in process. In many ways the text reads like that of an inexperienced composition student: Aristotle put in everything he knew (even if some of the things he put in differed from other things that were already there), he repeated himself, he contradicted himself, he wrote many, many sentences whose intent we can only guess at, and he never got around to giving his text that seamless, *finished* quality that we professionals so desire.

What we have from his professional exegetes, in contrast, is a series of texts whose process has been hidden. The "standard theory" of the composition history of the *Rhetoric*, which goes back at least as far as Adolf Kantelhardt's 1911 Göttingen dissertation and was argued most forcefully by Friedrich Solmsen in 1929, shows what I mean. Thomas Cole calls it the "widely held and probably correct view" (156), and Jacqueline de Romilly builds her reading of Aristotle on it. Her explanation takes us back to the old ἀντίστροφος argument. De Romilly sees Book I, chapter 2, as having been written much later than Book I, chapter 1, and she regards the definition of rhetoric in chapter 2 as enriching rhetoric in that it synthesizes and critiques everyone from Gorgias and Plato to Isocrates, finally settling rhetoric "at the highest place among authentic sciences" (62–66). To get where she wants to go, de Romilly cuts off Book I, chapter 1, as well as all of Book III. She cuts off Book I, chapter 1, by arguing that it was an early draft that was later obviated by chapter 2. Then she dismisses Book III by arguing that it is "less essential to Aristotle's approach." This has the wonderful effect of insulating her reading of the *Rhetoric* from an attack by anyone using either Book I, chapter 1, or Book III. Book I, chapter 1, no longer counts because it is merely a now-rejected "first draft." And if anything in Book III calls her reading into question, then she can dismiss it because that book is not integral to Aristotle's approach. Of course, if Book III turns out to be spurious after all, or perhaps a different and utterly unrelated prior text, then it matters not because Book III is always already not integral to Aristotle's approach.

The standard theory, whether or not one accepts de Romilly's interpretation of it, has been refined recently by John Rist (85–86, 136–44) and Kennedy (*Aristotle* 299–309). In general, according to the standard theory, Books I and II (if one omits Book I, chapter 1, and Book II, chapters 23–24) seem to be a kind of loose confederation of ideas assembled, but not carefully revised, sometime in the 330s. Book III, however, seems to be a different work entirely, perhaps written during the Academy period, perhaps, as Kennedy would have it, written parallel to but separate from Books I and II and joined to them by Andronicus of Rhodes three centuries after Aristotle's death.[4] Only the most evangelical of the unified-text critics tries to find a way to justify including chapters 2–17 of Book II—the sections of the *Rhetoric* dealing with ethical and pathetic appeals—in a text introduced by Book I, chapter 1, which so bitterly attacks any sort of pathetic appeal. Aldo Scaglione, in his inscrutable way, perhaps succeeds better than anyone in describing the problem of understanding the relationships of the various parts of the *Rhetoric* by calling the problem a task of "delicate interpretation" (12).

In fact, the standard theory is little more than a lacuna that implies more agreement than exists. Rist, for example, has one idea of the "early core" of Books I and II, Kennedy another. As recently as the 1950s, Ingemar Düring (258–59) turned the standard theory on its head, arguing, albeit cryptically and based largely on the absence of Demosthenes from Book I and Book II, that both Books were written during the Academy period (between 360 and 355), an idea that Anton-Hermann Chroust (1.115) at least provisionally supports. William Fortenbaugh, working from Düring's notions of the sequence of composition, argues that Aristotle wrote Book I, chapter 2, *before* he wrote chapter 1, which obviously makes hash of de Romilly's theory of the development of Aristotelian rhetoric, and which, if proven, would refute Kennedy. At about the same time Düring published his ideas about the sequence of composition, Joseph Zürcher argued at length that the authorship of the entire "Aristotelian canon" is questionable, a notion that Chroust spends several pages rehearsing in his preface.[5]

Daemonstraitening the *Rhetoric*

Once one has access to the finished and cool voice of professional discourse, it is, of course, possible to dehumanize almost any text.

That, in my opinion, is what William Grimaldi and Eugene Ryan do, even though anyone who reads their scholarship cannot help being impressed both by its detail and by its range. Grimaldi and Ryan transmute the record of one human being's struggle with a notion that both attracted and repelled him into a finished and complete thesis-driven example of professional discourse.

Grimaldi is a good bit less canny in his dehumanization of the text than is Ryan. Grimaldi begins with two assumptions: (1) Plato is the greatest philosopher of all time; and (2) Aristotle has written a whole and consistent rhetoric that is thoroughly Platonic.[6] Grimaldi begins his argument by addressing the old claim that the *Rhetoric* is nothing more than students' notes reorganized and stitched together by some unknown editor. Then, using the enthymeme as his point of departure, he tries to demonstrate that the *Rhetoric* is "a unified structure open to no major contradictions." Through a proper understanding of the enthymeme, he contends, we can situate ourselves in a manner similar to that described by Kennedy above, a manner through which "text statements which appear to militate against the unity and coherence of the text are susceptible to interpretation which makes them both intelligible and acceptable as essential expressions of Aristotle's rhetorical theory" (28–52).

Throughout his demonstration of the *Rhetoric*, Grimaldi's professional voice remains secure and confident. Grimaldi even calls his text a "demonstration," and he claims that his "demonstration" does what a demonstration always does: it offers "a correct understanding" (29–30). So clear is Grimaldi's demonstrative language that he can state with full self-confidence that "In this attempt no pre-conceptions about any theories of language were brought to the text." The "only question put to the text," he continues is "What do you mean?" The security of his professional question allows Aristotle's text to professionalize itself. "The more Aristotle's text, together with its many interpretations, was studied, the more it began to emerge that the text became tractable and understandable with the explanation offered here, even though this explanation with its strongly organic theory of language may sound to some more modern than ancient" (57–58). So tractable does the text become, so strong and clear its demonstrated meaning, that Grimaldi, like de Romilly, does not even need to address Book III, which is not "necessary for the purpose of this study" (49).[7]

Twelve years after Grimaldi published his monograph demonstrating the organic wholeness and consistency of the *Rhetoric*, Eugene Ryan published his own book, effectively accomplishing the same purpose. In meticulous detail, Ryan goes back through all the "Yes, it is! No, it isn't!" arguments about the textual integrity of the *Rhetoric*. After foregrounding all these arguments, Ryan enables his own demonstration by announcing that Aristotle himself put the treatise together; hence, "we can well expect to find in the finished work an attempt at synthesis" (19).

Ryan's book reveals the great power of professional discourse, especially as it works its demonstrative magic for the professional humanist. Such discourse has the power of settling any question inside the borders of the professional interpretation itself. Grimaldi can settle the question, as can Ryan, Kennedy, Vickers, Elizabeth Blettner (49–54), and an endless host of others. Outside the settled and settling voice of each professional explication, however, the thing explicated remains ever in need of being resettled. Grimaldi and Kennedy settle an issue that Ryan resettles, Vickers resettles, and Kennedy resettles yet again. Then along comes James Berlin with a Marxist analytical strategy, and all the settlings need correcting. Berlin argues that the emphasis on enthymeme and rational proof in Book I as opposed to the emphasis on audience in Book II results not so much from the fact that Aristotle wrote different parts of the *Rhetoric* at different times but rather from the fact that Aristotle failed in his "attempt to address the class conflicts of his time, conflicts that represent important ideological differences." Book I, according to Berlin, reflects the world of educated, responsible aristocracy. Book II, in contrast, deals with the reality of a popular democracy. This class split leads to "a contradictory division of rational and emotional proofs that reflects and reproduces, rather than resolves, the major contradictions in Athenian class structure." The *Rhetoric*, Berlin concludes, remains "a hopelessly conflicted text." Though Aristotle attempts to resolve the conflict between aristocracy and democracy, he fails because he "remains committed to an elitist politics while offering enough contradictory concessions to the democratic polis to give support to those who later appropriate him in the service of an egalitarian rhetoric" (Aristotle's *Rhetoric* 1–13).

Aristotle's (All Too Human) Beard

Looked at from the perspective of composition studies, the textual history of Aristotle's *Rhetoric* occupies a place of importance similar to that of contemporary chaos studies. No one thinks that composition teachers could do their jobs better if they mastered the mathematics that make the study of chaos possible, though everyone would probably agree that a passing knowledge of chaos studies— at a level somewhere near that of James Gleick's popular book— would be useful. By the same token, no one (or at most only a few diehards) thinks that composition teachers could do their jobs better if every composition teacher in every classroom had a fully articulated and defensible notion of the sequence in which Aristotle wrote what we now call the *Rhetoric*. Because of the *Rhetoric's* importance to the history of the teaching of writing, however, we can learn a good bit from it about the very human way in which early writing always works, as well as a good bit about how professional discourse manages the trick of seeming to escape from the human. The extant text of the *Rhetoric* records a long-term struggle, a struggle far from resolution. Almost without exception that sort of struggle stands behind every written text. Any modern writer can use writing to mask the struggle, to conceal the uncertainties, the lacunae, and the outright ignorance that motivated and limited the text from the moment the writer (or writers) knew that a text was occurring. Most modern writers do just that, especially in academic writing, the sort supposed to convey knowledge. Clearly Kelly Mays used writing this way in her composition class at Emory. After all, if we foreground the process of writing, we expose the ontological implications of writing and begin to ask who "we" are, as Earnestine Johnson does throughout her essay. Any professor who allows a discussion of who "we" are runs the risk of losing both professorial and professional authority. When that happens, the professor becomes nothing more than an experienced student, someone with a little more time in harness but someone in harness nevertheless—someone in exactly the same sort of harness as everyone else in the room. No one gets to stand behind the team and drive. Anyone can pose the question "Who are you?" to anyone else.

As, for example, one might ask of Aristotle. Who was he? Like the text of the *Rhetoric*, the biography of its author is an aporia. Was Aristotle a lifelong political agent, a member of the Macedonian CIA? Was he a traveling medicine man? A drug dealer? A dissolute, illiterate, and dissipated thug who squandered his patrimony and turned to philosophy at age thirty when all his resources were gone? Was he, as Peter Green (working from Strabo, Diogenes Laertius, and Werner Jaeger) describes him, a foppish, balding, spindle-shanked, small-eyed man who "in an effort to compensate for these disadvantages . . . wore dandified clothes, cut and curled his hair in an affected manner, and spoke with a lisp"? Did he indeed flaunt his wealth by wearing too many gaudy rings, giving an overall effect "rather like the young Disraeli at his worst" (54)? Was he indeed tutor to Alexander the Great? If he was, did he have great or little effect on the rising king? Was he Isocrates' pupil before moving on to Plato's Academy? Did Aristotle die of a stomach ailment? Of a broken heart? From the natural causes of old age? By suicide at Chalcis? Or (à la Socrates) by drinking hemlock in Athens?

None of these questions is answerable in any definitive way. They are all like Aristotle's beard, which, as we know from Al-Mubashir, was thick, and which, as we know from Usaibia, was sparse (see Chroust 1.62 for an introduction to these contradictory, unresolvable traditions). Of course, each of us is "ingenious" enough (as Kennedy would expect) to reconcile these descriptions by imagining that Aristotle had few hairs on his face but that each individual hair shaft was thick. Each of us is also ingenious enough, however, to know that our explanation has nothing to do with the degree to which a certain Macedonian of the fourth century B.C. who lived much of his life in Athens and probably wrote some of the most formative texts of Western culture was (or was not) hirsute.

The academic response to these questions—one might call it the humanistic as opposed to the human response—is that none of them matters. What Aristotle did for rhetoric (as well as for astronomy, biology, economics, philosophy, political science, etc.) stands on its own. If he participated in murdering the citizens of Olynthus, if he betrayed his own home city of Stagiros so that it could be razed more easily, if he helped to poison Alexander, even if he was the oddball, effete, extravagant, miserable wretch that Peter Green describes him as, his ideas still stand on their own. They are separable from the man, the lived life. They are, in brief, important texts in the humanities, not the texts of a human being. For composition studies, however, where most students still write as human beings, perhaps it is not a bad idea to dredge up the enigma with the name Aristotle, to remember the lived life from which our notions of communication emerged.

Both Chroust (1.120–23, 133–39, 141–72) and Green (54) argue that Aristotle's primary occupation throughout his entire adult life was as a Macedonian political agent. One might well compare Aristotle's role in the court of King Philip with John Milton's role in Oliver Cromwell's Protectorate or the role played by Benjamin Franklin and Thomas Jefferson after the American Revolution. After the Cromwell government executed Charles I, Milton undertook the intellectual defense of regicide and puritan theocracy and successfully battled the leading intellectuals on the Continent. During and after the revolution, Franklin and Jefferson undertook to explain in European terms why the revolution was necessary and why it would lead to a better world. "It would be unusual, indeed," Chroust argues

> if Aristotle, intellectually the most prominent Macedonian of his time, the best educated Macedonian conversant with Athenian and Greek conditions in general, and the close friend of King Philip and Antipater, should not have played an active and, perhaps, important role in the meteoric rise of Macedonia from a relatively insignificant and semi-barbaric mountain people to a cosmocracy within one generation—the generation of Aristotle. In keeping with his peculiar talents and interests, and by making use of his acquaintance with Athenian and Greek intellectuals, as well as consonant with his intellectual stature—qualifications which were extremely rare in Macedonia during the fourth century B.C.—it is only natural that Athens, the intellectual capital of the Hellenic world and one of the most important centers of Greek political activism, should become the place of Aristotle's political and diplomatic activities: He was dispatched to Athens in order to work for and, if possible, to facilitate the political aims and aspirations of Macedonia and, at the same time, to keep a watchful eye on any anti-Macedonian stirrings in Athens and throughout Greece. (171–72)

After a twenty-year stay, Aristotle probably left Athens in 348–47 for two reasons: first, Philip wanted him to go to the court of Hermias of Atarneus so he could work as a spy near the Hellespont; second, Philip had just enraged the Athenians by destroying the city of Olynthus, and Athens was rife with rumors that Aristotle had given Philip the names of the Athenian sympathizers there, betraying them to certain death. Thus it would have been dangerous for Aristotle to remain in Athens; besides, with his professional stature and his international experience, Aristotle could serve Philip more usefully by planning the invasion of Asia Minor than by trying to spy in a city where everyone suspected him.

Aristotle apparently used philosophy and science as a cover for his activities as a spy, and before his cover was blown, he managed to remain in the Hellespont until 343. From 343 onward, Aristotle's primary work was as an agent for the Macedonian court, and he did not return to Athens until Macedonian military might sent him back, "in the van of the conquering Macedonian phalanx," as Chroust puts it. Once again in Athens, after an absence of twelve years during which Macedonia had asserted itself as *the* dominant force in Greece, Aristotle was genuinely feared and hated as a foreign agent, "a particularly untrustworthy, treacherous and dangerous person," an "unwanted and suspected 'resident alien,'" according to Chroust (147–54).

It seems, therefore, that the human being named Aristotle, from his days as a student at Plato's Academy until his death (probably) on Chalcis, worked as a political agent. He stayed in Athens until the razing of Olynthus established Macedonia as a true power to be reckoned with and his cover was blown, and he returned in 335 only when Athens was under complete Macedonian domination. Then he fled Athens precipitously a second time in 323 when Alexander's death unleashed the winds of Athenian revolt against Macedonia. Chroust even goes so far as to hint that Aristotle could not have written much during his second Athenian stay (the period during which he is supposed to have taught at the Lyceum and written most of his important texts) because he was far too busy as Alexander's political agent.

S(h)aving Aristotle's Beard

It is easy to see how a professional would write about Aristotle. Every respectable library has thousands of books and articles on Aristotle that demonstrate the rules. But given the Aristotelian influence on all forms of written discourse, how should someone who teaches human beings how to write as human beings write about Aristotle? Is it safe to occupy the speaking position enabled by his rhetoric and to use the modes and the appeals defined by his rhetoric? Are those "rhetorical" strategies separable from human life? To what degree are they always already politically situated in such a way as to force reaction and struggle? After all, there is ample evidence that Aristotle began his studies in Athens at the feet of Isocrates and that he came to Plato as a sort of rebel against Isocratean rhetoric, against which he published a vitriolic attack in the now lost *Gryllus*?[8] Based on Isocrates' *Antidosis*, on the surviving hints about Aristotle's *Gryllus* and *Protrepticus*, and on Cephisodorus's four-volume *Against Aristotle*, which was an extended denunciation of Aristotle's attack on Isocrates, one can make a fairly good case that Aristotle was Isocrates' pupil before transferring to the Academy. Chroust even hints that the *Gryllus* may have been the price Aristotle paid for full admission into the Academy, as well as for permission to teach the Aristotelian version of rhetoric at Plato's school (114; see also 98–102). Aristotle was, after all, always a painfully self-aware outsider, a wealthy alien who could never own property, a distinguished scholar who could never succeed Plato because no alien could be the controlling force in the Academy. Whatever the degree of his fame, he had to use the public Lyceum area because of his inability to have a true school of his own. Apparently Aristotle wrote to Antipater in 323 as he was fleeing Athens for the second time that it had become "perilous for an alien to live in Athens" (Chroust 1.147). In fact, many aliens lived quite comfortably in Athens. Athens was dangerous only for a Macedonian alien who made his living as a spy and had a habit of providing information that led to genocide. Athenian—and indeed general Greek—acceptance of the Macedonian hegemony was always grudging because all the Greeks, and particularly the Athenians, regarded the Macedonians as upstart semibarbarians. Every time rumors of the death of Philip or Alexander hit Athens, the city erupted with joyous celebration. Because of Aristotle's reputation as a dangerous spy, he was particularly susceptible to the sort of treatment spies have received in all cultures at all times.

To what degree is the history of rhetoric, as far as Aristotle has shaped and influenced that history, partially the result of a political power struggle in which Aristotle lined up with Plato against Isocrates and all those other "alien intellectuals" living in Athens under the name created for them by Plato, the name "rhetorician"? One can, of course, write a history in which good wins out over bad, philosophy and philosophical rhetoric win out over nihilism and sophistical rhetoric, and Athens wins out over the relativist and atheistical linguistic manipulations of the aliens (Aristotle being a spiritual Athenian in this case). In large part that is the history we have lived now for twenty-five centuries. In this history, "sophist" becomes the label for any opponent. Once anyone can be labeled a sophist or any discourse labeled sophistical, both the person and the discourse have been dismissed completely.[9] Can we make any guess as to what kind of person the pedagogy growing from that history produces? Is it fair for me to name a few people whom we know the pedagogy produced? Alcibiades, Critias, and Plato, for example, or Aristotle and Alexander? When one ties education up with the instilled drive for ἀρετή, when one structures education so that it is competitive and agonistic at all times, when the wealth and class of a student's parents constitute *the* defining criteria for educability, when one evaluates students and publicly announces their relative success on a daily basis, when one uses education to single out the elite scholars who will be set apart from their peers for special treatment and special privileges, when one defines education as a laboratory agon intended to prepare students for the agon of life, when one conceives of education in all these ways, are the winners not likely to construe themselves as somehow superior, as people who truly deserve more than everyone else? Critias thought himself so superior to other Athenians that it was okay for him to rob them and even murder them if they got in his way. Alexander thought it was his heroic destiny to rule the entire world, so he murdered and ransacked his way from Greece all the way to India, all in an effort to establish himself as the true descendent of Achilles.

If one can believe Green, Aristotle's influence on Alexander was profound and enduring. Green argues that Aristotle's pedagogical relationship with Alexander carried "very special personal and political responsibilities"; that Aristotle's influence on Alexander was "fundamental" both in its xenophobia and its high-minded, philosophical asceticism (59–61); that Alexander's Homeric notion of ἀρετή, the notion of the great and powerful king-warrior, came from Aristotle; that much of Alexander's political acumen in dealing with Persia came from Aristotle (235, 299); that Alexander and his staff "took their fundamental notions on the geography of India from Aristotle" (404); and that Alexander kept up a correspondence with Aristotle all through the Asian campaign (458–59).[10] In fact, Green goes so far as to argue that Aristotle's concession in *Politics* (1253^a–1284^b, 1288^a28ff.) allowing for the great man with superior ἀρετή to transcend the collective political entity and become king was nothing but a construct created for Philip and then Alexander to fill. With this formative and continuing closeness in mind, what in the world is one to make of the fact that Plutarch (77.1–3), Arrian (7.27), Quintus Curtius (10.10.14–17), Justin (12.14), and Pausanius (8.18.4), in short, *every extant ancient source* of the life of Alexander agrees that Aristotle prepared the drug and participated in the plot to murder his former pupil (Green 476)? Would it make any difference at all if we could know for sure that Aristotle had as much influence on Alexander as a teacher can have on a pupil, that Alexander, in trying to live up to his mentor's notion of heroic, individual ἀρετή, became one of the most brutal military campaigners the world has ever known, and that for completely political reasons, Aristotle finally masterminded the plot to murder his own "creation"?

What kind of world, after all, did Aristotle live in, and how much did the dynamics of that world—the speaking positions that it offers, the notions of humanity that it creates, the values that it sends us—create ours?

If the extant literature and the leading intellectuals of fourth-century Greece can be believed (which, in my opinion, they cannot), the Athens that Aristotle knew was a veritable cesspool of mob rule and social disorder. All our sources are "out of sympathy with or actively hostile towards the Athenian democracy" (P. Jones 198).[11] From the beginning both the democracy and the function of rhetoric within the democracy came under attack. Herodotus, for example, writing a full century before Aristotle, praises the reasoned judgment of the Spartan king Cleomenes and condemns the gullibility of the Athenian democracy:

> Indeed, so anxious was [Aristagoras of Miletus] to get Athenian aid, that he promised everything that came into his head, until at last he succeeded. Apparently it is easier to impose upon a crowd than upon an individual, for Aristagoras, who had failed to impose upon Cleomenes, succeeded with thirty thousand Athenians. (V.97)[12]

When Thucydides picks up the narrative, the contempt for rhetoric and democracy grows stronger book by book throughout his text. In Book I (68–71), the Corinthian ambassador accuses the Athenians of being "by nature incapable of either living a quiet life themselves or of allowing anyone else to do so" (70). In Book II (65), Thucydides ridicules the Athenian democracy for its inconsistent treatment of

Pericles, calling the city a government by the "mob" and complaining
that after Pericles true democracy descended on the city, which
"naturally led to a number of mistakes." The clear implication is that
the democratic form of government itself led to the disastrous naval
expedition to Sicily in 415 and ultimately to defeat in the Peloponnesian War. In Book III (36–50), Thucydides presents the Mitylene
debate as democracy at its worst. The Athenians voted one day to
execute Mitylene's entire adult male population and to sell the
women and children into slavery; the next day they changed their
minds and had to send out a trireme on an all-night rowing mission
to overtake the first trireme and prevent the slaughter. For Thucydides, this does not represent a true change of heart, an act of vicious
anger mitigated by an act of genuine repentance; rather, it demonstrates yet one more example of the bumbling, ever-changing result
of rule by the mob. In Book IV (21 and 28) where he takes up Cleon,
whom he regarded as a "mere rhetorician" rather than a true "first-
citizen," Thucydides makes clear his contempt for states governed
by the will of the people and especially for "politicians-rhetoricians"
who aim at trying to please the people by doing what they think
the people want.[13] In Book VIII (67–68) where he describes the vote
for the oligarchic coup of 411, Thucydides makes clear his attraction
to Antiphon, whom he regarded as a great leader largely because
the Athenian people distrusted and disliked him so intensely.

Herodotus and Thucydides do no more than speak their class
prejudice. "Aristocrats and members of the upper classes in general,"
Donald Kagan points out, "regarded democracy as a novel, unnatural, unjust, incompetent, and vulgar form of government" (*Pericles*
101). In the fourth century, the attacks grew more strident as the
aristocrats articulated their social theories more fully. Nearly every
Athenian intellectual opposed the democracy. By the time Aristotle
returned to Athens at the head of the conquering Macedonian occu-
piers in 335, most Athenian intellectuals supported the idea of a
Macedonian hegemony simply because it offered the only available
means of destroying the democracy. Faced with a choice between
democracy and a king from the boondocks, the intellectuals clearly
preferred a bumpkin king. Without question, all four of the major
fourth-century intellectuals (Xenophon, Plato, Isocrates, and Aristotle) opposed the democracy (see Hornblower 141, Strauss 232,
and Kagan, *Great* 147).[14]

I rehearse all this for two reasons. First, I want to remind the field of composition studies the degree to which Aristotle's education and his mature theorizing are situated in antidemocratic ideology, and second, I want to foreground the nature of professional discourse, a discourse begun for us by Xenophon, Plato, and Isocrates and brought to fruition by Aristotle. This professional discourse, with all its clinical precision and analytical power, exists only in writing, and it always situates the writer outside and above the lived experience of the community. Professional discourse allows its speaker to "know" life and to "plan" life in a way that no one caught up in the vicissitudes of quotidian process could ever have the perspective or the vocabulary to do. "In no community whatsoever," Plato has The Stranger say to Young Socrates in *Statesman* (297b–c), "could it happen that a large number of people received this gift of political wisdom and the power to govern by pure intelligence which would accompany it. Only in the hands of the select few or of the enlightened individual can we look for that right exercise of political power which is itself the one true constitution." The Stranger makes clear that the state must be run like a ship, with the leader as captain determining what can and will happen, what cannot and will not happen. The crew exists (and is happiest!) when it receives orders from an enlightened captain. With such a ruler in place, a ruler freed from written law and responsible only to his own elevated moral and ethical code, "no wrong can possibly be done."

Writing about the notion of "equality" in *Laws* (757a–d) near the end of his life, Plato rearticulates this notion of human value and social hierarchy. In a well-run state, the Athenian explains to Clinias, "There can never be friendship between the slave and his owner, nor between the base and the noble." The wisdom of Zeus always "assigns more to the greater and less to the lesser, adapting its gifts to the real character of either. . . . ever awarding a greater share to those of greater worth, and to their opposites in trained goodness such share as is fit." And once again we are in Silver City, Mississippi, where the discourse attributes oligarchy and social injustice to divine intent. Only in the *Republic*, however, does Plato vent the fullness of his spleen against democracy. One can see the curl of Plato's lip as he lets his Socrates say that in a democracy the city is "chock full of liberty and freedom of speech," a place where everyone "has license to do as he likes" (557b). A democracy is "anarchic and motley," Socrates continues a few lines later (558c), "assigning a kind of equality indiscriminately to equals and unequals alike!" The democrat indulges

> the appetite of the day, now winebibbing and abandoning himself to the lascivious pleasing of the flute and again drinking only water and dieting, and at one time exercising his body, and sometimes idling and neglecting all things, and at another time seeming to occupy himself with philosophy. And frequently he goes in for politics and bounces up and says and does whatever enters his head. And if military men excite his emulation, thither he rushes, and if moneyed men, to that he turns, and there is no order of compulsion in his existence, but he calls this life of his the life of pleasure and freedom and happiness and cleaves to it to the end. (561d)

This democratic orgy leads inexorably to social decay, the "climax of popular liberty" in which "the purchased slaves, male and female, are no less free than the owners who paid for them." Then with his patriarchal watchdogs at full howl, the Platonic Socrates charges democracy with the ultimate: women demand the right to speak as men and sexual control breaks down. "Without experience of it," Socrates shakes his head sadly,

> no one would believe how much freer the very beasts subject to men are in such a city than elsewhere. The dogs literally verify the adage and "like their mistresses become." And likewise the horses and asses are wont to hold on their way the utmost freedom and dignity, bumping into everyone who meets them and who does not step aside. And so all things everywhere are just bursting with the spirit of liberty. (563b–c)

This complaint about excessive freedom of women, slaves, and thetes became a refrain, almost a mantra for the Athenian upper classes. It appeared long before Plato in the "Old Oligarch's" *Constitution of the Athenians* (1.10–12), where the anonymous author complains that "you can't hit a slave in Athens, and a slave will not stand aside for you."[15] You cannot hit slaves, he complains, because they are indistinguishable from true citizens, and they will not stand aside for you because they have come to think of themselves as having human rights roughly equal to those of citizens. After Plato, this old saw appears again in Aristotle's *Politics*: in radical democracies, Aristotle complains citing a play by Euripides, "everybody lives as he likes, and 'unto what end he listeth' " (1310ª30–36). And this is not the only place in the *Politics* where Aristotle essentially quotes Plato. In Book VI (1317ᵇ), for example, Aristotle accuses democracy of depending on "equality according to number, not worth," a claim identical to the one in *Republic* 558c, and then he condemns democracy as nothing more than the liberty "for a man to live as he likes," a claim identical to the one made by the Old Oligarch, Euripides, and Plato all three. Perhaps more to the point, in the *Republic* Plato argues that democracy can begin only after the rabble kill or exile their betters and that it can end only in tyranny. Aristotle lets this teleological notion of democracy pervade all of his *Politics*. In effect, "Aristotle wished to teach others what he already knew, that Athenian democracy was inherently bad and bound to pursue mistaken policies" (Strauss 232). In his classbound way, Aristotle seems incapable of viewing democracy as anything other than those of "low birth, poverty, and vulgarity" overthrowing those of "high birth, wealth, and education" who are the natural masters (*Politics* 1317ᵇ38–41). His political theory merely reinscribes the system of social distinctions based on supposed "worth."

Even when Aristotle tries to be evenhanded and fair-minded about democracy, he never really succeeds.[16] Each time he tries to deal fairly with democracy, he falls back into the language of his prejudice. His longest and most sustained defense of democracy occurs in *Politics* (1281ª39–1282ª25). "It is possible," he admits,

> that the many, though not individually good men, yet when they come together may be better, not individually but collectively, than those who are so, just as public dinners to which many contribute are better than those supplied at one man's cost; for where there are many, each individual, it may be argued, has some portion of virtue and wisdom, and when they have come together, just as the multitude becomes a single man with many feet and many hands and many senses, so also it becomes one personality as regards the moral and intellectual faculties.

The key to this passage, of course, is the verb in the first main clause ἐνδέχομαι, which, as it appears here in its impersonal form, comes into English as "it is possible that." The obvious rejoinder, of course, is "How possible is it?" According to Aristotle, not very, for immediately after admitting the above possibility, he continues by explaining that "this collective superiority of the many compared with the few good men" cannot be expected in "every democracy and every multitude" only in some multitudes (τι πλῆθος). After all, Aristotle asks rhetorically, "what difference is there, practically, between some multitudes and animals?" After a bit more casuistry, Aristotle reaches the point he wants to make, which is that "it is not safe" for "freemen, the mass of the citizens" to "participate in the highest offices." Rather, they should be admitted no further than jury service and the general processes of ensuring political accountability, processes where being an amateur actually has a few advantages. Aristotle offers two reasons for allowing freemen to play such limited roles in government. First, a large number is more difficult to corrupt than a small number, and second, no oligarchy is safe if it excludes too large a percentage of its population from all governmental operations.

The other places where Aristotle offers praise for democracy (*Athenian Constitution* 41.2–3 and *Politics* 1286^b26–35) repeat the advantage of large juries because such juries are difficult to corrupt: "just as the larger stream of water is purer," Aristotle explains, "so the mass of citizens is less corruptible than the few." In general, however, Aristotle regarded democracy with contempt. In the *Rhetoric* (1415^b7), for example, as he discusses the usefulness of an introduction to a speech, he undercuts his praise for democracy when he says, with clear disgust, that democratically appointed judges will listen to anything that the speaker can bamboozle them into hearing. In other words, while they may be more difficult to corrupt through bribes, democratic juries are also more easily led astray, which, finally, is cheaper than paying them off and just as effective. When the noun δημοκρατία appears with a modifier in Aristotle's notion of politics, the modifier, as Hansen (60) and Strauss (213) have pointed out, is usually derogatory.[17] To begin with, in his teleological notion of politics, Aristotle, like Plato, regarded the inevitable completion of democracy as tyranny ἡ δημοκρατία ἡ τελευταία τυραννίς ἐστιν (1312^b6, 1298^a29–35 and 1312^b33–38). When he treats democracy, modifiers such as the following almost always slip into his language: δεσποτικά (despotic), οὐ πολιτείαν (falling outside the parameters of normal civil society, negating such roles as "citizen," "government," and "statesmanship"), φαῦλος (insignificant, easy, slight, trivial, paltry, petty, sorry, poor, the most vulgar and degraded sort of people), οὐθέν ἔργον μετ᾽ ἀρετῆς (none of the work done by these people has any vestige of virtue, goodness, nobility, or manliness about it), ἄτακτος (undisciplined, disorderly, and lawless). The bad news for the democrats is that democracy cannot endure; the bad news for people of wealth and birth is that democracies are hostile to aristocracy.[18]

For Aristotle, as he makes clear in *The Athenian Constitution*, the term δημαγόγος was a pejorative term.[19] "From Cleon onward," he complains, "the leadership of the People was handed on in an unbroken line by the men most willing to play a bold part and to gratify the many with an eye to immediate popularity" (28.4). In fact, as Aristotle makes clear in *Politics* (1278[a]7–8), "the best-ordered state will not make an artisan a citizen."[20]

A Bearded, Philosophical Description

Somewhere between the death of Herodotus in 425 and the death of Aristotle in 322 (as Eric Havelock, Walter Ong, and many others have shown in such detail) written professional discourse emerged in the West, creating the possibility of the culture we now inhabit and at least in some ways, determining how that culture could and would develop.[21] No one enjoying the privileges, security, and convenience of modern life can possibly fail to appreciate what this discourse has done for all of us. Nevertheless, those of us who teach the discourse must keep it under constant scrutiny, for its power and privileges come only at a price. Professional discourse grew up in a democracy, but it was created and nurtured in opposition to that democracy, in large part, I believe, because it offers the "professional," the "expert," the "one who knows," a speaking position that seems to extract that person from the blinding desire of life itself, allowing that person to "know" life and to determine both how it ought to be lived and who ought to make the decisions about how it ought to be lived.

In light of the way our prose comes to us, in light of its intimate connection with an oligarchy of the "ones who know," it is important to remember that the "professional philosophers," who represented only a tiny fraction of the population, saw a rather different city from the one all the other "human beings" in Athens saw. Though we must look from a distance of twenty-five centuries, it seems clear that the philosophers' attraction to oligarchy was, as Eli Sagan has recently argued, really nothing but prejudice against poor people (137–38). And by the time Aristotle picked the prejudice up, it was very old indeed. Herodotus's oligarchic speaker, Megabyzus, for example, a speaker whose discourse was written a century before Aristotle and attributed by Herodotus to a period two centuries before Aristotle, condemns democracy in much the same terms that Aristotle would use in the fourth century:

> The masses are a feckless lot—nowhere will you find more ignorance or irresponsibility or violence. It would be an intolerable thing to escape the murderous caprice of a king, only to be caught by the equally wanton brutality of the rabble. A king does at least act consciously and deliberately; but the mob does not. . . . The masses have not a thought in their heads; all they can do is to rush blindly into politics like a river in flood.

In the standard maneuver, of course, every oligarch defines himself as one of the elect. Megabyzus, for example, concludes this little speech in the typical, oligarchic manner, asking that he and his friends "choose a certain number of the best men in the country, and give *them* political power." "We personally," Megabyzus adds in all innocence, "shall be amongst them" (3.81). At the very root of professional discourse, therefore, a niche outside of and above the common masses already exists.

The Old Oligarch makes much the same case. The Athenians, he fulminates, have a habit that all right-thinking persons find reprehensible:

> they everywhere assign more to the worst persons, to the poor, and to the popular types than to the good men; in this very point they will be found manifestly preserving their democracy. For the poor, the popular, and the base, inasmuch as they are well off and the likes of them are numerous, will increase the democracy; but if the wealthy, good men are well off, the men of the people create a strong opposition to them. . . . And everywhere on earth the best element is opposed to democracy. For among the best people there is minimal wantonness and injustice but a maximum of scrupulous care for what is good, whereas among the people there is a maximum of ignorance, disorder, and wickedness; for poverty draws them rather to disgraceful actions, and

because of a lack of money some men are uneducated and ignorant. (1.4–5)

Note the morality, lawfulness, and generally superior perspective
on life that the Old Oligarch attributes to the select few among
whom, of course, he situates himself.

    While Aristotle occasionally seems more judicious in dismissing
the poor, his judiciousness smacks of a Machiavellian sort of pragmat-
ics. Aristotle's advice to include poor people in a limited way in
government grows out of his alienated, self-protective way of dealing
with the world. The poor must have some limited role in government
so that they are seemingly included in the system that in fact excludes
them. If they have no involvement at all in government, they are
too likely to revolt; thus, the polis rests on a shaky foundation and
can neither guarantee oligarchic fortunes nor safeguard the agnatic
transmission of property.

A Clean-Shaven, Democratic Description

    The philosophers—particularly Xenophon, Plato, and Aris-
totle—wanted the state to shape its citizens in a mold settled on by
those with great "ability and wealth." The problem, apparently, was
that the Athenian population did not believe in the superior man,
the one Aristotle describes in *Ethics* (1129^b26–1130^a9), the one able
to behave justly toward himself and, when in power, toward others.
The Athenian experience had been that all too often such superior
men, upon achieving great power and being left to their own devices,
turn those devices into great personal gain and terrible general
suffering. Plato, Isocrates, and Aristotle all decried democracy as a
tyrannous exercise of power by the poor over the rich, a way to
despoil the rich and silence them in the running of the government.
Apparently, however, the philosophers could see a truth that few
living in Athens at the time or studying Athens today could or can
see. Kagan calls Plato's assault on Athenian democracy "a travesty"
(*Pericles* 269); Strauss argues that Aristotle is just plain wrong about
Athenian democracy (228–29). Professional discourse, it seems, always runs the risk of discovering truths so brilliant, so utterly apparent that these very truths blind their seer to the lived experience
of human beings. The citizens of Athens, it seems, had a pretty
good notion what life would be like *outside* Plato's cave. They voted

consistently that a life of equality inside the cave was a safer, better bet. Shadows on a cave wall may not be "real," but they do not murder you and your family in order to enjoy your wealth.

Although no one would deny that the Athenian democracy behaved badly on occasion, compared with the Athenian attempts at oligarchy, the democracy was as pure and innocent as an angelic host. The oligarchic coup in 411 was bad enough, but the one in 404, the one everyone in fourth-century Athens remembered most clearly, the one that neither Plato nor Aristotle can possibly have been ignorant of, was led by as despicable a bunch of self-seeking thugs as ever walked the face of the earth. The fact that most of them were Socrates' students means absolutely nothing—except perhaps that Socratic philosophy, at least for some of those who experienced it firsthand, did not necessarily lead to generosity of spirit or kindness of heart. The fact that the 404 oligarchs came from "the finest families in Athens" means nothing—except perhaps that when Aristotle or Plato or any of the other "great Greek thinkers" uses a phrase like "the most noble" or "the best of the people" they refer to a bloodthirsty, self-aggrandizing, vicious, and merciless group of murderers and thieves.

Admittedly one can charge the Athenian democracy with a freebooting kind of piratical intimidation in its treatment of friend and foe alike throughout the Aegean. And people frequently do that; but when Plato and Aristotle praise oligarchy, they seem to imply that it leads to a better, more ennobled form of government. One could defend the Athenian oligarchies, and especially the one set up in 404, by saying that Athens's neighbors received better treatment from the oligarchies than from the democracy. The reason, however, was that the oligarchies were so busy murdering and plundering their fellow Athenians that they had no time to go beyond the bounds of Attica.

Xenophon describes the 404 oligarchs in unstintingly brutal terms (*Hellenica* 3.3–4). They began their rule by executing all those who had offended against the wealthy, but after consolidating power, they began to act like money-hungry thugs. "Thinking they were at length free to do whatever they pleased," as Xenophon puts it,

> they put many people to death out of personal enmity, and many also for the sake of securing their property. One measure that they resolved upon, in order to get money to pay their guardsmen,

was that each of their number should seize one of the aliens residing in the city, and that they should put these men to death and confiscate their property. (2.3.21–22)

The 404 oligarchy ended up killing 1,500 Athenians and banishing another 5,000. In about eight months they managed to kill or exile approximately one-fourth of the citizens and wealthy metics in the city. A comparable outrage in the United States would require the murder or exile of 25,000,000 people, roughly the entire population of California. "For the sake of their private gain," as Cleocritus puts it, the oligarchs "have killed in eight months more Athenians, almost, than all the Peloponnesians in ten years of war" (*Hellenica* 2.4.21–22). To gain their own advantage, the oligarchs sold Athens out to Sparta. Critias, the savage and ruthless leader of the coup, publicly called the Spartans "our preservers" (τοῖς περισώσασιν ἡμᾶς) and praised them for having "the best of all constitutions" (2.3.24–34).

To get the full flavor of the holocaust the 404 oligarchs unleashed on their own people, however, one must read Lysias's "Against Eratosthenes." As wealthy metics, Lysias and his brother Polemarchus were especially vulnerable, and indeed the oligarchs came to Lysias's home, killed Polemarchus, tried to kill Lysias, and took every shred of family property, even the earrings out of Polemarchus's wife's ears. The oligarchs, Lysias explains pitifully, "thought nothing of putting people to death, but a great deal of getting money" (7).

Aristotle does not flinch in recounting the horror of the oligarch's rule. Once they were in power, he explains, repeating both Xenophon and Lysias, the oligarchs "kept their hands off none of the citizens, but put to death those of outstanding wealth or birth or reputation, intending to put that source of danger out of the way, and also desiring to plunder their estates" (*Athenian Constitution* 35.4). Having rewritten the constitution so that it covered only those whom they, on a whim, decided it would cover, the oligarchs killed off all their leading enemies, including Theramenes, who had at one time been one of them. After they changed the constitution and killed Theramenes, "their proceedings," Aristotle concludes dispassionately, "went much further in the direction of cruelty and rascality" (37.1–2). Perhaps the most astonishing thing about the coup, however, was not its voracious, greed-driven viciousness but rather the leniency with which the restored democracy forgave the oligar-

chy and allowed almost all its members to return to Athenian society
with little or no penalty. Given the outrageous bloodletting of the
eight-month coup, the generous amnesty offered by the restored
democracy was truly remarkable, especially in a society where violent retribution for wrong was customary and expected (Starr, *Birth*
57, Xenophon, *Hellenica* 3.3, Plato, "Seventh Letter" 325).

Does the behavior of the 404 oligarchs give Aristotle even the
slightest reason to rethink his support of oligarchy? No, it does not.
I have already complained about Aristotelian obtuseness on the
slavery issue. I want to press that matter again, because Aristotle
himself, in his matter-of-fact, "Dragnet" way explains the 404 coup.
It depended on "the notables," (*Athenian Constitution* 34.3) who
were divided into two camps: those who were members of exclusive
men's clubs (ἑταιρεῖαι) and "were eager for oligarchy," and those
who were not members of such clubs and were "merely cowed and
were forced to vote for the oligarchy."[22] The noun Aristotle uses to
refer to the oligarchs, both active and passive, is οἱ γνώριμοι. This
is the same noun he uses throughout the *Politics* to refer to that
special core of society that must have final political control.[23] It is
the same noun that he uses in the *Organon* where he sets up the
intellectual system of which rhetoric is a part. It is the noun that
names those whose "generally accepted opinions" found both rhetoric and dialectic. No matter how unpleasant it may be to admit,
Aristotle could both point out the horrid behavior of the 404 oligarchs
and, using the very same term by which they were identified, identify the elite corps of society that should rule, the elite corps whose
opinions should ground all public and private discourse.[24]

Aristotle, in short, wrote in a situation that glorified a small
percentage of "nobles" (γνώριμοι) while holding in contempt the
grubby, smelly population at large. He, like his teacher and his
friends, saw his own society through a lens that showed them a
picture quite different from what we see today. To begin with, as
Sinclair explains, "the oligarch's conduct in 411 and more particularly
the success of the thirty (Tyrants) in 404 discredited oligarchy as a
practical alternative to democracy" (43). After 403 no public argument for yet another oligarchy could be expressed in Athens. The
citizenship had suffered too much, too recently. Diogenes Laertius
(5.9) quotes Aristotle as saying just before his flight to Chalcis after
the death of Alexander that "I will not let Athenians offend twice
against philosophy." Clearly he alludes to the execution of Socrates

in 399. Since the bloody and vicious oligarchies in the last decade of the fifth century were all led by those closely associated with the "philosophical schools," one can, through the actions of the Assembly, see the Athenians anticipating that riposte by saying implicitly that Athens would not let the philosophers offend *three* times against democracy.

Admittedly, nearly everyone currently writing about ancient Greece lives in and supports some form of democratic society. Admittedly, those of us who look back at Athens as the cornerstone of an edifice that needs deconstructing do so from an ideology of our own, one that has come to valorize democracy. Admittedly, the very analytical modes for deconstruction come to us *from* the Greeks. Nevertheless, the Athens that we can reconstruct seems rather different from the one that we would infer from the texts through which our professional and analytical prose was invented.

Working from Aeschylus's plays *The Persians* and *The Suppliants*;[25] Otanes' speech in defense of democracy in Herodotus (3.80–81); Pericles' "Funeral Oration" in Thucydides (2.34–46); Lysias's "Funeral Oration for the Men Who Supported the Corinthians"; Demosthenes' "Against Leptines" (106), "Against Meidias" (67), and "Against Timocrates" (59); and Aeschines "Against Ctesiphon" (6 and 69); one can construct a fairly good notion of what democracy was and how it worked in Athens. If one adds to these texts Aspasia's fictional funeral oration in *Menexenus*, Protagoras's explanation of democracy in *Protagoras* (320d–322d), and Aristotle's *Athenian Constitution*, one gets a fairly clear picture of how political life operated in Athens. Although it was certainly more populist and more radically democratic than any of today's nation-states, it was hardly the vulgar and ridiculous place the philosophers so roundly condemned, and it was light years ahead of the two oligarchies that tried to subvert it in 411 and 404.

To begin with, the democracy was conservative and stable. The society it enabled from the reforms of Ephialtes in 461 through the coup of 322 was gently graded from top to bottom, with a small group of very wealthy citizens and a much larger group of laborers— some who worked in "genteel" professions, others who did manual labor of the most exhausting sort. From beginning to end, the democracy "stood for the rule of law and the protection of property" (Jones, *Athenian* 93), and it enjoyed its greatest security during the period 403–322, when Socrates, Xenophon, Plato, Isocrates, and Aristotle brought written, professional discourse to fruition and used it to create what we now think of as the West. Though the franchise was limited to adult males of native parentage, within those guidelines it was universal, and it "granted full and active participation in every decision of state without regard to wealth or class" (Kagan, *Pericles* 1). At least from 461 until the coup in 322 political influence at all times depended on the ability to carry the Assembly (Sinclair 48; P. Jones 25). Athenian officeholders swore an oath "to prosecute anyone who subverted the democracy or aided an attempt at tyranny,"[26] and the vast majority of Athenians, whatever the remaining literature may say, "were proud of their constitution and deeply attached to it." All three of the coups that surrounded Aristotle's life (411, 404, and 322) were carried out by small extremist groups and were short-lived (Jones, *Athenian* 42).[27] Demosthenes ("Against Timocrates" 149) quotes the Athenian juror's oath, which includes the following democratic and conservative principles:

> I will not vote for tyranny or oligarchy. If any man try to subvert the Athenian democracy or make any speech or any proposal in contravention thereof, I will not comply. I will not allow private debts to be canceled, nor lands nor houses belonging to Athenian citizens to be redistributed.

According to Aristotle (*Athenian Constitution* 56.2) the Eponymous Archon, on assuming office each year, had to proclaim the following oath: "all men shall hold until the end of my office those possessions and powers that they held before I entered into office." Though there was, as Jones (90–92) points out, "at all times a small group of wealthy intellectuals who hated democracy" (Socrates' pupils Alcibiades, Critias, and Plato being the most famous), they had little support most of the time, even from the very wealthy who preferred the stability and predictability of the democracy to the rapaciousness of Alcibiades and Critias. In spite of the claims by Plato, Isocrates, and Aristotle that the democracy despoiled the rich, the democracy was run at all times by wealthy, educated citizens (Strauss 225, A. Jones *Athenian* 50, Starr *Birth* 36–37, Sinclair 123–24, 209). Although it was theoretically possible for any citizen to speak in the Assembly, in fact few—usually the same famous few—were the only ones who did. Demosthenes ("Against Androtion" 30–36) says of both the Council and the Assembly that "the majority of you do not exercise the right to speak." Throughout the fourth century there were never more than thirty leading rhetors at any given time, and at any given Assembly meeting, a gathering whose size could grow to six thousand, there were probably no more than three hundred who had ever undertaken to speak on any occasion. Indeed by the 320s the Athenian system very much resembled a modern representative democracy (see P. Jones 201–3).

In sum, the claim made by Isocrates (*Antidosis* 159–60), Plato (*Republic* 565a), and Aristotle (*Politics* 1304^b–1305^a and 1320^a) that the Athenian democracy was a rabble led by rabble-rousers who plundered the wealthy was not even slightly true.[28] The only real plunder of the Athenian wealthy came under the rule of Socrates' pupil and Plato's friend Critias during the 404 oligarchy. And there is no doubt that Critias (as well as the equally unspeakable Alcibiades) *was* Socrates' pupil for several years. "Among the associates of Socrates," Xenophon writes, "were Critias and Alcibiades; and none wrought so many evils to the state. For Critias in the days of the oligarchy bore the palm for greed and violence: Alcibiades, for his part, exceeded all in licentiousness and insolence under the democracy" (*Memorabilia* 12). Aeschines confirms the association. In attacking Demosthenes he poses the following question: "Did you put to death Socrates the sophist, fellow citizens, because he was shown to have been the teacher of Critias, one of the thirty who put down the democracy, and after that, shall Demosthenes succeed in snatching companions of his own out of your hands" (*Against Timarchus* 173).

Instead of economic and social leveling and in complete contradistinction to the sort of government offered by the oligarchs, the Athenian democracy meant equality of opportunity, individual liberty, equality before the law, the right to vote, the right to hold office, and the authority to hold public officials accountable for their actions. As Protagoras argues so eloquently in Plato's text, the Athenians recognized clearly that "political science" was neither a divine gift nor a true science; rather, it was the art of living together peacefully, which, except for those times when the democracy was overthrown, the Athenians managed to do quite well for almost two centuries. Though Plato claims in his "Seventh Letter" (324–26) that the excesses of the 404 oligarchs coupled with the baseness of the restored democracy drove him to a life of philosophy (a claim that may well be true), in fact, most of his friends and relatives, the sort of people who would have been his natural allies, were so thoroughly compromised that few in Athens would have listened to anything any of them had to say. Plato and his friends had about the same credibility in the fourth century that the Nazi Party has had since 1945 in Germany.

While it is true that the leaders after Pericles, though they were all rich, "could not trace their ancestry back through many generations of nobility," that they "made" their money (often by exploiting slaves) from small factories, and that they gained access to power through education in such fields as rhetoric, finance, and maritime administration rather than through right of inheritance; it is pure hogwash to argue that by the mid-fourth century they were drawn from what the philosophers liked to call "the rabble."[29] However ironic Plato may have meant Aspasia's description of Athenian democracy (*Menexenus* 238c–d), it accurately describes the actual conduct of affairs. Since the inception of the democracy, she explains

> our government was an aristocracy—a form of government which receives various names, according to the fancies of men, and is sometimes called democracy, but is really an aristocracy or government of the best which has the approval of the many . . . authority is mostly in the hands of the people, who dispense offices and power to those who appear to be most deserving of them. Neither is a man rejected from weakness or poverty or obscurity of origin, nor honored by reason of the opposite, as in other states, but there is one principle—he who appears to be wise and good is a governor and ruler.[30]

The shift from a Pericles of the ancient and distinguished Alcmaeonid family to a wealthy slave factory owner such as Cleon was subtle at best, something like the difference between an old-money Rockefeller, whose money was made in the nineteenth century, and a new-money Kennedy, whose money was made in the twentieth. Part of the shift led to a separation between political and military leaders. As fourth-century audiences, in the wake of widespread education in rhetoric and finance, became more sophisticated, the military leaders increasingly had to rely on rhetoricians to carry the Assembly until finally rhetoricians became politically more important than the military leaders—rather like the shift from a Washington to a Jefferson. The attraction of the great military leader never seems to

go away completely—witness Ulysses S. Grant, Dwight Eisen-
hower, and (for a brief, euphoric moment) Stormin' Norman
Schwartzkopf. But when cooler heads prevail, most democratic soci-
eties recognize that the majority of the population fares better when
military leaders work for political leaders rather than the reverse.

The Unfortunate Agony of an Unobscured Face

Of course, I do not wish to argue that the Athenian democracy
was all sweetness and light. I recognize the danger of echoing Donald
Kagan's voice as he praises Protagoras, Prodicus, and Gorgias. All
three, he argues, were honored citizens in their home cities and
lionized in Athens for their support of democracy and conservative
social principles. Unfortunately, there is a dark side to what we in
rhet/comp have come to call the democratic political theories of the
"sophists." No one, in my opinion, can avoid being troubled by the
dark similarities between the Athenian democracy and our own.

As with everything about ancient Athens, estimates of population and voting franchise vary wildly, but one can with some security
accept Starr's estimate that the franchise in a total resident population of 230,000 extended to about 20 percent. In response to those
who claim that such a limited franchise does not constitute a democracy, Starr points out that Lincoln was elected president in 1860 in an
election that consisted of 4,700,000 ballots in a nation of 31,443,321
people. But 4,500,000 of those living in the United States could not
vote because they were slaves, 13,471,660 could not vote because
they were women, and 7,409,413 could not vote because they were
children, leaving a total electorate of 6,062,248, or 19 percent of the
population, with only 15 percent actually exercising their franchise in
the election. In other words, the voting patterns of the United States
in 1860 reflected those in ancient Greece almost exactly, even down
to the percentage of women and slaves excluded.

Like ours, the Athenian democracy was very much dominated
by the middle class. One can see the power of the middle class (τί
μέσον) at the end of the *Politics*, Book IV, as Aristotle explains
its pivotal importance. The middle class in fourth-century Athens
determined whether power would flow along democratic or oligarchic channels. Christian Meier (171), Kagan (*Great* 149), and Sagan
(113) all call fourth-century Athens a great middle-class democracy,

with Kagan going so far as to claim that "in the fourth century Athens was ruled by the bourgeoisie." Unfortunately, middle-class democracies have always been, in Sagan's words, "compatible with the existence of slavery, imperialism, insane warfare, and abject poverty." Frank Wallbank (50) has cataloged the rigid, cruel exclusiveness of Greek democracy in general and Athenian democracy in particular and shown the degree to which acquisition and protection of private property was the driving force in political matters, and Peter Jones (43) and I. F. Stone remind us that the trial of Socrates shows "how profoundly conservative the Athenian democracy was, how suspicious of innovation and change." The dominant political figure during Aristotle's second stay in Athens, after all, was Lycurgus, a wealthy former student of Plato and an admirer of Sparta who worked hard to push Athens as far right as possible given the need to pay lip service to democratic values. One cannot help drawing a comparison between Lycurgus's Athens and the Reagan/ Bush era in the United States.

One can give in to the temptation of praising Athens, as Kagan does, and lionizing such early democratic theorists as Protagoras and such public projects as the Parthenon.[31] In this gesture, one conceives the Parthenon as a balance between Protagoras's metaphysics and Pythagoras's mathematics, a civic symbol based on the Protagorean notion "that at the center of religion is not the divine *per se* but the human act of piety." In this gesture the Parthenon achieves "visually what [Pericles'] funeral Oration aimed at orally: the depiction, explanation, and celebration of the Athenian imperial democracy." In this gesture the Athenians create the notion of allotting power to all, and they place the obligation of civic, public education on themselves and all who follow them (*Pericles* 161–67).

The catch, of course, is the adjective "imperial." Athens, like the United States, did not have a democracy; Athens had an *imperial* democracy that spread its military adventures throughout the Aegean. As our Gulf War troops struggle to reintegrate themselves into civil life (many of our Vietnam veterans never having managed that feat), it cannot be lost on any of us that our democracy has been almost continually at war or in preparation for war throughout this century. Like the Athenians, we are prone to conduct our business through force, not diplomacy. Manuel Noriega may be despicable, the Mexican doctor who helped kill an American DEA officer may be equally despicable, but no one can deny our high-handed, holierthan-thou demeanor as we invade other countries in order to bring such "despicable people" to trial in our own country. If any other nation on the globe invaded the United States in order to seize an American politician, no matter how corrupt, or to abduct an American medical doctor, no matter how evil, the action would almost certainly lead to war. As was true for Athenians throughout their democracy, some form of military adventure or threat has been a constant for a century now in the United States. The Athenian leaders, from the great ones like Pericles and Lycurgus to the cut-throats like Alcibiades and Critias, all occupied what Sagan (using Freud) calls "the average, expectable paranoid position," a position that accepts racism, imperialism, social inequality, and violence as ordinary, unavoidable aspects of individual and political life (365–72).

In analyzing the ecological effect of Athenian democracy, James Mackin explains what I mean. He argues that Pericles' "Funeral Oration," though effective at generating consubstantiality in Athens, "damaged the ecological ground of that community, the larger sphere of Greek city-states." In building community in Athens, Pericles cut Athens off from its necessary ecosystem. Mackin implores us today to be more "ecologically aware" as we use rhetoric to build community. We must recognize that community building usually occurs as an act of exclusion. All too often we discover to our own detriment that what we have excluded is indeed necessary in the ecosystem where we have built our community.

The democratic franchise in its extraordinary power and glory carries with it the gestures that allow us to imagine "Others" as somehow outside. Thus the Serbs try to cleanse their territory of all but Serbs, the radical Arabs make cleansing the Middle East into a seemingly necessary mode of political discourse, and we send the Haitians "home" by the boatload, all the while cleansing ourselves by fleeing to suburban enclaves where we can "be safe" from the "threats" of contemporary life. Without a doubt, democracy, in its First World self-conception, has always operated within the notion of an inside and an outside. Those outside, like the Haitian boat people, for example, or the Korean merchants in south-central Los Angeles, are beyond the pale—the excluded ones through whose exclusion we can include ourselves.

Inside the charmed circle, however, there is no peace. Agony reigns supreme. It was spread across the landscape of ancient

Greece, and it is the way we conceive ourselves today. An agonal, competitive quality, Kagan praises the Athenians, "marked Greek life throughout the history of the polis and has played an unusually prominent role in Western civilization" (*Pericles* 4). The Olympics, the dramatic and literary competitions, the internal political struggles, the ongoing fight for cultural and financial hegemony, all these struggles show the Greeks' "powerful commitment to agon, the competition between individuals that allowed the winner to achieve excellence, fame, and heroic stature" (12). All the Greek aristocrats, culminating in the provincial world-beater Alexander *the Great*, were "deeply imbued with the Greek ideal of competition to achieve excellence, public recognition, and the glory that it carried. The battle to gain these rewards was always fierce" (19; see also Sinclair 175). Demosthenes, one of the "winners" in the agon accepted its rules with pride: "In an oligarchy," he says of Sparta in *Against Leptines*, "harmony is attained by the quality of those who control the State, but the freedom of a democracy is guarded by the rivalry with which good citizens compete for the rewards offered by the people" (107–8). "Even if you are better than the common run of men," he says in his "Erotic Essay," "seek to be superior in some respect to the talented remainder, and deem it the highest purpose to be first among all" (61). "Where the rewards of valour are the greatest," Pericles ends his "Funeral Oration," "there you will find also the best and bravest spirits among the people" (Thucydides 2.46). Glaucon, in the *Republic* (359–63), conceives even such abstract conceptions as "justice" as, in Socrates' mocking words, "the competition for the prize as if it were a statue." The drive for both honor (τιμή) and publicly acknowledged manly excellence and virtue (ἀρετή) was profound. One can see it throughout Aristotle, and particularly in the *Ethics* (see especially 1095^{b}14–31 and 1159^{a}16–25), the *Politics* (see especially 1302^{a}31–^{b}18 and 1283^{b}16–22), and the *Rhetoric* (see especially 1361^{a}28–^{b}2).

All Athenian culture was shot through with such language, and Athenian culture, right down to its alphabet, is at the root of our own. One can, for example, easily imagine, the first paragraph of the JACT's chapter on Athenian values appearing in a letter from any major university athletic director to the coaches in the athletic department. The only necessary editorial change would be to remove the first word of the quote and replace it with the word "American":

Greek cultural values—those rules of behaviour transmitted from generation to generation—can be usefully seen in terms of team games. (1) Games are competitive, but there is a permanent tension in a team game between the self-display of the individual and the needs of the team. (2) There is no doubt about the identity of the opposition. (3) You treat the opposition as people to be defeated, and you expect them to do the same to you. (4) Where games are played under the public eye, the game is an arena for conspicuous displays of success; excuses count for nothing and results for everything. (5) Finally, it is generally the case that the nearer the top a team reaches, the more difficult it is to stay there and the more dedicated the opposition is to defeating it. (132)

So deep goes the Greek notion of struggle, of agon, that in the *Physics* Aristotle defines his notion of matter as a kind of agon between matter and privation, good and evil (192^a).

So Much Depends on a (male)Face(re)
Do You Shave It, Trim It, or Let It Grow Wild?

There are, as anyone can see, a variety of ways to end this chapter. It could end with a plea for humanity and human writing. In this ending, I would argue that professional writing dehumanizes and desensitizes by focusing the writer's attention solely on the job at hand.

Or I could argue for some sort of writing that is a professional-human blend; I could even give this sort of writing the catchy name, "pro-human." In this ending, I would ask writing teachers to help their students become human beings before making them become professional beings. Professional writing would still have the most important place, but writers would be encouraged to remember their humanity and to remember the limited, uncertain, and incomplete human processes from which the finished products of Aristotelian demonstration arise.

Or I could end in a visionary mode by arguing that a deconstruction of professional discourse should be an educational experience, not a revolution. In this ending (perhaps as a rhetorical ploy or perhaps not), I would explain that a deconstruction of professional discourse does not imply either a destruction of or an escape from such discourse. Rather, it implies an attempt to recognize how professional discourse developed in the first place—not as a narrative of human accomplishments but rather as a series of power distributions, resource allocations, and role creations. This ending would lead to a plea that we try to imagine the human conditions generated by each distribution of power, each allocation of resources, and each role that someone might be required to fill.

Any of these endings would suit me fine, but, perhaps because I was raised on a steady diet of Old Testament prophecy, I prefer to end with a series of warnings. I articulate these warnings primarily for my own education, but I am happy to share them with anyone who has traveled a road similar to mine or who tills a garden with similar flowers and weeds.

First warning: The field of composition studies runs a real risk as it professionalizes itself. Obviously as someone who has contributed in a small way to this professionalization and benefited greatly from it, I recognize the need for professional behavior, professional standards, and all the other trappings of professionalism. I fear, however, that in the new millennium the voice of professional discourse will so dominate composition studies that all the other voices will be silenced. If we professionalize ourselves to that degree, composition studies will have found a way to empower itself and to protect its members, but it will have lost its ability to deal with human beings *as* human beings. I fear that Earnestine Johnson's essay will look unprofessional to those trained as professionals. When I use the essays by Mays and Johnson in faculty workshops for Vanderbilt's writing-across-the-curriculum program, a program in which most of the courses are taught by professorial faculty drawn from about a dozen different departments, Mays's essay almost always gets a universal B+. (Vanderbilt faculty members give the essay a B+ because they are wary of exposing themselves to the scrutiny of an announced A; in fact, not even those who despise New Criticism would really give Mays's essay anything below an A in a first-year writing course. After all, the pictures of Cleanth Brooks and Robert Penn Warren, Donald Davie and Allen Tate look down from the walls in the room where I hold workshops.) Johnson's essay, with incredible predictability, receives an A from those faculty who bring a feminist or cultural studies ideology to the workshop, but everyone else gives the essay a D or an F. Those who assign the D always explain at length that the essay deserves an F; they assign a

D because they do not wish to discourage a diligent student who seems to have some ability, even though the ability remains crude. Then we always have a big fight over the essay, the sort that anyone who has ever conducted such a workshop will be all too familiar with. This scenario occurs with such regularity because the vast majority of college faculty, in all disciplines, expect professional discourse from their students. They have no idea at all about what to do with human discourse. In my opinion, it would be a shame if composition studies lost its ear for human discourse.

Second warning: Democracy cannot be trusted to ensure that we look through human eyes at human situations. Democracy does not have and since its invention by the Greeks never has had a reliable conscience. For every Mitylene-like reversal of bad behavior, numerous other occasions show bad behavior that went unchecked. Democracy can operate quite peacefully even though its citizens experience wildly different opportunities and economic circumstances. Worse yet, democracy has the remarkable quality of drawing boundaries, and once the boundaries are drawn, those outside the charmed circle assume an ontology entirely different from those inside. Any Haitian detainee at Guantanamo Bay will tell you as much, as will the survivors of the "Japanese" internment camps of World War II and the African Americans who were forced to play Jim Crow as recently as the 1960s.

Third warning: The call of academic elitism through which we arrogate superior aesthetic and ratiocinative powers is practically impossible to resist. Every university professor hears that call. All of us listen to it and find it charming. It teaches us to professionalize ourselves as a way of escaping the human, as a way of protecting our superiority through the ferociousness of our language. Given his own privileged situation, Dan Quayle reveals himself as a simple-minded jerk when he concocts an imaginary cabal of Hollywood cognoscenti and college faculty and then calls the cabal "elitist." He is not bright enough and his handlers cannot create a simple enough script for him to articulate the way in which those in faculty lounges really are elitist. We are elitist because we generate discourses that cut us and our students off from the ongoing processes of human life, not because most of us support legal abortion, or gay rights, or whatever bugaboo Mr. Quayle has been sent out to attack in any given week. We are elitist because we have mastered a professional discourse and then given it moral standing. Such moralizing in the field of composition studies takes its rankest and most degraded form when a teacher construes a "grammatical mistake" or a "usage error" as a violation of moral rectitude, but every one of us is guilty of attributing a superhuman power of understanding to our professional discourse.

Fourth warning: It is crucially important that we as writing teachers keep our focus clearly on the history and operation of our texts of culture. Those texts are almost always texts that were still in process when their authors died. Aristotle's canon is an excellent, but by no means singular, example. We can, of course, turn Aristotle's human situation into a professional one, and there is no reason why we should not do so if we can remember that a professional discourse has been constructed for a reason and that it grew out of an entirely human discourse. We must not forget that when we write demonstrative discourse we are fleeing from the human into the professional, and we must remember that most people do not wish to take that flight. We must, in short, relearn the lesson Earnestine Johnson has to teach us, and we must relearn it every term. There must be some place for people to write like Aristotle wrote— as a human being trying to live through dangerous and frightening times.

Final warning: Because we know how to make ourselves appear professional, because professional discourse offers the secure authority of professorship, and because professional discourse pays so well, we in composition studies will be (are being) tempted to forget that we ever were human. When I began teaching writing in 1971, every English teacher I knew wanted essays like the one by Kelly Mays. I can teach some students to write such essays, and I am sure that Earnestine Johnson is one of those who could learn. In that context, I hear the complaint of the unhappy job candidate with whose story I began. What am I to say to him? How will it change my pedagogy? Without question I must admit my own failure. I should have trained him to be a sophist (clearly I myself am a sophist). As a sophist, he would have known how to make himself acceptable to any sort of audience, no matter how hidebound or ridiculous. Instead, I trained him as a moralist. I taught him my highly professionalized process pedagogy as if it were a moral imperative, not a choice one might make.

I would like very much to find some safe place to stand, some professional identity and pedagogy to embrace. Above all, I would like to discover a history with which I could affiliate myself. But even Lysias—the man ridiculed so wildly by Plato in *Phaedrus*, the man so bitterly attacked by Critias and his pals, the man who studied with Tisias, the man who throughout his life was a passionate democrat, the man who had his own school of rhetoric, the man who had the reputation as *the best* prose writer in Athens, the metic who lived his whole life as an alien in Athens, the one who was given citizenship and then almost immediately stripped of it, the one who looks for all the world like a rhet/comp person, the one who almost died at the hands of the oligarchs, the one who should have known better—even Lysias owned the largest known slave factory in Athens. He inherited it from his father, and he owned at least 120 other human beings. Given his intelligence, his politics, and his situation, surely Lysias should have been able to hear the sophists' arguments against slavery. And that is what worries me most. Perhaps he did hear those arguments. Chances are good that he made those arguments himself. But if he did, he made them in professional discourse. Then he went home to a house supported by slave labor and a dinner cooked by a slave cook. The discourse itself allowed him to see the injustice and to articulate why the injustice was wrong; alas, the discourse also allowed him to separate his professional ability from his lived experience, and he ate his dinner in peace.

4

IN THE HEART
OF THE HEART
OF THE *RHETORIC*

For Aspasia

Situated Writing I: In the Chair Where I Sit

The Simi Valley jury has just returned its verdict, and South Central LA has exploded. The images I see on TV are simultaneously so real and so unreal that I cannot stop watching; instead, I stop working and spend half a day buying a splitter and some coaxial cable so that I can set up an old TV in my study. Now I can watch TV while I work on this book. I have never been good at watching TV and writing. In fact, I have not tried to do both since I was a college freshman in 1965; oddly enough, LA was in flames then too. I do not remember watching any of the 1965 riot on TV. I cannot decide whether I should allow TV coverage of the 1992 riot to appear in this book. The media and the messages keep intertwining themselves in unexpected, often unpleasant ways, and I know full well that the 1992 riot will be a dim memory long before this book appears in print.

CNN plays the Rodney King and Reginald Denny tapes so often that they begin to have a hallucinatory normalcy about them.

Watching them is like listening to an old rock song whose lyrics and rhythm I can lip sync with no conscious effort. Occasionally, the CNN cameras cut to what used to be Yugoslavia where the various ethnic factions have begun to use infanticide and gang rape as part of the "normal" political process. Bad as LA must be right now, Sarajevo is worse. A reporter tries to interview a wounded woman who is clearly in shock. Her face and voice have a serene numbness about them. She was holding her baby in her arms when a stray bullet split open the baby's head before lodging in her own breast. Had she not been holding her baby, she would surely have been killed. I wonder in horror what it would be like to hold my daughter in my arms and watch her head explode. How would a parent live a life spared by the rupture of a child's head? As a former soldier myself, I know that the man who pulled the trigger would shrug, curse, and say, "There's a war going on here." Chances are very good, however, that he has no idea where his bullet went.

On the second day of the LA riot, according to Harold Myers, "The white city girded for violence." In a canyon

near the center of Hollywood, residents enrolled themselves in an ad hoc militia after spying gang members cruising through the canyon's lower stretches. . . . As one resident recounts it, a canyon filled primarily with "film industry and theater people" managed to come up with an amazing array of guns. An uneasy coalition of '60s liberals and survivalists then blocked off the mouth of the canyon with cars, and stood guard there all night (and the following two nights as well), brandishing rifles and bats on the several occasions when cars carrying young black men drove by. For the '60s lefties, it was a profoundly disorienting ordeal. "I always assumed that if I was going to be on the barricades," one resident told me, "I'd be on the other side." (25)

As a sixties lefty myself, I look down the peaceful street of my carefully zoned, suburban neighborhood in the high hills of south Nashville and wonder what I would do if "rioters" came driving up the street. I am ashamed of myself as the notion of buying a gun flits through my mind.

Serbia, it seems, has decided that all areas where Serbs live must be "cleansed" so that Serbian ethnic purity will run no risk of being defiled. Unbelievably, the Serbs seem to have set up Auschwitz-like concentration camps. "The blood from the Balkans is seeping under Europe's door," says the lead editorial in the *New York Times*.[1]

A week into their dawn-to-dusk coverage of the riot, the networks have said nothing about Louis Watson, Dwight Taylor, or Gregory Davis. Watson apparently participated in looting the Vermont Square Shopping Center on the evening of April 29. During the melee, he failed to notice two gang members who were angry at him for refusing to join their gang. They shot him dead, killing Taylor and Davis entirely by accident. I assume that none of the networks mentions this particular event because no one managing a network considers it "news." The murder of one black, male teenager by another black, male teenager, even when other black males are accidentally shot in the process, happens far too often for any national network to notice.

In 1988 my wife and I were living near Chicago and going through the process of adopting a child. Somehow one of the private, for-profit "placement agencies" got our name and sent us a fee schedule. I will never forget opening and reading the letter. It was elegantly printed on expensive, thick, cream-colored paper. For $20,000 plus expenses, it told us, we could get a white infant in six months, for $10,000 plus expenses a Hispanic infant in six months, for $4,000 plus expenses a black infant in four months.

The May 25, 1992, *New Republic* arrives. It has a solid black cover, a red masthead, and is covered with the white lettering of the first paragraphs of the editorial. Given the events in LA, this white on black with a spilling out of red gives the cover an eerie look, which the designer must surely have intended. Since I am writing a book on fourth-century Greece while watching the LA riot on TV, I find it weirdly unsurprising that a random issue of one of America's leading intellectual weeklies is devoted almost exclusively to two subjects: the LA riot and a long defense of the study of ancient Greek culture.

Everywhere I look I see continuing repetitions of tribalism, violence, hatred, segregation. I do not blame the ancient Athenians for this anymore than I blame myself. But I worry increasingly that rhetoric is at the heart of human behavior, that it was invented for the West by the ancient Greeks, and that we now have a symbolic system of persuasion that always already codifies, solidifies, and immortalizes the racism, violence, and hatred that everyone in urban America—as did their predecessors in ancient Athens—accepts as an unavoidable way of life. Late last night a drug deal here in Nashville went sour, ending in a shootout. One of the stray bullets crashed through the storm door of a nearby house, killing eighteen-month-old Terrell B. Banks as his father was putting him to bed. What was horrifying in Sarajevo is baffling here in Nashville. Blood is seeping under my own front door.

There are villages in Somalia during this summer of 1992 where the inhabitants are so near starvation that they have begun to eat their clothes. I look at my jeans and try without success to wonder what that might be like. Very soon, the children in Somalia will have no blood at all. They will simply wither and blow away.

The standard rhet/comp response to each repetition of the con-flagration is to say, sadly, "Another failure of rhetoric." Speaking in the wake of Burke and Rogers, we see our discipline as the means through which people become consubstantial, as the process through which writers learn to inhabit the perspective and the discourse of an opponent, as the way that students grow into responsible and decent academic citizenship. "For rhetoric as such," Burke argues in a quotation that we have turned into a cliché, "is rooted in an essential function of language itself, a function that is wholly realistic, and is continually born anew; it is the use of language as a symbolic means of inducing cooperation in beings that by nature respond to symbols" (*Rhetoric* 43). "Rhetoric," Burke continues a few pages later as we all nod our heads in assent, "becomes primarily the process whereby a community comes to share a symbolic discourse" (49). Rhetoric, I. A. Richards urges in another of our now-clichéd formulas, "begins with Aristotle," and should "be a study of misunderstanding and its remedies" (1–3).

"During the afternoon," Ari Posner writes in the aftermath of the LA riot, "I go with several friends to South-Central for the cleanup. Only four days ago I would never travel this far in, but thanks to the influx it's safe today" (20). The key word is "in." It rings of science fiction, of the zone where a protagonist goes only reluctantly, only when some desperate mission demands the journey. Once inside the zone, "normal rules" of education, civilization, morality, and behavior no longer apply. Once inside the zone, rhetoric ceases as a possibility. Skin color, accent, wardrobe, and tribal affiliation determine how and when one resorts to violence. Violence as the first and only resort is, in a Lethal Weapon-Terminator-matter-of-fact way, beyond question.

The last time LA exploded, composition had just begun its progress toward academic respectability, a progress that began, as fate would have it, in LA. In 1936 Richards had written that rhetoric

> is the dreariest and least profitable part of the waste that the unfortunate travel through in Freshman English! So low has Rhetoric sunk that we would do better just to dismiss it to Limbo than to trouble ourselves with it—unless we can find reason for believing that it can become a study that will minister successfully to important needs. (1)

Three decades later, what we now call rhetoric and composition "appeared—or reappeared—on the scene" at the 1963 CCCC convention in LA, where Wayne Booth and Francis Christensen stood to read "important papers" (Corbett, "Teaching" 444–52). In the wake of Watts, 1965, came the Great Society, the War on Poverty, and the attempted transformation of American class structure. Part of that attempt—admittedly a small, poorly planned, and low-profile part—was the transformation of college composition. By 1960, composition had deteriorated to the point that its only purpose in most colleges was to screen out all first-year students who could not spell and use punctuation marks properly. By the mid-seventies, however, even though writing teachers were routinely fired at tenure time, composition had become an enabling course, a course intended to help poorly prepared students succeed. Now we are in the nineties, and composition studies has gained considerable stature as a research field. Composition specialists who publish no longer risk being fired. We are very far *in* the academy indeed.

Perhaps during the early seventies I spent so long feeling misunderstood and persecuted that I cannot now live comfortably with the privileges that have befallen composition studies so unexpectedly in the last decade. I hope, however, that my discomfort at being so far *in* grows out of the commitments I made early on as a teacher, not out of some sort of perverse delight in being a righteous martyr.

Obviously I regard the 1992 LA riot as a personal failure. Because composition is the doorway subject, the enabling, authorizing agent, and because the LA riot grew directly out of alienation and despair, I must confront the responsibility I bear for not having found a way to deliver my pedagogy to those who need it most. The difference between me and my colleagues in other fields is professional, not personal or social. Every person living in America must bear personal and social blame for the unspeakable racism and poverty that plague the inner cities, the places most of us do not dare go very far *in*. One can, however, continue to work as a mathematician or even as a sociologist without necessarily feeling the burden of amelioration. With the teaching of writing, amelioration *is* the purpose. If people who do not write at all never begin, if people who write poorly do not improve, if people who write well do not continue, then the teaching of writing ceases to exist as it has configured itself in the last three decades, and it ceases to interest me as a worthwhile human endeavor. It retains its intellectual, inside-the-university attraction, but that attraction is entirely professional. It has little to do with the way most human beings live their lives.

Situated Writing II: In the Chair Where We Sit

I do, of course, know that the world has been vindictive and violent for centuries. At the height of his power as head honcho of the 404 coup, for example, Critias, according to Xenophon, set out to get even with his old teacher, Socrates, who had embarrassed Critias by comparing him to a pig (*Memorabilia* 1.3.31). Since Critias could think of no other way to attack Socrates, Critias passed a law making rhetoric and philosophy illegal.[2] Xenophon's text leaves the clear impression that Critias and his oligarchic pals were not afraid of rhetoric or philosophy. The τέχνη of the λόγος did not frighten them in the least. Critias merely wanted to retaliate against Socrates, so he outlawed the activity that Socrates enjoyed most. From the very beginning, it seems, rhetoric has depended on a prior sense of community. Those who exist within the charmed circle of rhetoric have already agreed to forego random, unexplained violence against each other: not, of course, against those *outside* the circle, only against those who have achieved full standing *within* the circle. As long as individuals retain the right of random, unjustified violence, rhetoric cannot function. In other words, if the second "speaker" shoots the first "speaker" while the first "speaker" is still drawing breath, rhetoric has been preempted. Admittedly the execution of someone outside the circle may have rhetorical value for those inside the circle. No doubt both the gang members who shot Louis Watson and the oligarchs who killed Lysias's brother, Polemarchus, saw their act as an expression of solidarity and manliness.

The flip side to this argument, of course, is that rhetoric does not offer much of an opportunity for expanding a community beyond its own preexisting boundaries. No one thinks the West "persuaded" the Soviet bloc to disintegrate. There was nothing rhetorical about the bullet that killed the baby in Sarajevo or the one that killed Terrell Banks here in Nashville. The conversations between Louis Watson and the gang members who tried to recruit him were in no sense rhetorical because the gang members reserved the right to kill Watson if he declined. The racist discussion in Silver City, Mississippi, in contrast, was rhetorical in every way, but no matter the outcome, the result for African Americans in Humphries County was the same, for the African Americans in Humphries County had no voice in the debate. Critias and his crew had nothing to fear from the "art of words," because they reserved, and frequently exercised, the right to kill those whose words displeased them. No doubt Critias and his twenty-nine friends behaved rhetorically among themselves as they decided whom to kill and which property to plunder. No doubt the gang members who killed Louis Watson behaved rhetorically as they decided whether and when to kill him. In dealing with those outside the circle, however, in dealing with people like the metic Lysias or the outside bystanders such as Dwight Evans and Gregory Davis, rhetoric ceases as a possibility. The people who leave Haiti on a boat bound for the United States find themselves outside the zone of rhetoric. The Coast Guard merely picks them up and takes them back to Port-au-Prince. They have no voice through which to be heard by those inside the discourse of North America. They have, as former Secretary of State James Baker said, "no legal standing and no right to inflict themselves on the American taxpayer."

Given the enormous divisions in the American community, how are we in composition studies to speak across the boundaries? Hardly any (I am tempted to say "no") longtime dues-paying member of CCCC accepts violence as a form of persuasion. Given that so many of our fellow citizens see violence as the *only* meaningful form of persuasion, how do we proceed? Research on the history and ontology of rhetoric, after all, has nothing to do with a riot—not in LA, not anywhere. Such research has to do with the generation and protection of a professional discourse, a discourse around which an amorphous group of people has gathered in order to indentify themselves as professional and to define and protect their professional behavior. In order to be themselves, such people need to write books that will be published by university presses and articles that will be published by scholarly journals. Most of them need to teach a few classes on the side, but that has little to do with their professional advancement. Questions such as "What is rhetoric?" "What is the history of rhetoric?" or "How are the canonized rhetorical texts to be interpreted?" have no answer. No one expects, or even wants, any of the questions answered because the answers would put the field of rhetorical studies out of business. Stephen Hawking can claim that he wants to have a Grand Unified Theory that would "solve" physics, but I do not think anyone, including Hawking himself, really expects it (74–79).

The professional discourse about Aristotle's *Rhetoric* "demonstrates" what I mean. When this discourse takes the form of history, it usually makes one of the three following claims: (1) Aristotelian rhetoric has dominated Western discourse theory, (2) Aristotelian rhetoric has had practically no influence on Western discourse theory, or (3) Aristotelian rhetoric has had enormous influence on Western discourse theory, but all those who were influenced by Aristotle misunderstood him. Although the three available claims may seem contradictory, in fact, they are the required sub-formulations of the following, all-encompassing professional formulation:

> Rhetoric is an important field of scholarly endeavor, and Aristotle's *Rhetoric*, as the most complex extant early rhetorical text, must be kept alive and continuously critiqued as part of that field.

Once the term *rhetoric*—like such other professional terms as *literature, psychology,* or *medicine*—becomes a site for professional discourse, a charmed circle grows up around it, and the professional process of disputation and reconciliation begins. Within the charmed circle, professional scholars must establish a canon, set out rules for interpreting that canon, and organize the lines of debate. The most

obvious kind of debate deals with preeminence and power. From
the beginning, Aristotle's *Rhetoric* has been in the thick of that fray.

Larry Arnhart offers the *Rhetoric* not only as the method for
political science but also as the foundation of all rational discourse.
James and Lita Baumlin call it "the most influential treatise in the
history of rhetoric" (248). Patricia Bizzell and Bruce Herzberg explain
that "Aristotle reduced the concerns of rhetoric to a system that
thereafter served as its touchstone. To speak of classical rhetoric is
thus to speak of Aristotle's system and its elaboration by Cicero and
Quintilian" (3). Thomas Cole contends that the *Rhetoric*, coupled
with the *Phaedrus*, laid the foundation for discourse theory well
into the modern period (12). "The Rhetoric not only of Cicero and
Quintilian," Lane Cooper states, but also that "of the Middle Ages,
of the Renaissance, and of modern times, is, in its best elements,
essentially Aristotelian. There is no book on the subject since Aristotle's that is not at least indirectly indebted to his" (xvii). "This textbook," Ed Corbett says of his very influential *Classical Rhetoric for
the Modern Student*, "is so much indebted to Aristotle's theory that
it can be regarded as a mere restatement, with some modifications
and extensions, of the *Rhetoric*" (599). Sharon Crowley sees Aristotle
as pivotal in the history of rhetoric because the strategy he used to
"finesse the impact of the Platonic charges against mimetic art" set
up a history in which rhetoric would be a forever unstable union of
idealistic mimesis and sterile formalist technique ("Rhetoric" 17–
31). "All the main theories after Aristotle," Jacqueline de Romilly
argues, "can be traced back either to [Aristotle] or to Isocrates, more
generally to both" (75). The rhetoric deriving from Aristotle, Richard
Enos contends, has an influence and offers benefits that "need not
be argued" ("Classical" 286); "classical rhetoric," he says elsewhere,
"has been, and once again is a dominant theory for writing instruction" ("Review" 97). Only a true philosopher, according to John
Henry Freese, could have rescued rhetoric from the rhetoricians
and made "a systematic and scientific 'Art' of Rhetoric" available to
other true philosophers (xxii). Aristotle's *Rhetoric*, according to
James Golden, Goodwin Bergquist, and William Coleman, "is the
most important single work on persuasion ever written" (30). Win
Horner waffles only slightly in saying that "the *Rhetoric* is probably
the most important early treatise on the subject" (5). Aristotle's
"voice," says Susan Jarratt, "has dominated the current revival of
rhetoric as a historical study," because "his *Rhetoric* is the most

complete ancient treatment of the subject" (xvii). For Christopher Johnstone the entire field of rhetoric after the fourth century B.C. is and must be "intrinsically ethical because the nature and function of the art are conceived against the background of Aristotle's ethical theory" (10–12). Since Aristotle wrote his *Rhetoric*, Thomas Kent complains, "rhetoric has been dominated not by social pragmatic conceptions of language-in-use, but rather by epistemologically-centered conceptions of language as system." The boundaries of this system "from antiquity to our time have remained remarkably stable" (492–93). According to George Kennedy, most of the famous twentieth-century rhetoricians—including Chaim Perelman, Kenneth Burke, Stephen Toulmin, and even Edwin Black—were all heavily influenced by Aristotle, whose work has always served as the basis for modern ideas about communication and rhetorical criticism (*Aristotle* ix–x). "Aristotle's influence," Jim Kinneavy explains at the beginning of his *Theory of Discourse*, "has dominated rhetorical theory for twenty-three centuries" (18). "By establishing rhetoric as the *antistrophos* or corollary of dialectic," Andrea Lunsford and Lisa Ede argue, "Aristotle immediately places rhetoric in relation to other fields of knowledge, and these relationships are painstakingly worked out in the *Organon*." Aristotle's canon, they continue, "established a theoretical relationship among belief, language, and action; Isocrates, Cicero, and Quintilian all adapted and acted out that theory." No contemporary theorist has articulated a rhetoric so elegant, useful, and coherent as Aristotle's, they contend, and they ask for a contemporary rhetoric rebuilt on Aristotle ("Classical" 78–97).

And the eighteen alphabetically chosen and arranged citations in the above paragraph take us no farther than the twelfth letter of the alphabet.[3] One need not turn to such Aristotelian evangelists as William Grimaldi and Eugene Ryan to fill a choir with voices claiming the seminal power of Aristotle's *Rhetoric*. Though the key signatures, rhythmic patterns, orchestrations, and even the vocalists for that choir change constantly, the choir will sing for as long as a professional discourse operates on the site of the term *rhetoric*.

The two counterpoints to this melody (that Aristotle has had no significant influence or that the great number he has influenced all misunderstood him) are sung softly by a much smaller chorus, but the voices in this counterpointed chorus are some of the discipline's most illustrious—something like having Battle, Pavarotti, Ramey, and Te Kanawa singing offstage while the chorus sings in full view. Aldo Scaglione harmonizes nicely with the main chorus, calling the *Rhetoric* "the earliest and most illustrious of the extant treatises," but his melody and rhythm introduce a slight variation when he adds that the *Rhetoric* has had "limited direct impact . . . on the rhetorical tradition through the centuries." Only "the most responsible proponents of the art," he claims, have allowed themselves to follow an Aristotelian orientation or to build on an Aristotelian foundation (14). Other voices introduce more vigorous disharmony. Michael Halloran, for example, after agreeing that Aristotle was "the most sophisticated of the classical writers on rhetoric" goes on to argue both that Aristotle "is less informative than provocative to the modern student" and that "in order to understand classical rhetoric as a cohesive and enduring tradition, we must define it in a way that makes it largely incompatible with modern rhetorical and communication theory" ("Tradition" 234–39). Kennedy, in contrast, says "the most famous discussion of rhetoric in Greek is surely that by Aristotle, but it was just as surely not rhetoric as described by Aristotle that was taught in schools for the next two thousand years." Not until the twentieth century, says Kennedy, did rhetoricians begin "to cite Aristotle's work on a regular basis as a fundamental statement of rhetoric" (*Classical* 3, 81). Grimaldi (*Studies* 115–17) offers a similar complaint. He agrees with the main chorus that everyone who studies rhetoric reads Aristotle, but he worries that none of those readers really understands Aristotle; hence, they end up truncating and impoverishing the greatest of the rhetorical texts. "A reading of Spengel's commentary on the *Rhetoric*," Grimaldi laments, "reveals a fairly consistent failure on the part of technographers to understand Aristotle's work" (68–69). Kathleen Welch, however, contends not only that classical rhetoric did not begin with Aristotle but also that he was not the prime mover and shaper of the classical system, a role she assigns to Gorgias and Isocrates ("Electrifying"). Thomas Conley demonstrates considerable breadth of knowledge about the history of rhetoric in arguing that the *Rhetoric* was largely neglected between the sixth and twelfth centuries and that Aristotle was to Byzantine scholars about as important as Hermogenes is to the twentieth century ("Aristotle's"). In reviewing Kennedy's *Classical Rhetoric*, Conley complains that Kennedy devotes too much time to Aristotle because Aristotle did not "have much influence, due partly to an accident of history, perhaps, but mainly to the fact that his *Rhetoric* was found to be comparatively useless by the speakers in the courts, the preachers in their pulpits, and the scholars in their studies." Aristotle's *Rhetoric*, he continues his assault, "is no philosophical rhetoric but a 'Rhetoric' with a few philosophical asides which reveal an interest in discriminating between sound dialectical arguments and paralogisms." The classical tradition, Conley concludes, "is virtually identical to the Ciceronian tradition"; thus, historians of rhetoric such as Kennedy should recognize that "Cicero's influence deserves more careful treatment than it gets" ("Kennedy" 208). Thomas Sloan also promotes Cicero at the expense of Aristotle. Rhetoric in both speech departments and in composition studies, Sloan argues, has been heavily dominated by Aristotle to the detriment of both. In Cicero, he continues, "debate is the process that defines rhetorical thought." Ciceronian invention is the pro and contra process of analytical argumentation, a process that is far richer and more complete in Cicero than in Aristotle. In responding to repeated calls for a revival of classical rhetoric, Sloan laments that "the revival is incomplete and, to borrow a phrase from Erasmus, utterly contaminated by Aristotle" (461–73).

Obviously Aristotle's *Rhetoric* generates considerable ink, considerable dissension. These apparent disagreements, however, are disagreements only at the surface. One can argue that Aristotle was the most influential rhetorician in history, or that he was the most influential rhetorician in history but that his influence has been pernicious, or that his great and pernicious influence results only from the inability of his exegetes to interpret him correctly, or that he was not influential at all, or that he was tremendously influential but that someone else (Cicero, for example) should have been more influential, or that he was influential for two millennia but that his influence has waned (whether for good or ill) in the modern world, or that he was not very influential from the time his manuscripts were lost in the third century B.C. until recently but that the twentieth century (again whether for good or ill) has seen him become the most influential rhetorician. One can argue any of these theses, but the apparent disagreements they generate are nothing more than the required moments of professional discourse inside the field of "rhetoric."

Conley, for example, argues that Aristotle's *Rhetoric* has been "comparatively useless" to public speakers, that for centuries it was largely ignored, and that it is not philosophical; thus, one might be slightly confused by his demand elsewhere that rhetoricians learn

Greek so that they can read Aristotle in the original language. Conley makes the demand because, in his opinion, Aristotle's "*Rhetoric* is recognized by everyone who knows or has some interest in rhetoric as the very foundation of the discipline. Anyone who proposes to say anything about the subject must have at least that work in mind, for despite attempts to supersede it or get around it, the *Rhetoric* is still both dominant and definitive" ("Greekless" 74). After giving several examples to show how translators introduce problems that do not exist in the original, Conley concludes that as long as most rhetoricians cannot read Greek, "contributions in our discipline to the understanding of the *Rhetoric* are not likely to come to much" (74–79).[4] Conley's thesis, of course, is that no responsible scholar, no legitimate speaker of a professional discourse, can afford to be ignorant of the texts in the disciplinary canon, and anyone who cannot read Greek is, by definition, ignorant of the rhetorical canon because the forefathers of rhetoric, Aristotle being the most powerful of the lot, all wrote Greek. De Romilly, who, as I have shown, sees Aristotle as *the* formative figure in the history of rhetoric, shows the exact boundaries I am discussing. There has always "been a living tradition of real oratory," she explains. She does not articulate the conclusion I believe to be implicit in her statement, but it seems clear that the actual practice of making speeches and persuading people has, at least since Plato, lived a life of its own, a life utterly unconnected with the field of rhetoric, which has professionalized itself as a discourse through which only the trained and licensed can speak. This discourse has little to do with persuading other people or with developing a pedagogy that will train better speakers and writers; rather, the professional discourse is about itself.[5] In his study of Lysias's canon, K. J. Dover articulates the distinction I am making when he defines "oratory" and "rhetoric" as different things:

> By "oratory" I mean speaking to a group of people with the intention either of persuading them to take a decision, adopt a mode of thinking or pursue a course of action, or of evoking in them a favourable aesthetic reaction to one's own speaking. By "rhetoric" I mean what the Greeks meant by ῥητορική, the intellectual study of the procedures of oratory, with or without the communication of the results of this study to "pupils." A failure to distinguish between oratory and rhetoric imposes on us, unnecessarily, difficulties such as the evolution of our language has

imposed on us in respect of the word "history," which means both "the past" and "the study of the past" (175).[6]

In my opinion, the day Aristotle transferred from Isocrates' school to Plato's Academy, rhetoric's fate was sealed. The key move comes in Book I, at the end of chapter 1. Then at the beginning of chapter 2, Aristotle repeats the move. Since this move appears in each of the first two chapters, one can with some safety argue that it indicates a notion of rhetoric that Aristotle held throughout his life. Whether Aristotle wrote chapter 1 during the Academy period and chapter 2 during the Lyceum period, or vice versa, makes no difference in this case since the same idea seems to have been part of each formulation. The "work of rhetoric is not persuasion," Aristotle writes at the end of chapter 1 (1355^b10–11), "but in each case to see the existing means of persuasion."* In the first sentence of chapter 2 he repeats this formulation, "Let rhetoric be," he writes, "in each situation the ability to see the possible means of persuasion."* And forever after, *rhetoric* as a term in the West is transformed from the name of a place of human discourse to the name of a field of professional discourse. After this definition, one may be a rhetorician without ever giving or intending to give a speech. Rhetoric, rather than a pedagogy that promises to make one a more persuasive speaker, becomes an academic field in which professionals debate two things: first, the exact nature of rhetoric, and second whether and how any given discourse is, was, or might be rhetorical. In Book III, where he takes up the process of making rhetoric urbane and witty, Aristotle explains that the abilities to be urbane ($\dot{\alpha}\sigma\tau\varepsilon\hat{\iota}\alpha$) and to create phrases that people will like ($\varepsilon\dot{\upsilon}\delta o\kappa\iota\mu o\hat{\upsilon}\nu\tau\alpha$) result either from natural genius or extensive practice. His study, however, deals with neither the nature of genius nor the pedagogy of practice; quite the contrary, "the function of this inquiry," he explains, "is to show what [smart and popular sayings] are" (1410^b6–9). Aristotelian rhetoric is almost entirely an analytical, academic undertaking. Though Grimaldi almost certainly would not have approved of the use to which I put his argument, in effect, he makes the same point I am making. Three times (*Studies* 3, 27, 85) he argues that rhetoric does not effect persuasion but rather discovers "in the subject those things which are suasive to others." "Rhetorical discourse," he argues later, "is discourse directed toward knowing, toward truth."[7]

Plato had prepared the ground for this sort of transmogrification of rhetoric near the end of *Phaedrus* where Socrates and Phaedrus conclude that the rhetoricians of the fifth century—including all the sophists that we in composition studies have been so intrigued by in the last ten years—knew nothing. Plato's Socrates invokes Adrastus and Pericles, who then urge Phaedrus and Socrates to be

> lenient, if certain persons who are ignorant of dialectics have been unable to define the nature of rhetoric and on this account have thought, when they possessed the knowledge that is a necessary preliminary to rhetoric, that they had discovered rhetoric, and believe that by teaching these preliminaries to others they have taught them rhetoric completely. (269b)

In *Sophistical Refutations*, Aristotle repeats this notion almost verbatim in attacking the models-based rhetoric of Gorgias. Clearly Aristotle conceives his own rhetoric as so new and different from its predecessors that it is entirely a different enterprise. Though he allows a kind of grudging credit to the history of Greek rhetoric, beginning with Tisias and continuing through Theodorus and Thrasymachus, when he comes to his own work, he writes,

> Of our present inquiry, however, it is not true to say that it had already been partly elaborated and partly not; nay, it did not exist at all. For the training given by the paid teachers of contentious argument resembled the system of Gorgias. For some of them gave their pupils to learn by heart speeches which were either rhetorical or consisted of questions and answers, in which both sides thought that the rival arguments were for the most part included. Hence the teaching which they gave to their pupils was rapid but unsystematic; for they conceived that they could train their pupils by imparting to them not an art but the results of an art, just as if one should claim to be about to communicate knowledge for the prevention of pain in the feet and then were not to teach the cobbler's art and the means of providing suitable foot-gear, but were to offer a selection of various kinds of shoes. (183^b32–184^b1)

By the time Cicero writes, this notion of rhetoric has taken on the quality of a truism. "To my thinking," he writes in *De Oratore*,

the virtue in all the rules is, not that orators by following them
have won a reputation for eloquence, but that certain persons
have noted and collected the doings of men who were naturally
eloquent: thus eloquence is not the offspring of the art, but the
art of eloquence. (1, chap. 32, n. 146)

Though her reading of Aristotle is more sweeping and in every way
more professional than mine, de Romilly reads Aristotle in much
the same way as I do, arguing that his effort to make rhetoric academically respectable depended on his strategy to make it a τέχνη,
which he accomplished by stripping out the magic, the irrational
inspiration, and making rhetoric into an analytical mode (58-88).
Cole reinforces this point with his incisive comment that Aristotle
"provides no instances of his own skill [in rhetoric] at all, confining
himself to analysis and, when examples are required, to excerpts
from the published writings of others" (129). Farrell does the same
when he says, "Aristotle nowhere says that the aim of rhetoric is to
be persuasive. . . . the aim of rhetoric is to *practice* judgment (to
enact *Krisis*) where certain sorts of problematic materials are concerned" (185). And Hugh Lawson-Tancred makes the same point
when explains that Aristotle "saw the task of rhetoric not as the
production of persuasion but as the discovery of the latently persuasive in any subject" (56).

The power of this reformulation of rhetoric can hardly be over-
stated. Through it, Aristotle creates a place in professional discourse
where one can be a professional analyst who claims no skill at all in
doing the thing the analyst analyzes. Few who teach public speaking
or composition in American universities, for example, believe themselves to be persuasive as public speakers or effective as professional
writers unless they can confine themselves within a thoroughly academic setting, a setting similar to that at the Lyceum. Even fewer can
offer their own texts as generally approved and acclaimed examples of
what students are to learn to do. This transformation of rhetoric
from a how-to course intended to guarantee successful public-speak-
ing ability into a discourse about discourse allows apprentices who
have never written or spoken a professional word outside the academy to play the role of analyst/teacher (a role Aristotle himself played
in his early years at Plato's Academy). No student would ever think
to ask such apprentices for samples of their own successful writing
and speaking. More importantly, the role of nonperforming profes-

sional analyst allows tenured faculty to play the role of authority, even though they have no texts of their own to show as examples; or, if they do have texts, most of the time they themselves construe their own texts as wholly inappropriate as pedagogical examples. A large majority would be embarrassed to show what they write to their students because their students would not be able to read it. While I certainly believe that one can become a better composition teacher by studying Aristotle, I also believe that Aristotelian theory, if followed to its teleological destiny, takes one out of the classroom entirely, impelling one toward the life of a pure research scholar.

The how-to rhetoric that Aristotle dismisses with such contempt had resulted from the political circumstances prevailing in several Greek city-states. In those places where how-to rhetorics developed, all citizens enjoyed equality before the law, freedom of speech, and the democratic responsibility of speaking for themselves. This highly democratic rhetoric was a rhetoric in which there were no "enthymeme masters," a rhetoric that purported to teach nothing more than successful public speaking. Professional rhetoric after Aristotle, in contrast, has the primary task of getting itself straight. It operates inside itself in a self-reflexive way. It creates a space in professional discourse where exemplary scholars like Eugene Garver can define the subject matter and set the boundaries of rhetoric, each gesture being absolutely indispensable for the playing out of demonstrative discourse, each gesture being absolutely necessary before a professional discourse can know itself by developing its jargon and defining its turf. "Aristotle has found," Garver explains, "a subject-matter for rhetoric and rhetoric alone." Until that essential task was performed, rhetoric could neither present itself as a professional discourse nor begin to operate as demonstrative language in a scientifically circumscribed arena. Aristotle's "instructions to legislators," Garver continues, "restrict rhetoric to those subjects for which there is no better method, about which rhetoric therefore is not a second-best method. With respect to those subjects, there is no appeal outside rhetoric, no 'right' answer that the rhetorician, or the audience, might or might not fail to assert" ("Work" 9–10). Aristotle shows modern rhetoricians how to have a professional discourse that obviates questions about where it came from and what it should accomplish; no external discourse precedes and enables the getting straight of rhetoric inside rhetoric. Inside the boundaries of this discourse, Garver can claim to "show how important a correct interpretation [of Aristotle's *Rhetoric*] is" ("Sciences" 383). No doubt Garver does not expect, or even desire, that other rhetoricians cease to offer interpretations of the *Rhetoric* now that he has presented his "correct" interpretation. What he expects is for rhetoricians to continue to argue about the correctness of his—or anyone else's—interpretation, a task that remains self-satisfying, self-obviously necessary, always better than it used to be, and unending. In this way, rhetoric, which is not and cannot be science, becomes a self-enabling site for scientific knowledge, a site that can forever reknow itself as if it had never known itself properly before. On this site, Friedrich Solmsen can claim in 1929, after twenty-four centuries and millions of analyses of the *Rhetoric*, that no one has really given a full accounting of the enthymeme; Grimaldi can say in 1972 that "post-Aristotelian rhetorical study toward an understanding of the enthymeme is non-existent" (68); and Ryan can claim in 1984 that though the enthymeme has received some attention, "no one that I have been able to discover has attempted to investigate thoroughly the entire theory of argumentation as it is found in *Rhet*" (10). Not one living person who has any experience at all with professional discourse would have expected Ryan to be the last to claim that no one has given a full and correct explication of the enthymeme. In fact, any attempt to settle dispute over a major piece of turf within the geography of a professional discourse has the same effect as turning up the heat under a kettle of boiling water. The molecules do not slow down, they speed up. In the same year that Ryan published his book, Conley published an essay on the history of interpretations of *enthymeme* ("The Enthymeme in Perspective"), and Michael Hood published a bibliography dealing solely with treatments of the Aristotelian enthymeme in the modern period.[8]

One can choose almost any term in the Aristotelian rhetorical lexicon and find the same ongoing contestation. Such words as $\tau\acute{\epsilon}\chi\nu\eta$, $\delta\acute{\upsilon}\nu\alpha\mu\iota\varsigma$, and $\pi\acute{\iota}\sigma\tau\iota\varsigma$ are obvious examples in that border wars and definitional skirmishes go on in and around them all the time,[9] but even less obvious terms such as $\phi\rho\acute{o}\nu\eta\sigma\iota\varsigma$[10] and $\acute{\epsilon}\xi\iota\varsigma$[11] name sites of contention. In one century E. Havet argues that Aristotle's definitions of sign, necessary sign, and probability are hopelessly confused (57); in the next, Grimaldi replies that these definitions are quite clear (*Studies* 105). Grimaldi, in turn, offers careful definitions of $\epsilon\emph{i}\kappa o\varsigma$ and $\kappa o\iota\nu o\grave{\iota}$ $\tau\acute{o}\pi o\iota$; two decades later Cole replies that a meaningful definition of such terms cannot be made (152–53). And enthymeme's companion term, *example*, has attracted almost as much attention as its more famous twin. In the last twenty years, for example, William Benoit ("Aristotle's Example" and "On Aristotle's Example"), Scott Consigny ("The Rhetorical Example"), Gerard Hauser ("The Example in Aristotle's Rhetoric," "Aristotle's Example Revisited," and "Reply to Benoit"), Michael McGuire ("Some Problems with Rhetorical Example"), and James Raymond ("Enthymemes, Examples, and Rhetorical Method") have carried on a lively debate on the site of that term.[12]

Inside rhetoric, as the contemporary literature shows quite well, one finds an endless series of crucially important disputes. While these disputes may seem trivial to anyone outside the discourse, to those inside, nothing could possibly be more important. Inside physics, the dispute over whether light is a particle or a wave has generated reams of literature, as have disputes over whether certain quarks have charm, top spin, or bottom spin. Those of us outside the discourse can do no more than watch with amusement. Inside, however, careers, endowed chairs, enormous grant subsidies, and extravagant perks hang in the balance. As examples of what I mean, I will summarize two small subdisputes over the ontology of rhetoric.

In 1977 Carl Holmberg argued that there are two kinds of rhetoric. The first, dialectical rhetoric, descends from Plato and has the following two characteristics:

> (1) Speaking and writing are to be clear and correct if truth is to be ascertained; therefore, rhetoric as style (*lexis*) has to do with clarity of expression and simplicity of syntax. (2) If there should be various experiences of reality, only one of the experiences, if any, can be correct; therefore, rhetoric as persuasion will aim at the conversion of experiencers who are "incorrect" to the "correct" view.

The second rhetoric, according to Holmberg, is rhetorical rather than dialectical and descends from Aristotle, bringing along the two following characteristics:

> (1) Speaking and writing are enthymematic; that is, the grounds of the connections of meaning are left undefined or ambiguous and the speaking and writing are open for various and equally

correct interpretations; therefore, rhetoric as style has to do with the duplicity or ambiguity of expression and nonconventional syntax. (2) If there should be various experiences of reality, any of them may be treated as potentially "correct"; therefore, rhetoric as persuasion becomes the converting of experience to such degrees that each different person can come to realize how "reality" is shaped for others and that, in turn, these alternatives are alike and viable. (238–39)

This notion of the two kinds of rhetoric was allowed to languish for a decade in the professional discourse, but in 1986 and then in 1989 it received two replies. Robert Gaines replied in 1986 with the absolutely necessary—for the professional discourse—reversal of Holmberg. Aristotle's rhetoric, Gaines, attempts to show, is not rhetorical at all; rather, it meets all the requirements for dialectic and is thus dialectical (194–200). Three years later Scott Consigny entered the fray, addressing first Holmberg's formulation that Aristotle's rhetoric is rhetorical and then Gaines's rejoinder that it is dialectical. "One may feel," Consigny concludes, "compelled to decide whether Aristotle's rhetoric is rhetorical, grounded in and affirming an indeterminate reality; or whether it is dialectical, relying on and articulating truths about a determinate reality." Behaving as a true professional, however, Consigny does exactly as one would expect, arguing that "Aristotle presents a third alternative, a rhetoric that enables the rhetor to discern persuasive elements of a given framework of beliefs while remaining free of such ontological commitments" (281–82).

So far as I know, no one has entered the fray since Consigny (though I do not pretend to cutting-edge acquaintance with the literature of rhetorical studies). If, indeed, the literature has been silent since Consigny, the likely strands of the conversation, when it is picked up again—as it almost surely will be—are fairly obvious. One could, for example, point out Holmberg's category error, an error in which such a thing as a "rhetorical rhetoric" can exist, an error in which something becomes a subset of itself or exists through having its own characteristics. Or one could join Gaines with Grimaldi and Ryan to make yet another pitch for Aristotle as the fountainhead for all that is good about public discourse in the Western world. Or one could join Consigny with those who see Aristotle as having changed rhetoric into a mode of (academic) analysis in which one can make studies without making ontological commitments. Or one could follow my pattern by agreeing with Consigny that Aristotle makes rhetoric into a mode of academic analysis; then, however, one would turn the reading against itself by arguing that no human being can act without making ontological commitments. Or one could pick up Holmberg's case, ally it with Heidegger and Stanley Fish, and argue passionately that a "rhetorical rhetoric" is by no means a category error. By using Heidegger's warning in *Grundbegriffe* against any attempt to identify the sphere of Being with that of rationality and then turning to Fish's contention that poststructuralist thought, with all its antifoundationalism, is "supremely rhetorical" (*Doing* 492–93), one could argue that "rhetoric" as a site of dispute has been so corrupted that the category "rhetorical rhetoric" is not only necessary but also clarifying.

Perhaps a better example of the operation of professional discourse is the rhetoric-as-epistemic dispute that ran its course from the late sixties through the early eighties. This dispute resembles the Holmberg-Gaines-Consigny argument, except that it extended over a longer period, included many more participants, and became prominent enough to be assigned its own name in the literature. Robert Scott started the argument in 1967 with his claim that rhetoric "is a way of knowing; it is epistemic." For a time, one could not attend conventions sponsored by the Speech Communication Association or the Rhetoric Society without hearing numerous arguments and panel discussions about the issue. In 1976, after Scott published his "On Viewing Rhetoric as Epistemic: Ten Years Later," the debate seemed to be everywhere. Thomas Farrell ("Knowledge, Consensus, and Rhetorical Theory") entered the fray in 1976, then Richard Cherwitz ("Rhetoric as a Way of Knowing") jumped in 1977, and in 1978, the peak year for the discussion, Lloyd Bitzer ("Rhetoric and Public Knowledge"), Walter Carleton ("What Is Rhetorical Knowledge? A Reply to Farrell—And More"), Michael Leff ("In Search of Ariadne's Thread"), Jack Orr ("How Shall We Say: 'Reality Is Socially Constructed Through Communication'?"), and, once again, Thomas Farrell ("Social Knowledge II") took up the debate. By 1982 Earl Croasmun and Richard Cherwitz could write a long overview of the various sides to the dispute, and then, in 1990, the *Quarterly Journal of Speech* could publish a "Forum" entitled "The Reported Demise of Epistemic Rhetoric" in which several of the luminaries in the debate could reflect on what they had meant all along.

Barry Brummett's "Eulogy" for the rhetoric-as-epistemic movement begins the *QJS* "Forum," with Brummett summarizing the history of the movement's "life" from birth in 1967 to death in 1990. He argues that rhetoric-as-epistemic died because it remained too theoretical; it never got itself tied down to lived discourse (69–72). Cherwitz and James Hikins speak second in the "Forum" and respond to Brummett's eulogy. While they agree that the phrase "rhetoric-as-epistemic," which had been everywhere from 1975 to 1985, had, by 1990, begun to disappear from convention programs and scholarly essays, they argue that it would be a "cataclysmic" mistake to turn away from theory and concentrate on practice. Rather than less theorizing, they ask for better theorizing, theorizing less dependent on Rorty, Feyerabend, Kuhn, Toulmin, Bernstein, Rescher, and others (73–77). Thomas Farrell, a major player in the discussions of the late seventies, speaks last in the "Forum," trying to mediate between the "It's dead" pronouncement of Brummett and the "We'll be back" response of Cherwitz and Hikins. Farrell's response reveals him as one of the most successful, widely read scholars of rhetoric in this half-century. He announces himself *as* a rhetorician, and then he offers his own "rhetorical reading" of the two preceding essays in the "Forum," thus making clear that such a thing as a "rhetorical reading" exists, that it can be performed, and that any professional can read the performance, extracting what it says. Finally, as any good rhetorician speaking about rhetoric must, Farrell defines his field: "Rhetoric, at least as interpreted by its traditions, is a collaborative manner of engaging others through discourse so that contingencies may be resolved, judgments rendered, action procured" (78–84).

Farrell's strategy is honest and professional. Explicitly he waves goodbye with one hand to the catchphrase "rhetoric-as-epistemic." Having generated a good deal of professional discourse, the phrase has lived its life and made its contribution. With the other hand, however, Farrell points back to the central concern ("What is rhetoric?") of the discourse by offering a definition on which one can build a reading of rhetoric or with which one can disagree. Certainly Farrell does not expect—or want—the SCA to publish his definition and in doing so cease to publish essays on "What is rhetoric?" Implicitly, Farrell restakes his claim to being a thoroughly professional, splendidly educated rhetorician, a claim that is, in my opinion, fully justified.

As with all such professional debates over a "name" for the field, the rhetoric-as-epistemic site for discussion did not vanish from the earth with its eulogy in *QJS* in 1990. The very next year, Daniel Royer added his voice to the waning chorus by trying to draw that debate more directly into the teaching of writing, and just last week I received from a journal for which I referee an essay dealing with rhetoric-as-epistemic. In effect, the rhetoric-as-epistemic movement merely served to embody the language of poststructuralism in rhetorical studies. At the time, most disciplines were reprocessing poststructural analysis in one way or another. Rhetoric-as-epistemic was rhetoric's way of accomplishing this academically necessary task.

Scaglione puts his finger on the matter I am trying to tease out, though his motive and his purpose differ from mine. Writing in the context of such splits as rhetoric versus philosophy, thought versus expression, and sophistic versus peripatetic, Scaglione concludes that "rhetoric was born as a *Janus bifons*, 'two-faced Janus,' since it had a 'logical' side, pertaining to the $\tau\epsilon\chi\nu\eta$ of persuasion, and an aesthetic, 'artistic' side, grounded in the doctrine of *ornatus* as the basic aspect of style" (11–13). I have but one difference with Scaglione. Whereas he seems to think the contradictions leading to so many splits in the attempted definitions of rhetoric grow out of the nature of rhetoric itself—as a divided, self-contradictory "thing"— I believe the contradictions grow out of the nature of professional discourse, which can only speak itself as a struggle to know itself, and which can enjoy such a struggle only if voices restate, elaborate on, differ with, enhance, and attack each other inside the charmed circle.

Situated Writing III: In the Chair Where Aristotle Sat

Aristotle, after all, created not only the place in which we could dispute what would, after him, be known as "professional, academic rhetoric" but also the notion of demonstration, through which one could behave professionally. And he created a fully legitimate inside for rhetoric, a place where rhetoricians could live, love, reproduce, and generally be happy. While rhetoric itself does not allow for demonstration, "rhetoric" as a field of discussion allows for little else. Scholars of rhetoric who write about Aristotle are not out to achieve temporary persuasion; they are out to explain the truth.

Because Aristotle cannot define rhetoric "by genus and differentia," Garver explains, he "must rely on the contrasts between rhetoric and its neighbors" to an unusual degree. Aristotle gives both a positive definition and an articulation of the boundaries between rhetoric and "sources of persuasion outside of discourse and hence outside the *art* of rhetoric." Garver treats the passage at 1358ª1–28 in detail. This is the passage in which Aristotle explains what happens when a rhetorician accidentally "hits on a principle." When this happens, "the progressive growth of knowledge" begins. Once knowledge (ἐπιστήμη) begins to develop, the discourse changes from opinion-based to knowledge-based; thus, rhetoric disappears because the discourse has moved from rhetoric to science. For rhetoric, Garver continues, "scientific discourse is no less a transgression than using the results of torture." The subtlety of this refiguration of rhetoric is easy to overlook. Aristotle assigns rhetoric to a place where science must be absent; as a result, rhetoric becomes a place where science works constantly to explain exactly how and why it is absent. The rhetoric that one might practice—that is to say any attempt to persuade an audience as quickly and effectively as possible—constitutes the never actually practiced outside of the inside in which rhetoricians work out exactly how persuasion might be or might have been accomplished—without, of course, any attempt actually to accomplish it apart from gaining a place in the discourse *inside* the profession. Rhetoricians inside rhetoric attempt correct interpretations and true histories because they are professionals. If they did anything else, in the terms of the Aristotelian system, they would not be professionals. Rather, they would be the amateur lovers of public discourse, anathema to any fully credentialed and ambitious professional. After Aristotle, rhetoric is no place for just fooling around, no place for the excess of a tour de force whose only goal is a celebration of its own excess.

Aristotelian rhetoric turns out to offer a nearly limitless site for disputation. Already in Aristotle, for example, one finds a field with an "inside" and an "outside" and a society peopled by a very small group of "those who really know about rhetoric" and a vast group of "those who don't know." Aristotle creates for himself an "in the know place" by contrasting himself with all those other "compilers" of rhetorics who do not know that the proofs (πίστεις) constitute the essence of rhetoric and thus foolishly "devote their attention to matters outside the subject." In a well-administered state, a state with properly written laws, such "out-of-the-know rhetoricians" would "have nothing to say" because they do not know how to teach mastery of the enthymeme. Those who do not know rhetoric try to lay down definite rules for "what should be the contents of the exordium or the narrative, or of the other parts of the discourse," thus "bringing under the rules of art what is outside the subject" (1354ᵇ16–19). As a result, these "misleading and ignorant" rhetoricians deal only with judicial strategies for putting the judge in the right frame of mind. They do not understand that within the confines of true rhetoric, the place where rhetoric is truly itself and not something else, one becomes "master of the enthymeme"; they do not understand that within true rhetoric, the true rhetorician is almost always someone who does not give and does not purport to teach others how to give persuasive speeches. Inside true rhetoric, the rhetorician knows how to dispute the essence and the ontology of rhetoric (1354ᵇ21–22).

After Aristotle, rhetoric becomes both a hierarchy and a body. In the hierarchy the logos reigns supreme, with every other possible appeal arrayed before it, awaiting its life-giving, enabling command. In the body, some organs exist essentially, others peripherally and expendably. Something can, in other words, be part of rhetoric without contributing to its essence because that nonessential thing, if omitted, leaves rhetoric still rhetoric, just as a person without tonsils remains a person.[13]

Once such a hierarchy and such a body appear on the scene, what we now call "rhetoric" can assume its name and know itself as its discrete and governable parts. It can equate reason with true being by relegating emotion (whether prejudice, pity, anger, or fear) to a penumbra somewhere between nonessential being and false being. It can create for itself a space where "speaking outside the subject" becomes a transgression against true being that every true being recognizes immediately (1354ᵃ21–24, 1355ᵃ1–2). Inside the inside of true rhetoric, inside the perception of true 'being', rhetoric takes up residence. And on that scene only the creations of true rhetoric, only the manufacture of true 'being' can claim ontological security. Anything outside the creative power of the enthymeme-mastering logos, anything that just any old person can easily see, anything that can claim "to be" outside the rhetorician's power to declare "let there be" (Ἔστω δή) really is not rhetorical.

Situated Writing IV: Rhetoric as Body

For rhetoric to inhabit the security of its inside, as Aristotle the taxonomist well knew, it must have a barrier/border between itself and all that is "not-rhetoric"; it must have an organized and efficient interior, an interior with its own discreet and independent parts; it must have clothing on the outside of its border/barrier; and, most important of all, in spite of its own "general" nature, it must have an object of study. In giving rhetoric 'being', Aristotle provides rhetoric with a border/barrier inside which it can be itself; next he describes rhetoric's interior, giving it its own taxonomy and hierarchy, a taxonomy and hierarchy that only those on the inside can hope to understand; then he defines rhetoric's object of study; and finally, with the border in place, the interior arranged, and the object of study in view, he sews the clothing that will cover and camouflage the exterior.

The border/barrier appears when Aristotle locates rhetoric in the realm of contingent reality where it deals "only with something whose essential being presents the ambiguous situation in which the thing may or may not occur. Anything whose essential being predetermines that it already is or that it inevitably will be, or anything whose essential being makes it impossible lies outside the scope of rhetoric."** Rhetoric deals only with those things within human control about which humans may disagree (1359^a30-^b1). Where there is no doubt, where no judgment can be made, Aristotle repeats later, no rhetoric can occur (1391^b7-8). More importantly, rhetoric cannot present a discourse about any specific thing, because then it would become a science; rather, rhetoric must forever remain discourse about discourse itself (μόνον λόγων 1359^b12-16, see also 1355^b8-9, 33–34). Within that mandate, rhetoric is universal in that it seeks to discover in any situation how persuasion might occur and to articulate in any situation the difference between real persuasion and persuasion that merely seems real (1355^b8-17).[14] This set of specifications provides rhetoric with the epidermis that allows it to have an inside where it can be itself, behave like itself, and know itself as separate from all that it is not. Only in rhetoric, as Garver ("Work" 10), Vickers (5, n. 5), and Kennedy (*Classical* 15) have all pointed out, can one be successful and yet fail. Inside the protective barrier that allows rhetoric to organize itself, the rhetorician can fail to persuade an audience, indeed, can be laughably inept at persuading audiences, yet remain ontologically intact so long as that rhetorician can show to other rhetoricians the means available for persuasion and demonstrate mastery of the enthymeme. In other words, so long as one masters the professional discourse about discourse, one *is* a rhetorician. And in a perverse sort of way, rhetoric assumes itself as its object, for it can have no other object and remain itself.

Sheltered and defined by this protective barrier, inside its own skin, as it were, rhetoric can organize itself as a discourse about discourse. This discourse disallows only one thing: silence. Since silence cannot *be* for rhetoric to *be* (itself), the inside of discourse must be polyvocal, which it is in a variety of ways. Inside the enclosure of discourse about discourse, rhetoric appears in three different "particular states" ($\varepsilon\check{\iota}\delta\eta$ 1358^{a}36), "genres" ($\gamma\acute{\varepsilon}\nu\eta$ 1358^{b}7–8) or "ontological conditions" ($o\check{\upsilon}\sigma\iota$ 1358^{b}20–22), which Aristotle names deliberative, forensic, and epideictic. Each of these three forms has its own time and purpose, its own telos and value. Each telos constitutes itself as an essential tension: deliberative is the tension between the better and the worse, forensic between the just and the unjust, epideictic between the honorable and the disgraceful (1358^{b}20–29). The three forms of discourse then arrange themselves in a hierarchy. Deliberative and forensic exist first and second as a kind of permanent, hierarchically arranged opposition. Epideictic forever lags behind as a third form. Deliberative rhetoric, Aristotle explains (before he has gotten around to telling us that epideictic forms a third state, species, or ontological condition for rhetoric), "is nobler and more worthy of a statesman than [forensic]" (1354^{b}22–29). And this is just the beginning of the pairing between deliberative and forensic, for deliberative is more scrupulous, more broadly based, more personal, more easily focused on the facts, more disinterested, and more dependent on artistic proofs; while forensic is more unscrupulous, more narrowly based, more impersonal, more prone to pandering, more susceptible to emotional appeal, and more open to nonessential arguments. Epideictic, clearly the third-place form, is inferior even to forensic simply because the epideictic occasion lends itself to and depends upon showiness and verbal display. After all, the main topics for epideictic are amplification and glorification, topics that tend naturally toward display rather than toward intellectual analysis. The main topics for forensic and deliberative, in contrast, are the past, the possible, and the future, the sort of topics on which the intellect can truly exercise itself (1391^{b}22–1392^{a}7). The hierarchy of the three is clear in a second way. Deliberative is the most difficult because it deals with the making of the future. Moreover, deliberative offers few opportunities to wander from the topic, to waste time with nonessentials, or to stoop to an emotional appeal. Forensic, in contrast, has the easier task of interpreting the past. Equally as important, forensic, unlike deliberative, has the secure foundation of the written law, which offers forensic demonstrations a definite point of origin, thereby making forensic easier. Epideictic, in contrast to the clearly superior forms of deliberative and forensic, "should be varied with laudatory episodes" after the manner of Isocrates and Gorgias; thus, epideictic by its very nature, drifts toward sophistry, toward the "empty show" of style and delivery for their own sakes. In epideictic, the vulgarity of an emotional appeal and the gaudiness of a stylistic tour de force are practically impossible to avoid.

Thus not only does Aristotle provide for rhetoric a location and a border/barrier inside which to *be* and *do*, but he also gives it the hierarchy of genera, forms, or states that allow for the sort of polyvocality necessary to any professional discourse. At this point, however, even though the really complicated process of professional discourse formation has hardly begun, already Aristotle has laid out the geography of a site where professionals can dispute the borders of rhetoric: Where do the borders stop? What do the borders border on? Do they encroach on anything else? What threatens to encroach on them? Within these questions, rhetoricians can forever debate the various genera, forms, or states of rhetoric, discussing whether the list is finite, exclusive, and complete or infinite, inclusive, and always expanding. As long as people talk and write, this border-genera work can never be complete.

The true work of rhetoric in the Aristotelian frame of reference, however, is epistemological and ontological, and Aristotle knew full well that rhetoric, like any true being, requires an organizing, controlling center, a place where pure self-presence can know itself, command its resources, and make its decisions; a place, in short, where the νοῦς can know itself in a fully self-present, unself-conscious way. Of course, Aristotle also knew that essential 'being' requires nonessential 'being' in order to know itself; thus, he gave rhetoric both an essence and a variety of accessories. In rhetoric "it is necessary to state the subject, and then to prove it," he explains, just as a demonstrator must state a problem and then conduct a demonstration. Articulation of an essence allows "those who know" to see just how ridiculous (γελοίως) "those who don't know" are when they demand that optional parts such as introduction, narration, proof, refutation, and peroration be present in a discourse (1414ᵃ30–ᵇ18). Inside the border/barrier of rhetoric, therefore, the three forms of rhetoric have their two essential parts and their accessories. The two true and truly necessary "parts" command and employ the optional and unnecessary "parts."

Aristotle spends a fair amount of time offering very practical, very sophistical advice about the optional "parts." This has a double effect. On one hand, it gives his *Rhetoric* the feel of a genuine manual of rhetorical strategies—a sort of "here's how you do it" textbook. On the other hand, it protects the location, habitation, and operation of the νοῦς, the place where the proofs can let their hair down and just *be*. Take the introduction, for example (1414ᵇ19–1416ᵃ2). Though the introduction is the "way into" a speech (its ὁδοποίησις), it is not actually part of the speech: "we must not lose sight of the fact that all such things are outside the true essence of the logos itself"* (ἔξω τοῦ λόγου). On an epideictic occasion, the introduction "may be either foreign or intimately connected with the speech." It can function as nothing more than verbal pyrotechnics, "as flute-players begin by playing whatever they can execute skilfully and attach it to the key-note." In a forensic speech, the introduction plays the role of prologue to a drama or the prelude to an epic. If the subject of the speech is immediately clear, however, or if the matter is small and inconsequential, the speaker should not use any introduction at all. Since "deliberative oratory borrows its introductions from forensic," the introduction in deliberative oratory is optional, and, indeed, is rare, having no other function than ornament because the absence of an introduction often "makes the speech appear offhand," offhandedness (or at least the appearance of offhandedness) being a desirable quality in deliberative rhetoric. Just as the absence of clothing, depending on the situation, might make a person appear undressed, the presence of clothing in other situations might make a person seem overdressed. Either way, clothing itself is not an essential feature of humanity.

Aristotle makes clear that the introduction has nothing to do with the "speech itself." It exists only because of the hearer's weak-minded tendency to listen to what is beside the point. When the hearer is too clever or too well trained to be distracted by something beside the point, the introduction becomes more liability than asset. The introduction has an endlessly reversible function: it can justify or vilify, raise or lower seriousness, dispel or create prejudice, raise or lower importance, add elegance or bawdiness, and so on. In sum the "introduction" is dispensable, moveable, and reversible. Above all, it protects the logos by being outside of, unnecessary to, and dependent on the logos.

The narrative (1416ª14–1417ª24) and the epilogue (1419ᵇ10– 1420ª8), like the introduction, are dispensable, reversible, intermittent, deceitful, and, when used, purely functional. The epilogue has four functional capabilities: "to dispose the hearer favourably towards oneself and unfavourably towards the adversary; to amplify and depreciate; to excite the emotions of the hearer; to recapitulate." The narrative is dispensable in epideictic because the actions of the situation exist outside rhetoric, its νοῦς, and its λόγος. The narrative is intermittent because the speaker needs different narratives in different places to show such different qualities as courage, wisdom, and righteousness. It is rare in deliberative "because no one can narrate things to come." It is reversible in forensic because accusers make much of it to construct their attack, while defendants use little of it, and use it differently, to defend themselves. It is deceitful because it has the function of giving the speech and the speaker the appearance of "moral character" rather than the appearance of sharp intellect. Oddly enough, though, the *appearance of* moral character requires a sharp intellect. Only a rhetor with a sharp intellect can use that sharp intellect both to create the "appearance of" moral character and to efface the sharp intellect itself. Sharp intellect, in other words, must be sharp enough to conceal itself and seem to be the pure and simple honesty of moral character.[15]

Having dispensed with all of the "accessories" at this level of the being of rhetoric, Aristotle can turn his attention to the place where rhetoric is truly itself. Rhetoric can be itself, he argues, only when it functions demonstratively in the pure serenity of its two essential parts: the statement of the subject and its proof. The statement of the subject is so utterly obvious that, beyond its self-evident self-annunciation, nothing else needs saying. The proofs, on the other hand, are the essence of both rhetoric and the *Rhetoric*. And what an essence! It is just the sort that a field of professional discourse needs, for in the heart of the heart of rhetoric, demonstrative reason-

ing can work forever, always making the essence and operation of
rhetoric clearer than it was before, always rescuing rhetoric, like a
damsel in distress, from those who would pervert or misuse it.[16]

The previous compilers of rhetoric, Aristotle complains in his
second paragraph, in the process carefully separating himself from
"those who don't know," "have provided us with only a small portion
of the art, for proofs [πίστεις] are the only things in it that come
within the province of art; everything else is merely an accessory"
(1354[a]11–16).[17] These rhetoricians "who don't know," he continues
his delineation, "give no account of the artificial proofs [τῶν
ἐντέχνων πίστεων], which make a man a master of rhetorical argument" (1354[b]21–22). These "artificial proofs" turn out to be just as
complicated, just as unsettled and unsettling as one would expect
inside a professional discourse.[18] To begin with, the proofs, which
we already know to be the "essence" of the inside of rhetoric, turn
out to be neither stable nor univocal. The proofs themselves turn
out to have an "essence" of their own, a "body" as Aristotle calls it.
And this body that constitutes the essence of the essence of rhetoric,
this place where the minimum set of ontological specifications (the
DNA, one might say) for rhetoric are inscribed, has its own accessories whereby it can know itself as essence and not accessory. The
"body" (σῶμα) of the proofs is the enthymeme, outside of which
everything else is "mere accessory." Inside the essence of the essence
of rhetoric, however, inside the very cavity of its "body," the professional rhetorician does not find a nugget or a foundation or a name.
Rather, the professional rhetorician finds an ever-shifting set of oppositions and hierarchies as rhetoric plays out the founding of itself
forever.

In the first opposition, the proofs know themselves by differing
from rhetorical strategies that seek only "to put the judge in a certain
frame of mind:" In the second opposition, they know themselves
by being artificial, by being proofs that the rhetor-who-knows knows
how to invent. In the third opposition the proofs extract their identity
from the language of philosophy. In this set of oppositions, rhetoric
functions as the receiving side of a copula, where it draws life in
the following ways (1355[a]4–18):[19]

> an artistic rhetoric "*is* about the proofs"
> "proof *is* a kind of demonstration" (ἀπόδειξίς τις)
> "rhetorical demonstration *is* an enthymeme"

> "the enthymeme *is* a kind of syllogism"
> "the study of every kind of syllogism in a similar manner *is* dialectic"
> "the one who has the greatest ability at theorizing on how and from where syllogisms arise *will also be* the best master of the enthymeme"
> "the abilities to see the truth and to see those things that resemble the truth *are* the same ability."

And there is yet one more opposition. In this last opposition the proofs operate as the antitheses of themselves in that they conduct their business either through enthymeme, which we already knew, or through example, which we do not learn until the middle of chapter 2 (1356^b). In keeping with the logic of the other oppositions, the opposition between enthymeme and example reveals that rhetorical induction is not the full induction of dialectic, ἐπαγωγή, but rather its simplified inferior, παράδειγμα, just as rhetorical deduction is not the full deduction of syllogism but rather the truncated and simplified "rhetorical" deduction. This particular opposition is especially complicated because it never ceases to function as its own self-reversal or undoing in that example (or induction) leads up to the point at which enthymeme (or deduction) begins and can never cross over that point, just as enthymeme begins at the point where example leaves off and can never reach back beyond that point. One can even argue that example serves not only as the twin of enthymeme but also as its parent. Example functions as parent because example (or induction) constitutes the process both prior to and necessary for enthymeme (or deduction). By giving enthymeme a partner (or twin) whose process has clear parental overtones, Aristotle may appear to have used imprecise terminology or even to have contradicted himself. Actually what he has done is to give system and method precedence over happenstance and accident. Enthymeme must have priority of place so that it can discover its own origin in induction. "Let there be rhetoric" (ἔστω δὴ ῥητορική) appears in the West as an already formed and organized system. Once the logic and control of that system have been articulated, the induction that enabled the system can appear. Its appearance, however, comes on a scene already set and controlled by enthymeme. If the system began with induction, it would begin in the chaotic swirl of random phenomena, in a kind of primordial soup where the elements might coalesce in unexpected, even frightening ways. Things might even work out in such a way that the enthymeme master is not the master at all. If, however, induction appears after the organization of deduction has already stabilized discourse, the original primordial soup in which everything was up for grabs is always already history.

These complex and shifting oppositions do not, however, complete the essence of the essence of rhetoric. They merely form a new exterior inside the interior, giving this new interior of the interior a border/barrier of its own. Much as an the internal organ of a living being has its own walls, its own rules of organization, and its own physiological processes, the essence of the essence of rhetoric (its heart or brain one might say) has its own walls, rules of operation, and interior life. Inside the interior of the proofs, inside the essence of the essence of rhetoric, one finds a new arrangement, this time a complex and detailed hierarchy in which the proofs (still called the πίστεις 1356ª1–27) present themselves in three different forms. The first way the proofs can be themselves in this hierarchy "depends upon the moral character of the speaker, the second upon putting the hearer into a certain frame of mind, the third upon the speech itself." In keeping with the logic and operation of a hierarchy, this particular hierarchy gives precedence to only one of its self-manifestations, the logos. So powerful does that term become that we render it into English as "the speech itself," and we give its name to the very act of being reasonable. The logos has the authority to use itself to prove itself through an appeal to itself; in the interior of the essence of the essence of rhetoric, the logos finally has a place to be itself completely. If it wishes, since the logos is always in the situation of deciding and disposing, the logos can use an ethical appeal or even a pathetic appeal. This hierarchy gives the logos command of itself by giving it two other manifestations of itself whereby it can recognize itself as a "thing" both to command and to be commanded.

Once again, Aristotle may seem to have been imprecise or self-contradictory. After all, at the beginning of his attempt to articulate the essence of rhetoric, he defines true rhetoric as deriving from proofs and false rhetoric as nothing more than an attempt to "put the judge in a certain frame of mind." Now that he has reached the very heart of the heart of the proofs, however, he tells us that putting the judge into a certain frame of mind *is* a proof. If the logos that names itself and takes command at the very foundation of rhetoric has the power to furnish itself with a pathetic appeal, does this not insinuate the most degraded manifestation of false rhetoric into the very heart of true rhetoric? Well, yes, as a matter of fact it does, but not in a way dangerous to the ontology of rhetoric. What Aristotle has done is to bracket off the most degraded strategy of rhetoric so as to make his own rhetoric pristine and pure. Having done that, he can bring this degraded form back into rhetoric (a pathetic appeal is, after all, a *very* effective means of persuasion) by subordinating it to the logos. Aristotle allows the logos to furnish itself with itself, thus keeping it pristine, while at the same time furnishing itself with pathos and ethos, which are purified by the prior control and pristineness of the enabling, superior logos. George Bush can use the Willie Horton ad in his campaign without becoming a racist, Jimmy Swaggart can frequent prostitutes and remain God's spokesman to a sinful world, and the leader of the newly resurgent German Nazi party can both deny the existence of World War II concentration camps and declare that when the Nazis get their second chance they will not be so lenient and generous with the Jews as was Hitler (in other words, he can deny the existence of concentration camps during the Third Reich as a way of purifying that regime while at the same time promising them in the Fourth Reich as a way of accomplishing what Hitler failed to do, and he can do both these things without seeing the contradiction they embody).

Situated Writing V: Ethos and Pathos as Prophylaxis

The traditional way of interpreting Aristotle's use of the term πίστεις is to argue about whether he has been consistent. Grimaldi, as ever, finds Aristotle's use of the term understandable, coherent, and precise (*Rhetoric I* 349–56). For him, the proofs consist of enthymeme, example, ethos, pathos, and logos, which I have just rehearsed, as well as particular topics, general topics, probabilities, signs, and necessary signs, which, for the sake of brevity, I have ignored. All this explication allows Grimaldi to find a notion of rhetoric through which reason (or the logos) takes command of the soul, where it has access to all aspects of the inside of rhetoric (see especially *Studies* 144–47). Everything about the proofs is consistent and harmonious if only readers are astute enough to understand

Aristotle. Johnstone agrees, arguing that within the inside of the inside of Aristotle's rhetoric "the individual can act self-consciously, with an awareness of what one is doing and of why one ought to be doing it" (2–4). Ryan also agrees with Grimaldi about the coherence, clarity, and precision of the word "proofs," but as one would expect given the way professional discourse always operates, he thinks Grimaldi is right for the wrong reasons. Freese (6), though he offers no explanation, glosses the word "proof" as including enthymeme (in which logos is implied), example, ethos, and pathos.

Others, predictably, have been both less generous with Aristotle and less certain that his term remains consistent. Edward Cope, for example, argues that the proofs consist exclusively of enthymeme and example, and he opposes this sort of proof to ethos and pathos, which necessarily implies that Aristotle was inconsistent or careless. Cooper argues a similar interpretation, making clear that the "proofs" include only enthymeme and example and do not include ethos or pathos. Rhys Roberts and Kennedy, in contrast, waffle. Roberts admits (19, n. 3) that "a uniform rendering of the word is hardly possible," but he goes on to declare that whatever the "proofs" may be, they are not "fully demonstrative." Showing the sophistication of another half- century of professional discourse, Kennedy explains early in his new edition of the *Rhetoric* that the term *proofs* "has a number of different meanings in different contexts" (30, n. 9).

Obviously the dividing point in the debate is whether ethos and pathos are proofs. In fact, any well-trained Aristotelian rhetorician ought to be able to argue either that they are or that they are not. The interesting thing about either argument, however, is the form that the argument (the logos itself) must take in order to be itself. For example, in good Aristotelian form, any theoretical essay about whether pathos is a proof eschews any sort of pathetic appeal and depends absolutely on the demonstrative mimicry of the logos. Though Aristotle includes pathos as an aspect of discourse that a professional rhetorician can and should recognize, he excludes it from the repertoire of rhetorical strategies that any professional rhetorician might resort to. Pathos, after all, comes into existence only because there are audiences that cannot follow the rigors of dialectic, and no self-respecting audience of professional rhetoricians would ever agree to such a self-definition. In fact, those who pose and try to answer a question about whether pathos is a proof merely reify the way Aristotle actually used the term, for he uses it consistently as a prophylactic for the logos. By opposing his own notion of rhetoric against the pathos-based appeals of all prior rhetoricians (1356ª14–17), Aristotle protects the logos of his own system because he situates his logos so that it transcends and controls pathos. Thus, when Aristotelian rhetoric offers the never-used and already neutralized pathetic appeal as part of itself, it does so only after having vetted that appeal and sheltered it by the prior controlling logos. When Aristotle says that the audience determines the telos of a speech (1358ᵇ1–2), or that the most certain mode of persuasion is to appeal to the audience's self-interest (1365ᵇ21–30), or that no successful speaker can afford to speak without considering the prejudices and culture of the audience (1367ᵇ7–9), or that the one to be persuaded "is the judge" (1391ᵇ8–17), not one of these apparent sellouts affects the integrity of the proofs inside the inside of rhetoric, for the logos furnishes itself with such "sellouts," decides when and how to employ them, and because the logos is by definition the logos, it cannot use them inappropriately. Indeed the logos assumes such power of command and privilege that no one writing about pathos as a phenomenon in the history of rhetoric would dare (or even know how) to construct the essay as a pathetic appeal. Of course, every student failing a first-year writing course knows how to make a pathetic appeal. Such a student approaches the teacher with a heartrending, highly personal account of why the student should pass, in effect hoping to achieve through mercy what has not been achieved through mastery of the logos. The teacher recognizes such a pathetic appeal right away and (if the teacher is truly professional) pays no attention at all.

The professional literature about ethos constitutes an even better example of the point I am making about the way Aristotle's *Rhetoric* situates itself. Certainly there are those who argue passionately that ethos fits well within the Aristotelian system of proofs, that it plays a role on the inside of rhetoric under the guidance of logos and in the service of enthymeme. Ryan, for example, sees the entire text of the *Rhetoric* as an ethical document and argues that Aristotle saw his rhetorical principles

> as a means of shaping the ethos of a society. Speakers, using the art of rhetoric, would over a period of time have a great impact on the ethos or character of a society. In no way was it Aristotle's view that the ethos was completely determined by speakers, but

rather that it was developed by an interplay between speakers and hearers, hearers who on the one hand would be influenced by the speakers, and on the other hand themselves be such that Aristotle could write of them that they "are sufficiently disposed toward what is true, and most of the time they attain the truth." (191)

Kate Ronald argues that the whole of the *Rhetoric* is a builder of ethos; its entire text "can be read as a method of discovering choices in language, and being responsible to an audience for those choices" (42). Anyone who believes that the *Rhetoric* allows for an unethical manipulation of the audience's emotions, according to Johnstone, simply does not know how to read the text. A correct reading situates the *Rhetoric* inside its companion text, the *Nicomachean Ethics*. In this light, the passions must be in the "right condition," "amenable to rational guidance." Aristotle gives us what we need to avoid "warping the rule" (8–10). D. S. Hutchinson waxes almost euphoric in describing the wonders of the Aristotelian system on human ethics. He turns to both *Eudemian* and *Nicomachean Ethics* to offer a notion of "the life recommended by Aristotle as best for a man to lead." Such a life "will indeed be intrinsically attractive and it will subsume all the goods which matter to the man who lives it." In an epiphany Hutchinson concludes that Aristotle's system offers "a full life of activity undertaken in light of . . . excellent reasoning," such a life, he claims, "is the highest legitimate aspiration of men" (71–72).

Although I would not claim that I can make a case for ethos as well as do Ryan, Ronald, Johnstone, and Hutchinson, I can claim that I know how to make such a case. In effect, however, I am less interested in learning to speak with Aristotle's voice than I am in trying to hear what the voice sounds like. When Aristotle first addresses the matter of ethos, for example (1356^a1–13), he acknowledges that a speech by a believable, trustworthy speaker is naturally more persuasive than a speech by someone whose character is doubtful. Then, however, Aristotle adds what seems like an odd stipulation. The rhetor's confidence-building ethos "must be due to the speech itself, not to any preconceived idea of the speaker's character." In Book III, Aristotle repeats this principle in a more forceful, much more cynical way. He compares the rhetor to a character in a tragedy whose stage demeanor implies what the coming speech will say. "Present yourself from the beginning of the speech in the character you wish the audience to see," Aristotle explains, "But do not let your audience see what you are doing"* (1417^{b}8–12). This notion of ethos, articulated both at the beginning and at the end of the rhetoric, a principle that Aristotle apparently held throughout his life, has two rather striking implications. First, it separates rhetorical discourse from the lived history of its speaker. The rhetor can live any sort of life while using rhetorical discourse to generate the effect of a moral, reliable ethos.[20] Second, it situates ethos in a role subordinate to logos. The logos's ability to furnish itself with proofs together with its ability to present itself in the form of a finished speech create the ethos of the discourse, which already has nothing to do with the speaker's real lived life. In other words, Aristotelian ethos operates as professional discourse, discourse having nothing at all to do with the human discourse that the speaker would have to speak with a lifelong friend, a family member, or anyone who knows enough about the speaker's personal history to compare the discourse with the known events and behaviors of the speaker's life.

Once the logos in both its rhetorical manifestations—both the controlling reason that manages all aspects of the text and the body of the text itself—takes control of the ethos, then all aspects of ethos become effects of professional writing and speaking ability. Morality, honesty, reliability, and other such human traits that emerge into history only through the behavior of a lifetime, all these ethical issues become effects of the discourse. They have nothing to do with behavior or with the actions and events of human life. In the middle of Book I (1366^{a}25–27), Aristotle explains the nature of virtue and vice, the good and the shameful. In speaking about these opposed qualities, he mentions "the second proof" by saying, "our discussion will at the same time make plain the means by which a speaker may produce in his audience the impression that he is of such and such a character" (Cooper). In other words, virtue and goodness can be rhetorical effects, and by knowing how to produce these effects through the discourse, the rhetor can, as Hamlet says to Gertrude, assume a virtue not actually present in the rhetor's lived life; thus, when Aristotle takes up the matter of ethos in earnest at the beginning of Book II, he has already made clear that ethos is an effect of the speech, an effect having nothing at all to do with the speaker's actual behavior. "The speaker should show himself to be of a certain character," Aristotle explains, because a speaker "possessed of certain qualities" and "disposed in certain ways towards" the audience is more persuasive. The Greek phrase here ($\alpha\mathring{v}\tau o\nu$ $\pi o\iota\acute{o}\nu$ $\tau\iota\nu\alpha$) has the clear denotation of a form of self-making. In the speech the speaker makes up a self who seems moral, good, and reliable. When Aristotle writes at the end of the section on ethos, "the definition of how and through what means one ought to make speeches ethical should be complete" (1391^b20–21 Kennedy), clearly he means that he has explained how a discourse can give the rhetorical effect of having been delivered by a moral, good, and reliable speaker. The speech, of course, has nothing at all to do with the life of the speaker. The professional discourse is utterly separable from, and independent of, the human being who delivers it.

At the end of the section on maxims (1395^b1–19), Aristotle explains that maxims "make speeches ethical" because, by choosing maxims that the audience knows well and approves, the speaker appears to the audience as a moral person. In Book III, Aristotle spends considerable time (1416^a3–$^b14$) explaining how to deal with a prejudiced audience when that prejudice threatens the ethos of the speech, and a little later (1418^b23–32) he explains how to create "the element of moral character" by putting some remarks of self-praise in the mouths of others. Perhaps the most significant passage on ethos, however, occurs in the middle of the section on moral character itself (1417^a24–25). Aristotle tells rhetoricians to construct an ethos that seems to speak from lifelong ethical and moral principles ($\pi\rho o\alpha\acute{\iota}\rho\epsilon\sigma\iota\varsigma$) not from intellect. As with the effect of sharp intellect in narrative, however, the ability to create an ethos that seems to present itself on a foundation of lifelong moral principle is nothing more than an effect of the speech; "lifelong moral principle" as a rhetorical self-incarnation is both a product of and a function of intellect, even though such "moral principle" seems to be self-sufficient and self-sustaining. Of course the intellect must be sharp enough to do its work and efface itself at the same time so as to create the appearance of never having been there, never having done anything at all.

This notion of ethos as a function of and a product of the discourse, with no connection whatsoever with the speaker's lived life, informs all aspects of academic writing in the West today. In every composition course, the student essay is graded as a document entirely separable from its writer. So strong is this ideology of ethos, this notion of professional discourse, that we can use holistic scoring, take the writer's name off the text entirely, and treat the discourse as a measurable performance. No one would think of figuring any student's character into an assessment of that student's writing ability. Indeed, such a grading policy would almost certainly generate a lawsuit—if the teacher managed to keep a job long enough for a student to sue. Because of student loads and contact time, any possibility of "knowing" a student's character ends with high school anyway. While it is certainly not appropriate to "blame" Aristotle either for our decision to exclude "character" as a criterion for grading students or for our attraction to holistic evaluation, neither is it appropriate for us to blind ourselves to Aristotle's seminal role in a metaphysics that so easily accommodates both the exclusion of character and the use of holistic evaluation.

For me, therefore, in the situation where I write, Aristotle has set the terms of discussion in which we still operate. By making the pathetic appeal possible as he does, in effect Aristotle precludes it as a voice through which any serious professional might speak. By separating ethos from the life of the writer/speaker, Aristotle sets up a notion of professional discourse that, by definition, excludes any sustained reference to discernable behavior or lived experience. Only professionals, only those with voices that live and die within written texts, can speak the discourse of the professional.

Situated Writing VI: The Obscuring Clarity of Style

The proofs, of course, exist only as the interior of the interior of rhetoric. For rhetoric to have such an interior interior, such a true and self-present heart, as it were, obviously it must have an exterior, and Aristotle knew that well. With an external border/barrier in place, an essence (and even an essence of that essence) described, and an object of study identified, Aristotle could turn his attention to the outside of rhetoric, which he does in Book III. Like any body, it seems, the body of rhetoric must decorate itself in order to present the externality of its being to others. Not surprisingly, the decoration that rhetoric wears serves a double function. First, it "makes rhetoric pretty"; more importantly, it protects the integrity, priority, and independence of rhetoric by announcing itself from the beginning as external, secondary, nonessential, and even a little unfortunate. One can almost hear the regret in Aristotle's (or Tyran-

168 ARISTOTLE'S VOICE

nio's or Andronicus's) voice as he (whoever "he" was) makes the transition between Books II and III. "He" must cross the barrier between the inside of rhetoric, where rhetoric is truly itself, and the outside of rhetoric, where clothing, jewelry, and other adornments can be attached. "Since there are three things in regard to a speech," Aristotle (or his cipher) writes at the end of Book II, "let what has been said suffice for . . . what concerns the intelligence generally, the thought element (διάνοια)" (1403ª34–ᵇ3). Having devoted roughly three-fourths of the total space in the *Rhetoric* to the construction and operation of the logos, he can turn to "what remains," a "discussion of style and arrangement."*

At the beginning of Book III, Aristotle repeats the division between the inside of rhetoric—where one finds enthymeme, example, ethos, pathos, and logos—and the outside, but he has made his work easy by defining the field so that nothing he says about the exterior of rhetoric can penetrate or infect the inside, just as a soul remains unaffected by the color of a shirt or even the color of hair. The need to take up style at all, the requirement to "dress rhetoric up," causes a palpable sense of regret. Aristotle begins by repeating that his treatment of rhetoric conforms to the dictates of nature (κατὰ φύσιν). Just as rhetoric has its own telos, the treatment of rhetoric, too, has a telos, and in this telos such external matters as style and arrangement remain forever outside, forever accessory. Style itself consists of two different manifestations of externality, each serving as *nothing more than* adornment. The first, more mundane sort of externality is delivery. Those who are good at delivery, it seems, often win not only dramatic contests as actors but also political contests (that is to say they triumph in the most elevated form of rhetoric). Delivery assumes such power because politics have become so wicked, such a haven for rascals (μοχθηρία). The whole business of delivery is, after all, vulgar and degraded (φορτικός); in no way is the rhetorical phenomenon of delivery straight, upright, true, correct, or genuine (ὀρθός). But because "the whole being of rhetoric has to do with mere opinion, conjecture, fancy, and external appearance" (ὅλης οὔσης πρὸς δόξαν), no rhetorician can afford to ignore delivery. It is "necessary." In a just world, Aristotle shakes a remonstrating index finger, a speaker would present a case based entirely on the facts because "everything outside demonstration is superfluous."* Unfortunately, he continues in disgust, those who hear speeches are so corrupt and depraved that any rhetorical pedagogy must pay some attention, however reluctant, to style and delivery. Rhetoricians can undertake such a debased study just as long as they remember that "the necessity to pay attention to style" is "slight," that the difference made by style "is not so very great," and that such things as style and delivery are nothing but "outward show," nothing but rank attempts to placate a crude and corrupt audience. "Style, delivery, and acting," Freese glosses this line, "are of no use to serious students" (1404^{a}7–12). This sort of maneuver has the magical effect of allowing a serious student to be serious about rhetoric by bracketing off the logos, giving it priority, and then contemptuously stirring around in the mess that nonserious students mistakenly construe as the "thing itself."[21]

Cope (3.8) and Kennedy (*Aristotle* 218, n. 6) are doubtless correct when they claim that this nose-holding way of presenting delivery grows out of Aristotle's contempt for democracy. Plutarch, though indirectly, makes the case as clearly as anyone when he describes how Demosthenes learned the importance of delivery. After having failed in an early attempt to speak to the Assembly, Demosthenes was walking home dejectedly with "his head muffled up" when he met the actor Satyrus. As a way of teaching Demosthenes, Satyrus quoted a speech from Euripides, "accompanying it with the proper mien and gesture," thereby showing Demosthenes the importance of delivery. After reflection, Demosthenes apparently concluded not only that delivery is crucially important for an orator, but also that delivery carries with it political overtones. "To slight and take no care how what is said is likely to be received by the audience," Plutarch quotes Demosthenes as saying, "shows something of an oligarchical temper, and is the course of one that intends force rather than persuasion" (6–8).[22]

The legacy is clear. No one who speaks at CCCC or even SCA could possibly be judged on the quality of delivery. No matter how inept the speaker might be at matching gesture and tone, no matter how foot-shuffling-mumbly-voiced-monotoned the delivery might be, anyone who attacked a speaker at one of these conventions on the basis of delivery would be hooted down as both rude and anti-intellectual. Delivery is a thing that a professional rhetorician knows how to recognize and analyze, but it has nothing to do with the professional discourse inside the closure of professional rhetoric.

The second, less mundane sort of rhetorical adornment is λέξις, which, of course, we usually translate as "style."[23] As Cole points out, Aristotle was the first to separate style from the "thought-element," and Book III of the *Rhetoric* is the first full treatment of style as a separate and separable phenomenon.[24] Even so, the metaphysics informing Aristotelian notions of style come right out of Plato. One can see this Platonic metaphysics most fully articulated at the beginning of *On Interpretation*. "Words spoken," Aristotle writes there (16^a4–9) "are symbols or signs of affections or impressions of the soul." Written words, he continues, in a clear echo of *Phaedrus*, "are the signs of words spoken." Though writing and speaking differ from race to race, "the mental affections themselves, of which these words are primarily signs, are the same for the whole of mankind, as are also the objects of which those affections are presentations or likenesses, images, copies." "A noun," Aristotle explains a little later (16^a20–21), "is a sound having meaning established by convention alone." This does not mean that either perception or reality is socially constructed. Aristotle makes that clear in *Categories* where he explains that speech is nothing but a servant of the knowledge that precedes it and, in turn, of the reality that the knowledge "knows." Units of speech, he writes, "have no lasting existence. Pronounce them, and then they are gone, so that, since they pass out of existence, they cannot have place or position" (5^a33–37). To make his point, Aristotle turns to one of his favorite analogies, the slave-master relationship. "The existence of a master involves the existence also of a slave. If a slave exists, then must a master. . . . to cancel one cancels the other." As a result, Aristotle continues his argument, "the object of knowledge is prior to, exists before, knowledge. We gain knowledge commonly speaking, of things that already exist, for in very few cases or none can our knowledge have come into being along with its own proper object." If the "object of knowledge" is removed, however, "the knowledge itself will be cancelled," but if no knowledge exists about any object, "yet that object itself may exist." "Take away or remove the perception," Aristotle concludes, yet "the perceptible still may exist" (7^a29–8^a6; see also *Sophistical Refutations* 165^a3–38).

In short, reality exists. It's out there in its essentially true state whether anyone perceives it or not. And when it is perceived, the perceptions are the same for all people. Only the speech that conveys the perception varies from person to person or race to race. Writing, being nothing more than a secondary image of speech, unavoidably

degrades the essence of perception one degree further. This metaphysics protects not only "reality" and the "perception of reality"
but also the pure self-presence of the place where perception can
occur. As long as language can be brought under the strict control
of demonstration, it is okay. When rhetoric appears on the scene,
however, all sorts of interpretations begin; as a way of controlling
the absolute free play of persuasion that such wild interpretation
might allow, Aristotle imports this Platonic metaphysics into his
own theory of rhetorical style.[25] At the moment he considers style
(1403^b18–20), the metaphysics is clear. We considered the proofs
or "thought-element" first, he says, because that is what comes first
naturally. "In the second place," he continues, "one must consider
how to set these preexisting proofs out in language ($\lambda \acute{\varepsilon} \xi \varepsilon \iota$
$\delta \iota \alpha \theta \acute{\varepsilon} \sigma \theta \alpha \iota$)."** The poets were the first to pay attention to style,
he says a few lines later (1404^a21–23), "for words are counterfeits or
copies [$\tau \grave{\alpha} \gamma \grave{\alpha} \rho \, \grave{o} \nu \acute{o} \mu \alpha \tau \alpha \, \mu \iota \mu \acute{\eta} \mu \alpha \tau \alpha \, \grave{\varepsilon} \sigma \tau \acute{\iota} \nu$], and the voice, of all our
parts, has priority and is the best at imitation."** When Aristotle
takes up the practice of using popular sayings, little doubt exists
about what he means when he describes words as follows: "words
indicate, make known, point out, signify, announce, declare, or bear
the mark of their own meaning ($\grave{o} \nu \acute{o} \mu \alpha \tau \alpha \, \sigma \eta \mu \alpha \acute{\iota} \nu \varepsilon \iota$)"** (1410^b11);
nor is it surprising that he refutes the sophist Bryson, arguing that
reality is so strong and clear that one can judge the appropriateness
of a word by comparing it to the "thing" for which it stands:

> for it is not the case, as Bryson said, that no one ever uses foul
> language, if the meaning is the same whether this or that word
> is used; this is false; for one word is more proper than another,
> more of a likeness, and better suited to putting the matter before
> the eyes. (1405^b8–12)[26]

In the Aristotelian theory of language, style, by its very incon-
stancy and uncertainty, protects and ensures the proofs. To begin
with, style must be clear ($\sigma \alpha \phi \hat{\eta}$). If style is not clear, then it cannot
perform the work proper to it ($\tau \grave{o} \, \grave{\varepsilon} \alpha \upsilon \tau o \hat{\upsilon} \, \grave{\varepsilon} \rho \gamma o \upsilon$). This is a crucial
notion in the operation of Aristotelian rhetoric, for style must be
clear in order to show the workings of the inside of rhetoric. If style
is not clear, the proofs, the very essence of the essence of rhetoric,
may be distorted. Being clear, however, turns out to be rather more
complicated than one might expect, for clarity turns out to be the

midway point between two self-excluding opposites. Clear style
must not be low or base (ταπεινός), nor may it be too elevated
(ὑπὲρ τὸ ἀξίωμα). In fact, style must be (à la Goldilocks) just right
(πρέπουσαν). "Using words that draw their authority from being
part of the vernacular," Aristotle explains, "creates clarity"**
(1404ᵇ5–8). If the rhetor goes beyond the ordinary, however, style
takes on a proud or haughty quality. Of course, the rhetor wants
just a little of this sort of elevation, but not much, not nearly so
much as the poet, whose subject allows for more elevated diction.

The verb πρέπω (some form of which appears repeatedly as a
descriptor of style) prescribes style's self-presentation: "Style must
show itself forth as appropriate or beseeming"** (1408ᵃ10–ᵇ20; see
also 1404ᵇ5, 16, 18, 31, 1405ᵃ12, 14, 1406ᵃ12, 13, 32, and 1406ᵇ6).[27]
Style manages to "show itself forth as appropriate and beseeming"
by being plain and ordinary, which, in turn, allows the subject itself
to appear credible. Such plain ordinariness also contributes to the
ethical effect of the speech by giving the hearers the impression
that they share cultural and intellectual solidarity with the speaker.
Plain, ordinary language, Aristotle explains,

> makes people believe in the truth of your story: their minds draw
> the false conclusion that you are to be trusted from the fact that
> others behave as you do when things are as you describe them;
> and therefore they take your story to be true, whether it is so or
> not. (1408ᵃ20–24 Roberts)

Choosing the style for a logos, Aristotle explains a little later, is like
painting the scenic backdrop for a play. The painting is nothing
more than a calculated effect done in just enough detail and with
just enough finish to suit the situation (1414ᵃ8–18).[28] As long as the
scene convinces the audience to accept it as reality, the fact that
the scene is nothing but a painting matters not.

The mistaken notion that high-flown, poetical, extraordinary
language is appropriate to the logos appeared in Athens, Aristotle
complains, because of the excesses of Gorgias. "Even now," he
continues, "the majority of the uneducated think that such persons
express themselves most beautifully, whereas this is not the case."
Quite the contrary, style depends on the clarity of ordinariness.
When one uses words that are not ordinary, one runs the risk of
sounding poetical. And when the logos sounds poetical, as Aristotle

repeats in nearly every sentence (1406^a11–13, 30–31, 1406^b1, 10–11, 24–25, 1407^b31–32, 1408^b18–19), it no longer sounds ordinary, and thus its clarity and naturalness disappear: "those who employ poetic language by their lack of taste make the style ridiculous and frigid; for when words are piled upon one who already knows, it destroys clarity by a cloud of verbiage."* One must always "aim at the mean, for neglect to do so does more harm than speaking at random" (1406^a15–16).

The following attempt by the JACT editors to render some of Gorgias's style into English shows what Aristotle (and hence we) despise(d) so much:

If, then, the eye of Helen, charmed by Paris's beauty, gave to her soul excitement and amorous incitement, what wonder? How could one who was weaker, repel and expel him, who, being divine, had power divine? If it was physical diversion and psychical perversion, we should not execrate it as reprehensible, but deprecate it as indefensible. For it came to whom it came by fortuitous insinuations, not by judicious resolutions; by erotic compulsions, not by despotic machinations.

How then is it fair to blame Helen who, whether by love captivated or by word persuaded, or by violence dominated, or by divine necessity subjugated, did what she did, and is completely absolved from blame?

By this discourse I have freed a woman from evil reputation; I have kept the promise which I made in the beginning; I have essayed to dispose of the injustice of defamation and the folly of allegation; I have prayed to compose a lucubration for Helen's adulation and my own delectation. (*Helen* 19; see P. Jones et al. 286–87)[29]

Everything about this passage demands scrutiny. Any reader or hearer would recognize that something is afoot, some dazzling display of verbal pyrotechnics is under way. In this case, style calls absolute attention to itself. Aristotelian style, on the other hand, goes far beyond this sort of display, concealing itself so as to seem not to be there at all. In its seeming ordinariness, however, it is every bit as artistic, every bit as contrived as anything by Gorgias; indeed, I would argue that it is more contrived and less honest because it attempts to conceal itself by pretending not to be there, by pretending to be nothing at all while doing its work in secret.

The last stage in Aristotle's theory of style aligns nicely with his treatment of ethos as a rhetorical effect, an effect having nothing to do with lived experience. The ordinary, unadorned style so necessary for successful rhetoric, Aristotle blithely explains, not seeming to notice the archness of his categories, turns out not to be itself. That is to say it is neither ordinary nor unadorned. It is an artifice that merely *seems* ordinary and unadorned; in fact, it depends on complex and sophisticated art.[30] "Those who practice this artifice [of ordinary language]," he explains, "must conceal it and avoid the appearance of speaking artificially instead of naturally; for what is natural persuades, but the artificial does not." Art "is cleverly concealed," he continues, "when the speaker chooses his words from ordinary language" (1404^{b}15–25). This notion of naturalness as carefully crafted art seems to have been one of the primary tenets of the Aristotelian theory of style, for Aristotle makes the point again and again. In discussing epithets, for example, he warns that the artifice must be "stolen" ($\kappa\lambda\acute{\epsilon}\pi\tau\epsilon\tau\alpha\iota$) out of the logos so that it cannot be seen by the audience. The orator should not have all aspects of the speech correspond exactly because such complete correspondence will merely call attention to the fact that the speech's apparent naturalness is nothing more than a highly contrived rhetorical effect. The hearer "will see your artfulness, and be on . . . guard," as Cooper glosses this line. If, however, the speaker decides to present harsh language, harsh features, a rough voice, and all other aspects rough and harsh, such a strategy can be used only once in a speech. If the speaker uses such complete correspondence only one time, "the art escapes notice" (1408^{b}4–10). Finally, Aristotle explains that the diction for the logos cannot be metrical, for if it is, "it appears artificial" (1408^{b}21–23). The infinitive, $\pi\epsilon\pi\lambda\acute{\alpha}\sigma\theta\alpha\iota$, here translated as "artificial," is the root of the English noun *plastic*, and it has the connotations of something that has been consciously shaped in the mind, probably as a result of extensive education. This is the sort of artifice that the logos must have but must *seem* not to have. Naturalness, in other words, comes about through extraordinarily unnatural art that has the power to create what, once it is written or spoken, will seem to be its plain, unadorned, natural, spontaneous self. Indeed, the art of prose turns out to be even more complicated than the art of poetry. Though poetry requires great art, at least the poetic artist may allow the art to appear. Prose, in contrast, requires a kind of art that goes beyond art by concealing itself even though it is present. Rather than its simple self, the plain, middle style of prose turns out to be an art form more highly wrought and more exquisitely self-aware than poetry. Indeed, the plain, middle style must be self-aware (one might almost say vigilant) so that it can keep itself hidden.

The logos writer, Aristotle continues as he returns to the matter of diction, may not use strange, compound, or coined words, for this makes the language seem too elevated, too unnatural. The logos writer, who "has fewer resources" than the poet, may achieve the effect of clarity by using only two linguistic strategies: ordinary words and metaphors. Speakers who limit themselves to ordinary words and metaphors can achieve that desirable, slightly foreign quality while at the same time achieving clarity and concealing the art whereby all these effects come into existence. "And this is," Aristotle says triumphantly, "the chief merit of rhetorical language."

Since ordinary, vernacular words are just that—ordinary and quite usual—and since the prose writer in essence has recourse only to ordinary words and metaphors, metaphor gives the logos some of the things it needs in order to be itself: "Metaphor," Aristotle explains, "gives style clearness, charm, and distinction as nothing else can" (1405^a8–10). This is a fairly easy notion to overlook, but it is really quite astonishing, for the one thing above all else that Aristotle has demanded of the logos writer is clarity. He has already told us that clarity derives from a carefully balanced opposition between the low and the elevated and that the rhetor must obscure the art that was used to make art itself seem absent. Now he tells us that clarity, which depends in an absolute way on the ordinary, comes to know itself through metaphor. In other words, clarity suffers from a deficiency; it can be itself only through the play of the extraordinary, only through the play of substitution called metaphor, the linguistic process that Aristotle himself calls "a kind of enigma" (1405^b5). "Because strange words mystify us and because we already know ordinary, common words; metaphor is what pleases and informs us best"* (1410^b13). Because of the deficiency of ordinariness, the logos needs to be "citified," to be made witty, clever, playful, and refined. Metaphor alone can make up for this deficiency of ordinariness.[31] Of course, the logos must remain ever vigilant not to let the play of metaphor get out of hand; thus, the logos may not use a simile ($1406^b20-1407^a17$, 1410^b17-20), nor may it use metaphors that exceed "propriety." Rhetorical metaphors must occupy a situation just the right distance between the absolute ordinary and the obviously farfetched (1412^a11-13).

Metaphor mastery, therefore, is the technique that the logos master absolutely must have. Without it, effective style simply is not possible because the logos has only metaphor as a way of making the ordinary ordinary. With ordinariness "explained," one final turn of the screw remains. Because of Aristotle's social theories, the turn offers no surprise, but it remains troublesome. When Aristotle first takes up metaphor (1405^a6-10), he says two things: (1) that metaphor is the only thing that gives style clarity, pleasure, and surprise, the things style *must* have to be good; and (2) that the ability to use metaphor "cannot be learnt from anyone else." The second notion has an astonishing effect on Aristotelian rhetoric in general. Rhetoric depends after all, on style, and style depends on metaphor, and metaphor depends on an innate, unlearnable ability. In other words, rhetoric, though it may be a set of strategies that can be improved, depends absolutely on prior, innate ability. One either gets the gift from the gods or does without. And this seems to have been a notion that Aristotle believed deeply, for he says almost exactly the same thing in *Poetics*: "the greatest thing by far is to be a master of metaphor. It is the one thing that cannot be learnt from others; and it is also a sign of genius, since a good metaphor implies an intuitive perception of the similarity in dissimilars" (1459^a5-8).[32] With this gesture the arena of professional discourse that wears the name "rhetoric" finally completes itself. An orator, after all, succeeds because of a divine gift.[33] A rhetorician, on the other hand, needs no divine gift, for the rhetorician in the Aristotelian frame sets out to critique and describe a gift given to others. Rhetorical pedagogy, as a result, teaches analysis, not performance. Performance cannot be taught or learned.

Situated Writing VII: In the Chair Where Aristotelian Rhetoric Sits

In nearly every writing class, we teach the plain, ordinary style as a simple, almost homespun American virtue. We wince when we read student essays that depend on a thesaurus or that strain to sound elevated and important. Such writing characterizes itself as

immature and tasteless. We are so accustomed to our own professional discourse that we cannot see it as more contrived, more
artificial, and *much* more difficult to write than Gorgian or Euphuistic
style, which are free both to call attention to their excesses and to
be awkwardly excessive. Few things are harder to learn than the
process of seeming to erase oneself. Of course, we know that the
apparently gone author of professional discourse is really there all
along, but we radically oversimplify the intellectual and discursive
strategies that allow that person to seem to be gone.

The analyst, after all, must play the role of someone extracted
from and disinterested in the "thing" being analyzed. In setting up
a syllabus, it is worth remembering that Aristotle, that figure who
towers over rhetoric, was only the most influential of rhetoricians.
He was never an orator, and he never pretended that he could teach
anyone how to influence Athenian society, which, for him and his
friends, was nothing but a cesspool of democratic style and delivery
anyway, the sort of cesspool that no self-respecting aristocrat, no
enthymeme master would deign to enter.

Like I. A. Richards, anyone who pays attention to Aristotle's
notion of metaphor cannot help wondering "how much influence
this remark has had," how much its "evil presence" has influenced
rhetoric and critical theory (89–90).[34] The most obvious evil is social
and educational elitism leading to the old cliché, "I can teach you
to write a B paper if you work hard, but A writers are born." In the
Aristotelian system, the genius for discourse, whether the discourse
of the logos or that of poetry, is an unlearnable gift. The Aristotelian
theory of metaphor, according to Richards, also leads to the notion
"that metaphor is something special and exceptional in the use of
language, a deviation from its normal mode of working, instead of
the omnipresent principle of all its free action." As a result, Richards
concludes, "throughout the history of Rhetoric, metaphor has been
treated as a sort of happy extra trick with words," a trick requiring
"unusual skill and caution," a trick that comes only from the gods
(90–91).[35]

More importantly, however, by building rhetoric on an innate
skill with metaphor, Aristotle accomplishes a remarkable double
function. First, he makes the division between the *act of* persuasion
and the *analysis of* persuasion natural and teleological. The ability
to persuade—and especially to persuade large groups—derives from
an unlearnable divine gift with metaphor. People like Cleon or

Jimmy Swaggart have such a gift, and naturally, such people are also gifted at, and uninhibited by, the demagogic excesses of delivery. The enthymeme master, on the other hand, the true discourse analyst, need not be very effective at persuasion so long as that person can analyze persuasion and communicate that analysis in professional discourse open only to other enthymeme masters. Second, and in Aristotelian terms much more importantly, Aristotle excludes rhetoric from serious uses of language. In *Posterior Analytics*, which is the place where he works his way through demonstration (ἀπόδειξις), Aristotle explains that a demonstrative definition must be "clear" (σαφές). This is the same demand, made using the same term, that he makes of rhetoric. The demonstrative definition must be clear because demonstration is the most rigorous, most elevated form of human inquiry. To achieve such pristine clarity, however, to be σαφές, demonstrative definitions must remain free from any taint by metaphor:

> Just as demonstration demands a completed inference, so definition demands clarity; and this will be achieved if we can, by means of the common features which we have established, define our concept separately in each class of objects . . . and so advance to the general definition, taking care not to become involved in equivocation. If we are to avoid arguing in metaphors, clearly we must also avoid defining in metaphors and defining metaphorical terms; otherwise we are bound to argue in metaphors. (97^{b}31–40)

In *Topics*, which is the place where he works his way through dialectic, Aristotle explains that a dialectical definition must not be unclear (ἀσαφές). Again he makes the same demand of dialectic that he makes of rhetoric, and again he uses the same term. To avoid such unclear language, the dialectician, like the demonstrator, must avoid using metaphors in a definition because metaphors create an opening through which an opponent can achieve victory, and more importantly, because metaphors make language unclear. Dialectic, of course, is the form of inquiry that intelligent, well-educated people use when there are no ignorant and boorish people around to require a reduction to rhetoric. A commonplace of dialectical dispute, Aristotle explains, is to discover whether one's opponent "has spoken metaphorically, as, for example, if he has described knowledge as 'unshakeable,' or the earth as a 'nurse,' or temperance as a 'harmony'; for metaphorical expressions are always obscure" (139^b33–140^a3). Aristotle's demand that demonstration and dialectic achieve clarity by avoiding metaphor must seem a little odd to anyone, like me, who happens to have read the *Rhetoric* first and then turned to those other, more traditional, texts as a way of rereading the *Rhetoric*. In the *Rhetoric*, after all, Aristotle explains at length on several occasions that rhetorical language must be clear and that the only way to make it clear is to rely on one's innate gift for metaphor. Thus, not only is metaphor permissible in rhetoric, it is essential. The demonstrator or the dialectician, in contrast, must avoid metaphor because the same linguistic strategy that makes rhetorical language clear makes demonstrative and dialectical language unclear.

By making rhetoric the place where style is important and metaphor appropriate, Aristotle has completed his system. In the Aristotelian intellectual system, rhetoric plays exactly the same role that style, and its degraded partner, delivery, play in rhetoric. Rhetoric is the prophylactic that demonstration and dialectic wear in order to protect their identities and their processes from the free play of linguistic transfer. Demonstration and dialectic need rhetoric in an absolute way. Without rhetoric the philosopher would have no place to send metaphor with all its destabilizing and unexpected effects. As a result, clarity becomes a situated term in Western thought. Professional discourses, the discourses of demonstration and dialectic, take on a clarity all their own, a clarity in which language functions as a noninhibiting conductor; thus, clarity inside a professional discourse, a clarity that is crystal clear to those who have learned the discourse, remains utterly opaque to those on the outside, a situation that Aristotle spent his entire life creating. More importantly, by describing rhetoric as he does, by giving it such a carefully crafted and deceitful exterior, Aristotle can think—and allow history to think—of demonstration and dialectic as having no exterior at all. The demonstrator or the dialectician, the seeker of either permanent or contingent truth, uses no style and remains free from any demand to consider delivery. The very existence of rhetoric allows demonstration and dialectic to appear as nothing more than the pure self-presence of the logos as it applies the syllogism in a fully unmediated way.

In describing rhetorical pleasure (1369^b33–1370^a18), Aristotle raises the notions "natural states" and "natural processes." These notions seem to have been structural in his world view. "One of the most conspicuous features of Aristotle's view of the universe," Ross says, "is his thorough-going teleology" (185). Rhetoric, like all extant things Aristotelian, *must* have its teleology.[36] It must *be* what it must *be*. And the result of the "discourse about discourse" that Aristotle leaves for us under the name "rhetoric" performs many functions. It creates a place where professional discourse about itself can speak itself forever, it sets apart a special place in language where the free play of persuasion, interpretation, and metaphor can have a specific home, and it allows the truly professional discourses of demonstration and dialectic to be free from contamination. It also causes me to wonder about the telos of composition studies. What, I cannot help wondering, is the inevitable "thing" that composition studies, because of its telos, must and will be. Rhetoric has, after all, been the discipline from which composition studies has learned the most and borrowed the most. Anyone would agree that, as disciplines go, rhetoric is centuries older, far better established, and much more coherent than its youthful and still ill-formed offspring ($\pi\alpha\rho\alpha\phi\upsilon\acute{\epsilon}\varsigma;$), composition studies. May we in composition studies exercise the non-Aristotelian option of having no telos at all? Can we, or do we even wish to, remain ill formed and undisciplined? If we speak as nothing more than human beings, will we remain forever infra dig? Or must we professionalize ourselves to save ourselves inside Plato's Academy? If we professionalize ourselves, the academy will not care what we choose as a subject for discussion. While it is certainly important that we gain enough adherants and make enough noise to achieve power and status in the academy, the academy itself will not care a whit what we quibble about, so long as our quibbles lead to university press books and refereed journal articles. The question, then, is not *what* we will argue about but *whether* we will argue as professionals.

Situated Writing VIII: Back in the Chair Where I Sit

Not having turned on the TV beside my desk for over a month now, I remove the splitter, role up the coaxial cable, and store them both in the attic alongside the no-longer-needed TV. Everyone who does not live in one of the burned-out LA neighborhoods has already forgotten the 1992 riot; the 1965 riot is now prehistoric. I cannot remember the last time I wondered what I would do if rioters came driving up my street. Rodney King has made the Nashville papers three times since the riot. Each time he had been arrested for something or other. I cannot remember what. Reginald Denny's name has begun to fade from memory, and such unimportant casualties as Louis Watson, Dwight Taylor, and Gregory Davis have vanished entirely from the memories of all but their families and close friends. Terrell Banks now rests in his little grave somewhere here in Nashville. Drug dealers will sell their wares on the streets near his old home again tonight. At the graveside service for some of the children killed by Serbian snipers, mortar rounds fell, badly wounding the dead children's grieving relatives. The Sarajevo airport was open just long enough yesterday for two planes to leave for Barcelona, one carrying the Bosnian Olympic team, the other the Yugoslavian team. The war goes on. Since geologists have discovered no oil in the Balkans, Western interest in the bloodshed remains desultory. So far, my response to each situation has been to watch TV and work on this book. Now that I can speak and write inside the discourse of composition studies, I find it increasingly difficult to speak or write any other way. Rhetoric as a self-enclosed discursive strategy goes on as it has for millennia. I wonder if it is possible for any human voice to speak at all there. Though composition studies is still green as a professional discourse, one can easily imagine it fifty years hence with a canon over which specialists fight endlessly and a conflicting set of methodologies about which professionals never cease arguing. I remember Stephen North's complaint in *The Making of Knowledge in Composition* about how hard it is to "get a handle on" the philosophers in composition studies (91). He felt that the people who work in composition under that rubric do not fit together with any homogeneity. Never once did it occur to any of us in 1987 that the problem might be with the category, not with those who supposedly do not fit into it. The taxonomizing of the field is already well advanced, and I begin to fear that Aristotle has taught us more than we wanted to know.

5

THE COMPOSITION OF SOPHISTRY AND THE SOPHISTRY OF COMPOSITION

For Bryson

Mere Rhetoric

It really is astonishing how much difference a τι can make. It can shift an interpretation from the positive to the negative, and as we all know, so much depends upon (not only a red wheelbarrow but also) an interpretation. One need do no more than compare Aeschines' *On the Embassy* with Demosthenes' *On the False Embassy* to see how excruciatingly different the same thing can be. "Those who discovered the beginnings of rhetoric carried them forward quite a little way," E. S. Forster translates lines 183^{b}28–32 of *Sophistical Refutations*, "whereas the famous modern professors of the art, entering into the heritage, so to speak, of a long series of predecessors who had gradually advanced it, have brought it to its present perfection." These lines follow Aristotle's description of how any discipline begins and how it develops. "The beginning of anything is the most important," Aristotle explains, "hence it is also the most difficult."

Once a group of pioneers has begun a discipline, their followers have a much easier time because followers do no more than add to. The beginning of a discipline, in contrast, "is very small in size and therefore very difficult to see," but beginning a discipline, Aristotle assures us, is worth the effort and the risk. The beginning "is very powerful in its effects" because the beginning founds and orients what comes after it. Such a powerful and orienting beginning "has happened," Aristotle continues, "with the rhetorical logos, and also with all the other arts."* Next follow the lines with which I began, the lines about the "progress of rhetoric." W. A. Pickard-Cambridge translates these lines rather differently from the way Forster translates them. Those who discovered the beginnings of rhetoric, according to Pickard-Cambridge, "advanced them in only a little way, whereas the celebrities of today are the heirs (so to speak) of a long succession of men who have advanced them bit by bit, and so have developed them to their present form." The differences between the two translations are obvious. According to Forster, the beginners of rhetoric developed rhetoric "quite a little way," and the "famous modern professors of the art" have brought rhetoric "to its present perfection." According to Pickard-Cambridge, in contrast, the beginners of rhetoric advanced it "only a little way," and "the celebrities of to-day" have developed it to its "present form." The question, in my opinion, has to do with where one puts the παντελῶς in relation to the τι, for the semantic location of those two words determines the frame of reference within which the translator considers the verb αὐξάνω. In translating αὐξάνω the translator must choose among these three options: (1) to increase or augment (making no judgment about the value of the increase), (2) to aggrandize (something that is being puffed well beyond its value, (3) to exalt or magnify (something that deserves exaltation or magnification).

In my opinion, Pickard-Cambridge chooses option two, thus making the "right" choice and the "correct" translation. Both the diction and the context of these lines tell me that Aristotle intended to denigrate not only the beginnings of rhetoric but also those who taught rhetoric in his own day. In my opinion, οἱ δὲ εὐδοκιμοῦντες ("celebrities of today" or "famous modern professors") is entirely sarcastic. No celebrity or modern professor in Athens at the time Aristotle wrote the sentence would have worn that οἱ δὲ εὐδοκιμοῦντες proudly. And I justify my preference for Pickard-Cambridge's translation by pointing out that Aristotle goes on to condemn wholesale Gorgian rhetoric and to claim that his own rheto-

ric is something utterly new to the world. His own rhetoric offers
a "new beginning." Obviously this allows him to arrogate a new
"power," the power of the one who begins a field, lays its foundation,
orients its vision.

Aristotle was not, of course, free to situate rhetoric *any*where;
nor could he give it *any* form. As I have tried to show in detail, he
was a situated being just like anyone else. He was a man born in
the northern boondocks; he was an itinerant (though wealthy) alien
most of his life. Nevertheless, he made choices. He chose to leave
Isocrates and study with Plato; he chose to spy for Philip and Alexander; he chose to teach Alexander the notion of ἀρετή that would
send Alexander tearing across the world seeking Achilles' mantle;
he chose to cast his lot with the slave-owning oligarchs (although I
recognize that it would have taken a monumental, perhaps superhuman, act of courage and freethinking for him to have become an
abolitionist democrat); he chose to define himself as a philosopher
rather than a sophist; and he chose to study and teach rhetoric. The
lines near the end of *Prior Analytics* (70^a2–70^b6) in which Aristotle
defines "probability," "sign," and "enthymeme" show what I mean
about choice, foundation, and orientation. The systematic reasoning
enabled by such technical jargon as "sign" or "enthymeme" constitutes Aristotle's great contribution to Western thought. To demonstrate the operation of the sign and the enthymeme, Aristotle offers
two examples in this passage. In the first, he links lactation and
sallowness with woman to demonstrate the notion pregnancy; in the
second, he links wisdom and goodness to demonstrate the nature
of Pittacus's character. And already a whole teleology is in place, a
teleology in which men have names and are judged on their wisdom
and goodness, while women are generic, nameless vessels to be
judged on the contents and the color of their bodies. Such an example
as this is surely the most innocent sort of παράδειγμα in the world.
I have already stretched to the breaking point the notions "historical
accuracy" and "scholarly fairness" by calling Aristotle a racist bigot.
Calling him a sexist would surely shatter those notions entirely, and
since those notions are useful to me, I will resist the urge. But while
resisting, I would like to point out how a teleology, any teleology,
works, and I will press my claim once again that one takes a great
risk in using the analytical language Aristotle offers us, for that
language does have a habit of throwing up the oddest sort of "utterly
innocent paradigm." The universal naturalness of a white man seems

to leap off every Aristotelian page. Perhaps more to the point, since adulthood implies a kind of teleology, we in composition studies may want to think twice about having our discipline "grow up."

I will not, however, resist the urge to foreground the notions "foundation" and "orientation," for I want to explore those notions in regard to composition studies. Almost like a "real 'being'," the amorphous and uncertain endeavor that wears the phrase "composition studies" so tenuously as a name is also situated. Anyone who attends a CCCC or WPA meeting can readily see the wildly idiosyncratic and inconsistent nature of that situation. For brevity's sake, as well as for ease of access, I will limit myself to the *MLA Newsletter* (Summer 1992) and *CCC* (May and October 1992), which, since I put my old TV back in the attic, just happen to be the three most recent professional publications I have had the time to read.

The *MLA Newsletter* (12–16) offers good news and bad. The good news is that jobs in "writing" now account for 18 percent of the total MLA listings in English,[1] making rhet/comp the single largest category of jobs available. It is ever so slightly larger than British literature (at 17.8 percent) but roughly twice the size of American literature (at 10.1 percent) and minority literature (at 9.1 percent). There is, however, bad news. Forty percent of all the non-tenure-track assistant professorships are in writing, and 71 percent of instructor and lecturer positions (positions that almost never offer any chance of tenure or permanency) are in writing. "Non-tenure-track positions," as the MLA puts it, "are more likely than tenure-track positions to be in writing. . . . Tenure-track positions, in contrast, are more likely to be in literature" (12–14). In other words, if rhet/comp has "come a long way, Baby," the gendered, diminutive "Baby" still applies, and something very like a cigarette may be the reward.

The May and October 1992 issues of *CCC* clarify anecdotally what these MLA figures show statistically. Lynn Bloom's (comically?) angry and resentful "I Want a Writing Director" merely summarizes what writing program administrators have suffered ever since American colleges have offered such positions. In effect, the writing program director continues to play the role of the 1950s housewife, except that departments can divorce their fifties-style wives with nineties-style family court efficiency, leaving those abandoned relics with none of the after-marriage support that the legal system usually offered to rejected, faithful fifties wives. The symposium on feminism in the composition classroom that leads the October *CCC* shows even more clearly both the degree to which composition plays the role of "woman" in the academy and the degree to which the academy resists any effort by its "woman" to speak with her own voice (see Eichhorn et al.).[2]

Robert Merrill's attack on the "Statement of Principles and Standards for the Postsecondary Teaching of Writing," which appears as the lead essay in the May *CCC* issue, reveals the psychology that generates the professional treatment that Professors Bloom, Eichhorn, Farris, Hayes, Hernandez, Jarratt, Powers-Stubbs, and Sciachitano describe so trenchantly. The essay itself is a remarkable piece of work.[3] It begins with the challenge that the CCCC "Statement of Principles" "cannot be supported by anyone who thinks through the consequences," and it ends with the apocalyptic warning that if the "Statement" is implemented it will destroy "English departments as we know them," a phrase that holds "life as we know it" in the palm of its "Statement"-threatened hands.

Merrill's ire stems from the effect that he believes the "Statement" would have on the English department at the University of Nevada at Reno, which he chairs. At present, this department employs nine lecturers who teach eight composition courses each year, roughly 29 percent of the department's total composition offerings. If the nine lecturers were replaced by tenure-track, noncomposition faculty, who could reasonably be expected to teach two composition sections per year, Nevada-Reno would need to create thirty-six additional faculty lines; if the nine were replaced by tenure-track composition specialists, who would teach five composition sections per year, Nevada-Reno would need to create about five new lines. Professor Merrill seems to regard the possibility of replacing nine nontenure-track lecturers with fourteen tenure-track composition specialists as a perverse, stupid, and evil notion. Instead of replacing the lecturers with tenure-track faculty, he suggests creating a "two-tiered system" in which the composition-teaching lecturers "continue to perform their current functions" while improving "lecturer working conditions as much as possible." While reveling in his realpolitik view, Professor Merrill argues that no honest, moral, right-thinking person could possibly suggest otherwise.

Anyone who has read this far in this book will already see both how to understand the "true world" that Professor Merrill administers and how one might make (a necessarily sophistical!)

response to the justness of his moral outrage. Before leaving his essay, however, I would like to make one final point about the way he sees the department he chairs. His diction throughout makes clear that he takes his proprietorship of his department quite seriously, for the department consists of those things that he owns and those that he does not. For example, he refers to the nine, nontenurable composition teachers on four occasions (in a four-page essay) as "my nine lecturers." He does, of course, claim ownership of other things in the essay. He refers to literature courses as "his," he refers to the forty courses that would be unstaffed each semester if "his" lecturers were fired as "his," and he claims ownership of his "own personal experience." Enlightened by the range and the security of his ownership, one cannot help wondering who does not get to have a "personal experience" so that Professor Merrill's "personal experience" can remain so clearly knowable, so unassailable, so righteous, and so correct.

These two short essays by Bloom and Merrill do not, however, bring new information into the world, nor does the symposium on feminism. Taken together, these three texts merely reiterate a metaphysics in which the teaching of writing does not occupy the same sort of academic respectability as other disciplines. For example, if Nevada-Reno were unable to afford professionally trained, appropriately paid literary critics or historians, Professor Merrill would not argue with such passion that history and literature be taught permanently by faculty on substandard appointments with teaching overloads. One could wish that Reno were less typical and Professor Merrill less emblematic, but each wish would be thwarted by the harsh "reality" by which Professor Merrill so enjoys being controlled. Like it or not, when a professional moves from the *teaching* of writing to the "teaching" of anything else, a real category shift occurs, and anyone who cannot see that category shift has not learned how to read the text of the American university.

Those of us in composition studies are, in other words, situated, and we are situated in wildly different economic and political constructs. The only "truth" that spans all thirty-two hundred postsecondary teaching situations in the United States is that the teaching of writing is (or was until *very* recently) in the history of any given institution a remedial, unfortunate necessity that can (or could) be staffed by an unprofessional faculty. And anyone who bothers to look can see that the vast majority of writing courses are still taught by faculty who have little or no training in the field and no long-term commitment to the field.

So what do we do? To begin with, we must acknowledge our situation and decide how we intend to live through it. The most obvious strategy is to try to make our discipline into a fully legitimate professional discourse. Of course this will take decades, and no one living today will see the time when composition studies (or whatever other label the discipline finally gives itself) enjoys the credibility of literature, philosophy, history, or even rhetoric. But the time will come, and when it does, we who initiated the discipline will be regarded with a mixture of awe and contempt: awe for having succeeded at all and contempt for having begun as we did. (The contempt will be unavoidable no matter how the discipline begins. Those who come later will necessarily regard their predecessors as heroically naive. Professional discourse cannot speak itself without a fully self-satisfied belief that it is always more sophisticated and accurate than it used to be.)

If we choose the full professionalization option (and I believe that we will choose this option even though it is not the one I prefer or can contribute to) our history can already be written. We will forever discuss the ontology and methodology of composition studies. The border wars will be fierce, as will the methodological wars. Aristotle has taught rhetoric well that a name begets an ontology. After each study of the ontology of rhetoric, the reader has the impression that something has been described and finished or, if not finished, at least furnished with a permanent foundation on which the finishing-up work can be built. Of course rhetoric does not work (never has worked) this way, but professional discourse does not allow for the scholarly contribution that makes no contribution; nor does it allow for the scholarly discipline that makes no progress and, in fact, has no discipline.

The argument between John Poulakos and Edward Schiappa over the origin of the term *rhetoric* in ancient Greece is a legitimate dispute within the history of rhetoric. In my opinion, it has nothing whatsoever to do with teaching anyone how to speak in public, but without a doubt it is part of the academic study of the history of rhetoric. Within the debate over the ontology of rhetoric, this argument sets the stakes quite high. It *matters* who wins. And as I have shown repeatedly, these disputes intensify themselves as they flow into and out of each other. If George Kennedy claims that Aristotle reduces rhetoric to dialectic (*Classical* 66), William Grimaldi responds that Aristotle's rhetoric is not a reduction at all; rather, it is the construction of an all-encompassing theory of language that includes everything but silent gestures (*Studies* 15, 54). And once begun, the argument over the ontology of rhetoric takes on a life of its own. James Kinneavy and Robert Connors reply to Grimaldi that the *Rhetoric* does not provide "a general theory of language"; quite the contrary, the *Rhetoric* offers nothing more than a guide to persuasive public speaking ("Grimaldi" 185; *Theory 212–18*; "Explanation" 190–91). Inevitably, Brian Vickers attacks the University of Wisconsin Press for defining rhetoric too broadly; attacks Vico, Kennedy, Hayden White, and Roman Jakobson for defining it too narrowly; and attacks Paul de Man, Jacques Derrida, and Kenneth Burke for perverting it entirely (439–69). Thomas Cole chides Burke and Chaim Perelman for stretching rhetoric too far and thus violating Aristotle's injunction (1359^b12) against making rhetoric into a science, and then he divides all of human consciousness into the "rhetorical" and the "antirhetorical" (20, 41–42). Carl Classen complains that those who "applique les regles de la rhetorique sur les mots écrits, fait une transgression dans un autre genre" (7–8) and in the same essay lays out the framework in which rhetoric can be applied to everything from writing and literature to speech, film, painting, politics, and advertising (12–17). Calvin Schrag makes a cultural divide between classical rhetoric and communicative rhetoric: in classical rhetoric "the rhetor as subject knows beforehand what the situation requires with regard to the best interest of the *polis* and is privy to the most effective means for achieving consensus"; in communicative rhetoric, in contrast, the rhetor "moves about within the intersubjective space of a collaborative 'we-experience' that is first opened up in the wake of a decentering of the rhetor and a decentralizing of his/her authority" (7–8). Cy Knoblauch and Lil Brannon go even farther than Schrag, claiming that classical rhetoric is "no longer supportable in terms of the epistemological assumptions of the modern world" (25). Then Reed Way Dasenbrock responds that classical rhetoric is not so bad; all we need to do is use modern theory as a way to correct classical "rhetoric's overemphasis on persuasive discourse and figurative language" (291–303). And this debate over the size, range, efficacy, and appropriateness of rhetoric leads back through all the other disputes and subdisputes I have discussed above at such length. Obviously, no one can miss the agonistic, maleness of all these disputes. If, for example, one adds all the speakers summarized under "enthymeme," "example," "How many rhetorics are there?" and "rhetoric-as-epistemic" in chapter 4 and then adds those "major theorists" mentioned in this paragraph, the total list of speakers comes to fifty-three (fifty-four if one counts me as a "speaker"). Of those fifty-four speakers, one (Lil Brannon) is a woman.

In composition studies we are just beginning to see debates such as this develop. If we are to be fully professional, such debates are unavoidable. The more carefully we taxonomize ourselves, the more sharply we will draw the boundaries of dispute. Choosing a situation in the professional discourse will soon be the most urgent and defining act a graduate student can make. For in professional discourse there must be winners and losers, there must be scholars who are right and scholars who are wrong. The world Aristotle left for us demands such agonistic competition, a competition that allows only a few audible voices, while all the others are relegated to oblivion. Even if collaboration becomes the research model, teams of collaborators will continue to compete, though each team may work harmoniously and noncompetitively within itself.

Mere Sophistry

One alternative to such professionalization is sophistry, which seems to be the place where I always end up. The most obvious way to become a sophist is to articulate and then inhabit the theory and the pedagogy of previous sophists. I have done a little of that myself, but Sharon Crowley, Richard Enos, Susan Jarratt, John Poulakos, and Vic Vitanza, to mention but a few, have done it both more thoroughly and more productively. Increasingly, I prefer a second, perhaps less obvious, way of seeking out a theory and a pedagogy with the name "sophist." And I find the second way more reliable and more productive than trying to figure out what Protagoras or Gorgias or some other sophist meant or thought. I prefer to inhabit the notions of "sophistry" created by Plato and Aristotle. Whether Plato and Aristotle described "sophistry" accurately matters little to me. What matters is that the theoretical frame (up) that Plato and Aristotle left for us exists through its exclusion of something that they called "sophistry." I wish to inhabit the (human) discourse that Plato and Aristotle excluded under the name sophistry, regard-

less of whether that excluded and debased discourse correctly reproduces what anyone else in ancient Athens may have advocated. As
"founding fathers" Plato and Aristotle located rhetoric in a certain
place and oriented it in a certain direction. I am not content either
with the place or the direction, and I would very much like to know
what happens when that foundation is moved and the orientation
turned.

Schiappa has done a good job raising questions about the validity
of any such category as "ancient sophistry." I agree with him that
the notion "sophist," which at various times includes everyone from
Socrates to Isocrates, is quite difficult to pin down, and I also agree
that it is probably impossible to articulate a notion of sophistry
that would include everyone from Antiphon, Thrasymachus, and
Protagoras to Gorgias, Lysias, and Isocrates.[4] More to the point, a
certain danger insinuates itself into any attempt to rehabilitate the
sophists (or any particular sophist). Sophistical education, in spite
of its democratic leanings, did nothing to transform Athenian class-
and race-based society. Although the education offered by the sophists did enable students to play the political power game in democratic Athens, that education was hideously expensive, open only
to the wealthiest young men (and in spite of the names Lasthenia
and Axiothea the students *were* all men; no shred of evidence indicates that the emancipation of women played any role at all in
sophistry).[5] Re-creating the notion "sophistry" from the works of
Plato and Aristotle, however, is not so difficult. I have already tried
to show that Plato is himself what he tries to exclude under the
name sophistry. One need do no more than read *Phaedrus* to see
both that Plato tries to exclude certain maneuvers under the name
sophist and that he uses each of those maneuvers in his attempted
exclusion.

Teasing out Aristotle's notion of sophistry is both less interesting
and less enjoyable than teasing out Plato's, but in many ways it is
more important. I think Plato knew exactly what he was doing as
he tried to steal writing and sophistry from the West. Plato "creates"
the foundation for his system (and hence the system itself) by placing
it forever beyond knowability. The way the Platonist "knows" that
the Forms exist is that they remain forever beyond human comprehension. Plato gets to eat his cake by not having it. By being a
sophist (of his own describing), Plato tries to fill that category so full
that no one else will ever again be able to enter it, use its voice, know

its knowledge. Aristotle's sophistry is a different matter entirely, for Aristotle is not a sophist; that is to say he does not use the strategies that he associates with sophistry in order to exclude those strategies. Aristotelian sophistry is more mundane and less brilliant than Platonic sophistry, because Aristotle's texts are so consistently "honest," so ploddingly "systematic." But Aristotelian sophistry is just as dangerous to the Aristotelian system as Platonic sophistry is to Platonism.

In *Topics* Aristotle lumps sophists in with slanderers and thieves to explain that the capability of doing evil does not make a person evil. Only evil actions make a person evil. Thus, a sophist, like a thief or a slanderer, becomes a sophist only because a sophist *practices* sophistry. All people are capable of sophistry; only bad people employ it. In dealing with sophistical opponents, Aristotle explains a few paragraphs later, one must be careful about how one assigns properties to things (133^b15–134^a4). If one is not careful, a sophist, who is so very tricky, will confuse all the clear and proper categories. Any right-thinking person knows that "what belongs to 'man' will also belong to 'white man,' " Aristotle says almost with a sigh of contempt over the need to make the point at all. "If there is a white man," he continues, "what belongs to 'white man' will also belong to 'man.' " (No, I am not kidding. That is Aristotle's example, and it is indicative of what his vision shows him when he searches the world for examples of his theories. The "white man" example goes on for a page.) Sophists, however, mix everything up, trying to create so much confusion that such clear and proper categories as "man" and "white man" are no longer synonymous; while dealing with a sophist, one runs the risk of not knowing for sure what "man" and "white" mean or how they relate.

What makes one a sophist, Aristotle explains in the *Rhetoric*, is lack of moral purpose (13551^b8–21). A sophist, after all, is one who does evil, works wickedness, deals basely, corrupts, and falsifies (1404^b38–39). Indeed, in the Aristotelian system, sophists take on almost demonic proportions, playing a role similar to that of Satan in Milton's *Paradise Lost* ("To do aught good never will be our task," one can almost hear the Aristotelian sophists chant, "But ever to do ill our sole delight"). Aristotle explains at length (*Sophistical Refutations* 165^a20–38) that the sophist actively seeks the appearance of knowledge rather than knowledge itself, preferring the sham to the truth. "Appearing wise," rather than being wise, "is the real purpose which sophists have in view."

Why are sophists so tricky and unscrupulous? What possible motive could they have for seeking the appearance of truth in preference to the truth itself? Money. They do their dirty work for money: "the sophist is one who makes money from apparent and not real wisdom" (165ª22); "the art of the sophist is a money-making art which trades on apparent wisdom, and so sophists aim at apparent proof" (171ᵇ25–30). The reason that sophists demand to be paid in advance, Aristotle explains in *Nicomachean Ethics*, is that no one would pay them in arrears because students who study with sophists do not learn anything:

> people who take the money in advance, and then, having made extravagant professions, fail to perform what they undertook, naturally meet with complaints because they have not fulfilled their bargain. Perhaps however the sophists are bound to demand their fees in advance, since nobody would pay money for the knowledge which they possess. (1064ª28–34)

Aristotle does not explain how a sophist stays in business after the graduates spread the word that they learned nothing. Presumably Aristotle attributed the extravagant success of the sophists' schools to democratic gullibility; democrats are so gullible that none of them can imagine the vacuousness of sophistical education without experiencing it, and once they have the experience, because they are so poorly educated, they do not have the logos necessary to warn others away.

The method of the sophist, according to Aristotle, is to seek out the unresolvable paradox in any given situation (*Sophistical Refutations* 172ᵇ9–14; *Nicomachean Ethics* 1146ª22–31). "The sophists," Aristotle charges in the *Ethics*, "wish to show their cleverness by entrapping their adversary into a paradox, and when they are successful, the resultant chain of reasoning ends in a deadlock: the mind is fettered, being unwilling to stand still yet unable to go forward because it cannot untie the knot of the argument." When such a paralyzing paradox cannot be developed, sophists seek to defraud the opponent by producing "the appearance of refutation, when, though they have proved nothing, they do not put the final proposition in the form of a question but state conclusively, as though they had proved it" (*Sophistical Refutations* 174ª8–12). "Sophistry," as Aristotle explains in *Metaphysics*, "is Wisdom in appearance only" (1004ᵇ18–21). Sophists focus their attention on accidents rather than facts and end up dealing "with what is non-existent" (1026ᵇ14–17). A sophist's only study is "unreality" (1064ᵇ29–30). Sophists attempt to perform the absurdity of separating a thing from its essence because they do not invest the intellectual effort required to separate the accidental from the essential: "In a sense the accident and its essence are the same," Aristotle explains, "and in a sense they are not; for the essence of white is not the same as the man or the white man, but it is the same as the attribute white." Only a sophist would try to mix all of this up, making it less than crystal clear (1031ᵇ19–1032ª12).

The reason that the sophist is such a vicious, evil, untrustworthy, destabilizing force in society is that sophists do not inhabit the system that reveals true knowledge. As a result of some strange perversity (perhaps a genetic defect), they go around doubting all the time. Not only do they believe nothing, they continually unsettle those who believe something. So utterly excluded are sophists and sophistry in Aristotle's system that both ἀπόδειξις and ἐπιστήμη know themselves as "unqualified knowledge" by being "contrasted with the accidental knowledge of the sophist." Real knowledge is the sort that "enables us to know by the mere fact that we grasp it," and we know such knowledge by knowing sophistry as the opposite of such knowledge, for sophistry offers the sort of knowledge that remains forever mixed up in contradictions and refutations (*Posterior Analytics* 71ᵇ9–19). The demonstrator knows knowledge in its essential, absolutely certain way, in contrast to the sophist who remains forever perplexed about whatever "knowledge" seems present (74ᵇ5–26; see also 73ª21–73ᵇ24 where, incredibly, "white" and "man" crop up again as examples, and *Topics* 162ª15–18 where a sophism is contrasted with a philosopheme and an epichireme). And thus, with a clarity far beyond the clarity of rhetoric, in *Metaphysics* Aristotle claims to have refuted Protagoras's contentious statement that "man is the measure of all things" (*Metaphysics* 1007ᵇ18–1008ª9), for Aristotle has shown throughout his works that the things that man can "know" are the measure of man. When Aristotle takes up Protagoras's radical relativism the second time in *Metaphysics* (1062ᵇ13–1063ª17), Aristotle shows how his system disables Protagorean (and all other forms of) sophistry. Man-in-general cannot be the measure of all things, because if man in general is the final measure, Aristotle explains, "it follows that the same thing is and is not, and is bad and good." Aristotle attributes such nonsense to "those who study human nature or nature in general"* (τῶν περὶ φύσεως). Such "natural philosophers" argue that "a thing does not become white which was before completely white and in no respect not-white." As a result, "that which becomes white must come from what was not-white. Hence according to this theory, there would be generation from what is not, unless the same thing were originally white *and* not white." It is not difficult to refute such logic, Aristotle explains, and he points to his *Physics* for the technical explanation. Here in the *Metaphysics* he resorts to a different kind of response. First, he calls the sophists self-evidently "foolish." Then he proclaims the (to him) self-evident truth that in any dispute "clearly one side or the other must be wrong." To exemplify the clarity of his understanding, he offers the sense of taste. If the same substance is sweet to one person and sour to another, then one of the persons suffers from an "injured or impaired organ." And if one of the persons has an "injured or impaired organ," then the person with a whole and healthy organ "should be taken as the 'measure,' and the other not." In other words, when there is a dispute over taste or interpretation, one of the two parties in the dispute has an impaired organ. All one need do is discover which party has the impaired organ and then name the other party the measure. How do we know which party is impaired? Easy, if the dispute is between a white man and any other sort of creature, well, need I say more? If the dispute occurs between two white men of high birth and philosophical training, we ask Aristotle.

So, if you join me in sophistry, here's what you risk:
1. Aristotle will think you are bad, immoral, wicked, evil, base, corrupting, tricky, and dishonest. In any disagreement over taste or interpretation, he will declare your organ to be "injured or impaired," and he will declare your opponent "the measure." In light of what we know about Aristotle, I will leave to you the decision about how much importance you wish to place on Aristotle's opinion, or on the opinion of anyone who continues to inhabit Aristotle's νοῦς.
2. As a habit of life, you will go around doubting all the time

and unsettling those who do not doubt. Anytime intellectual or cultural resolution seems imminent, you will seek out the paradoxes, contradictions, and silenced voices in order to unsettle that resolution.

3. You will never know any essential knowledge about anything at all. All your knowledge (Aristotle would say all your not-knowledge) will be provisional and transient. Thus in the "real" sense, you will have nothing to teach your students because—well, because you yourself do not *know* anything.

4. You will have no methodology for seeking the truth. Indeed, you will have an almost genetic predisposition to seek the apparent truth rather than the truth itself. Even when the truth is there in plain view and everyone around you can see it clearly, you will work to show the unresolvable contradictions and uncertainties of that clear and present truth. In every case, you will seek the accident and the unreal rather than the true and the real.

5. You will work for money. Unlike your colleagues in literature, philosophy, and history who do their work for the love of truth and would go right on working if their colleges stopped paying them, you will always have to live with the fact that you would stop working if your college stopped paying you.

6. You by your very existence will enable all the disciplines, all the scientists, and all the philosophers around you. By being the seeker of sophistical not-knowledge, you will embody the activity through which the seekers of true, scientific knowledge know themselves; they will know themselves because they will know that they seek the thing that you do not have and can never achieve. By seeking the contradiction, the uncertainty, the aporia, you will enable the true philosophical dialecticians to know themselves by distinguishing themselves from your nihilistic sophistry. Indeed, your presence on campus (or at least near campus) will enable the entire university, for you will embody the necessarily unfortunate and misguided activity that the university must differ from in order to discover the knowledge that it knows.

L(i)ability

Unlike Plato's Academy, which, according to Donald Kagan, "engaged in advising and training statesmen," Aristotle's "Lyceum was a research institute which provided scholars and teachers." As a true research scholar, Kagan continues, "Aristotle is remote and scientific to the degree that he can look at constitutions he disapproves, yet analyze their weaknesses and recommend means for their preservation and improvement" (*Great* 199). And as I have tried to show throughout this book, Aristotle's discourse allows him to extract himself from his culture and to justify or critique it in a way that no one caught up in the press of lived experience could hope to do. The power of the professional discourse he offers can hardly be overestimated. Who can imagine scholarship that presents itself as nothing but stylistic excess? Who can imagine a speaker or writer of any professional discourse publishing a text that depends even slightly on a pathetic appeal? Aristotle may not have "won the argument," but I do not think he was concerned about "winning the argument." He, like his mentor, wanted to set the terms in which argument would operate.

Some months ago, I heard Lynn Cheney give an address about the humanities. She spoke against everything that one might associate with the term *theory*. She said the humanities, and hence the National Endowment for the Humanities, should focus on those great thinkers and writers who transcend race, gender, class, and politics and deal with the "essential human condition." I think Lynn Cheney has read Aristotle and believed him. Anyone who becomes a sophist of the sort that Aristotle's system excludes will also read Aristotle. But sophists will know better than to believe him. The most liberating and troublesome result of such sophistry for composition studies, however, is that it does not produce scholarship. It produces sophistry. And every respectable scholar will know right away when a supposedly scholarly text is not behaving itself or when it is not generating any knowledge. Any good scholar will see that a sophistical text is a little too playful, a little too self-indulgent, a little too angry, a little too slipshod, a little too situated in the purely personal, a little too unsure of itself. It keeps coming apart all the time. It never seems to end or to know how it should end.

In contrast to sophistry, rhetoric (by which I mean the "never-practiced" theoretical construct created by Plato and Aristotle) is a great place to "be." Even though it occupies the lowest, most degraded place in Aristotle's system, it does occupy a place. If one can ignore or forget the contempt other scientists have for rhetoric and rhetoricians, one can forever behave demonstratively on the site of rhetoric. Sophistry, on the other hand, is nothing but l(i)ability.[6] An extra letter lives inside it, always turning it around to something else. If the sophist could eliminate that letter, then sophistry would operate itself indefinitely as chemical, physical, and biological change and breakdown. The extra letter, however, adds an element of obligation, responsibility, exposure, risk. Teaching writing, it turns out, is just that—obligation, responsibility, exposure, and risk all embedded in an unending process of physical, chemical, and biological breakdown.

One can speak or write professional discourse, I believe, by knowing Aristotle or any of his legitimate descendants. One can "know" professional discourse, however, only through sophistry. To those who do not mind speaking with a voice that any scholar will recognize as "injured or impaired," to those who do not mind being tricked into confusing the clear and proper categories (even if the whiteness of man loses a little of its magical luster as an innocent example), I can recommend sophistry. It will not produce knowledge, it will not "finish anything off," it will not create a foundation or add to an edifice. If you become a sophist, in the end you will never be able to claim more than Gorgias claims: to have pleased yourself. And no true scholar, no true speaker of a *real* professional discourse will ever forgive you for that. No true scholar will tolerate historicism when there is taxonomy to be done.

Michelangelo's *Night*, Medici Chapel, Florence.
Courtesy of Alinari/Art Resource, NY

EPILOGUE
The Writing of Situations

The most haunting aspect of Michelangelo's Atlas is that it cannot free its head. The agonistic struggle grips the viewer. Night, in contrast, has an elegant comfort about her. I like everything about Night. She is *so* beautiful, so calm, so complete. Her body looks like that of a natural athlete, one of those athletes who seem forever unconscious both of their rarity and of their blessing. Only by looking at Night from the back can one see that she, like Atlas, is still emerging from stone. The robe that drapes across her right leg, her buttocks, her left shoulder, and part of her back descend, finally, into stone. Unlike Michelangelo's *David*, which appears completely formed and utterly "free," Night has a back side that, for her purposes as a work of art, did not need finishing. Having spent my entire adult life in an agonistic struggle against both my education and my culture, I suppose I do wish to enter a "beNighted" state. I do not, however, want to escape or ignore my situation, beNighted though it may be.

Because my pedagogy depends so much on Aristotle, I have tried to articulate my situation as carefully and honestly as I can. Although I have never assigned Aristotle in any of my composition classes, I have taught almost all of those classes from within Aristotelian notions. As a point of departure in my classes, I foreground the ethical, pathetic, and logical appeals, and almost without thinking about the matter, I emphasize the logical while downplaying the pathetic. I teach invention, spend considerable time on arrangement, work constantly on style, and (now that my students write on computers that have multiple fonts, graphics, and sound capabilities) spend an increasing amount of time on delivery. On occasion, I even use the common topics, and I often depend on the sort of popular psychology that Aristotle articulated first in his *Rhetoric*. And these are just the most obvious ways in which Aristotle organizes my classroom. In a larger sense, Aristotelian theory organized the whole research university. As a result of this influence, my pedagogy demands that I scrutinize Aristotle, which I have tried to do by carrying out the five tasks that lead to the ontogeny of "a composition teacher."

First, through my study of Aristotle, I have tried to foreground the social and political implications of the sources of my pedagogy. As a result, I know that when I speak with Aristotle's voice or employ his notions of discourse, I take a terrible risk, both for myself and for the students who enter my classroom to learn from my pedagogy. My culture taught me to be racist and sexist, and it encourages class prejudice of all types and in every direction; moreover, the source of my pedagogy wrote the first systematic defense of slavery and sexism, and he embedded his rhetoric in that defense. Naturally, I feel like Atlas, like someone whose head has never been made and whose body remains partially unformed. The desperation of the necessary struggle, with all its agonistic, Greek overtones, cannot be denied. Night seems far away indeed.

Second, as a way of changing myself from Atlas to Night, I have tried to allow the Aristotelian system to unwork itself. Rather than attacking the system directly, which would be a military maneuver that would largely imprison me in the system, I have tried to overhear the oppressed and hidden voices of self-contradiction that the system includes. This reading allows me to see how and why the Aristotelian system degrades rhetoric and thus to understand why students in my classes are often so uncomfortable. My students anticipate an academic world that seeks either permanent (demonstrative) or contingent (dialectical) truth. In my classes, however, these students learn nothing more than the available means of persuasion. In my classes, truth forever resides in the effectiveness of the discourse on the intended audience. This reading also explains why my colleagues, whether demonstrative scientists or dialectical humanists, are so wary of anything merely rhetorical and so horrified by the overtly sophistical.

Third, I have tried to explore the "professional voice" that emerges from Aristotelian theory. This voice can easily trick a human being, even the human being who speaks through it. Analyzing the sort of person I must become to play my own role "teacher" and the sort of people my students must become to play the role I give them as "students," I immediately hear the voices of Kelly Mays and Earnestine Johnson, and I try to remember that they are both students. They are not different ontological states. They are (or were when they wrote the two essays I cite) merely two young women in college seeking a baccalaureate degree. Without question I know that my own voice sounds *much* more like that of Mays than like that of Johnson, and I know all too well that Mays can glide through the academy, as I have done, without changing a nuance, while Johnson's voice will be threatened in every classroom, every corridor. My analysis of Aristotle's (and hence my own) voice reminds me that professional discourse is nothing but human discourse with a lisp—just the sort of fantastical, dandyish lisp that Aristotle apparently affected in order to attract attention. Indeed, so powerful is that lisp in its idiosyncratic, self-liberating effect that the professional easily takes on the self-conception of "one who understands." The νοῦς, after all, was Plato's nickname for his star pupil.

Fourth, having read the Aristotelian system and listened to the Aristotelian voice, I have tried to read Aristotelian rhetoric as closely as I can. Admittedly, I learned my reading strategies from Plato and Jacques Derrida; thus, what I mean by "reading" has an antagonistic, faithless manner. Through this sort of reading, however, I see the operation of Aristotelian rhetoric as it loses itself in knowing itself and finally implodes into its own attempted valorization of the logos. Aristotle's texts, I have learned, do not tell the truth, either about themselves or about what they seem to reveal. Aristotle saw an agonistic world in which one speaker had to be right, the other wrong. His own maneuvering allows him to extract himself from that situation in order to articulate the general principles whereby rightness and wrongness are recognizable. Having read most of Aristotle's texts closely, I know that I do not want my students to write as he wrote or to think as he thought. Thus when I use his conceptions of discourse, I must always be careful not only to use them but also to use them against themselves.

Finally, I have tried to explain why I construe sophistry as the most effective response to Aristotelianism. This sophistry, because it never "knows" anything, always seeks out the undecidables that prevent the closure of understanding. Thus even when I feel myself "emerging," when I feel that my arm has finally pulled my head free and I can lie down like Night, I still fear the Aristotelian trap. For Aristotle (as Nussbaum has shown so well) *does* construct his system on the "appearances" (as opposed to the Platonic "realities"). As a result, I cannot help worrying that in the sanctity of my own self-present *voûs* the appearances appear correct. Sophistry teaches me that I can never cease the process of interrogating my own relativist and uncertain interpretations, for those interpretations have the oddest habit of shedding their "apparentness" and becoming "reality." Because I do not believe there is any discourse other than human discourse, sophistry is my way of remaining human. My reading of Aristotle's canon shows me how one of the West's founding fathers used human texts as a way of seeming to escape the human in order to speak through the professional. In responding to the archsophist, Protagoras, Aristotle argues that a human being must be measured by what that human being "knows"; thus, Aristotle makes humanity into an entity that can be measured, and he defines the Supreme Scientist, the most professional of professionals, as the one who is freed from the human condition and allowed to do the measuring. But as I have tried to show, Aristotle's texts are deceitful; they sound professional, but they remain human throughout.

The last question before I leave the Greeks is, "How do I go on teaching?" The answer is obvious. I go on doing what I have been doing. Even the newest, most inexperienced TA right out of undergraduate school can do it. The questions do not change; only the situations change. All teachers at all times can say to themselves: (1) What are the sources of my pedagogy? What role do those sources allot me? What role do they allot my students? Even if my sources consist of nothing more than my own experience as a composition student together with a departmentally assigned textbook and a writing program administrator who tells me what to do by mandating a syllabus, even those sources imply social and political conditions. Those sources allot certain roles to teacher and to student. (2) In the arena defined by the sources of my pedagogy, what counts as knowledge? What are the rules that determine whether discourse is legitimate? The most crucial and naive mistake I could make, after all, would be to believe that my pedagogy frees students to "be themselves." No such all-freeing pedagogy can exist because no teacher can be free from that particular teacher's situation. Like any teacher, I must study the sources of my pedagogy to learn what my own rules are. (3) What does my professional voice sound like? Where did I learn to speak as I do? What ontological commitments must I make to continue to speak with my voice? (4) Is there any difference between what my sources say about proper discourse and the actual behavior of my sources? In other words, do my sources tell me to tell students to do one thing while the sources themselves do something quite different? (5) How can I speak through the voice that my sources silence?

All this leads to one final criterion, a criterion unique to the field of composition studies. The composition teacher need not worry about being true to the subject matter. Unlike the calculus teacher who can give an exam or the literature teacher who has a canon and a reading methodology to protect or the physicist who must ensure that students can operate within the reigning paradigm of physical science, the composition teacher must remain true to pedagogy. Such faithfulness need not take the appearance of Atlas; indeed, as long as the teacher is caught in a heroic, agonistic struggle, the sort of sophistry I seek cannot begin, for my sort of sophistry is both self-indulgent and playful. Only in the comfort of Night can such sophistry begin. Of course, Night must never forget that she does have a back side, but then the teaching of writing has always been conscious of its nature as backside.

The difference between Aristotelian rhetoric and the composition of sophistry is both great and small. The only real changes are these: Whereas Aristotle conceived rhetoric as the lowest, most degraded discursive strategy, a composition teacher rereads that very conception as an unknown, unconscious act *of* persuasion. Whereas Aristotle sought to escape the human in order to live the superior life of the professional, a composition teacher never forgets the humanness of any professional voice. Whereas the Aristotelian rhetorician behaves demonstratively on the site named "rhetoric," always trying to get straight what is and what is not acceptably "rhetorical," a composition teacher behaves sophistically, trying to hear as many student voices as possible and trying to show the speakers of those voices both the strategies for, and the costs of, speaking in a world that believes itself to be professional. The Aristotelian rhetorician lives the life of Atlas, always caught in the agonistic process of self-definition. The sophist, on the other hand, lives a much happier, more peaceful Night-life. Such a sophist seems relaxed and fully whole to those who look at her, but she never forgets that she *was* made, that she was not fully made, that nothing like her could ever be fully made, and that her processes of being and becoming are the same.

NOTES
WORKS CITED
INDEX

NOTES

1. The *Rhetoric* and the *Politics* of Slavery

1. The name was a misnomer from the beginning in that people of all races were free to join. It was called the "black" party because the so-called Mississippi Democratic party did not admit black members.

2. *The Oxford Annotated Bible*, Genesis 9.20–27. Future English citations from the Bible are taken from this translation and will be cited by book, chapter, and verse, in the text.

3. Cope (1.60), Grimaldi (1.91), Roberts (35), and Freese (41) all offer translations supporting the interpretation that Aristotle subordinates rhetoric to the (ἀρχιτεκτονική) political science. Kagan (*Great* 202–4), Shulsky (77–78), and Vickers (8) also offer this interpretation. I should also note that the Greek comparative adjectives (ἐμφρονεστέρας and μᾶλλον ἀληθινῆς) are used to describe political science in a positive way (as being more intelligent, scholarly, or instructive and more exact, true, or real than rhetoric) rather than rhetoric in a negative way. My text implies the negative, but I do not think that violates the Greek.

4. I do not doubt Kathleen Welch's contention that the canons were in place in Plato's day and thus were not Aristotle's invention. The fact that Aristotle codified such things as the canons and preserved them for history as he did are the important points for me.

5. I accept the general judgment that Aristotle wrote the *Politics* during his second stay in Athens (335–22); thus, it reflects his mature and seasoned opinions about how society should be organized.

6. In the *Economics* ($1344^{a}23$–$1344^{b}22$) Aristotle, or one of his followers at the Lyceum, works through the business of slavery yet again, this time with the spin of how one manages and gets the most production from a slave. It is also worth noting that the notion of human "whiteness" appears so often in the *Categories* as to become a sort of fetish. Among other places see $1^{a}28$, $2^{a}1$–10 and 30–34, $2^{b}1$–22 and 35, $3^{a}20$, $4^{a}5$ and 20–30, $4^{b}14$, $5^{b}1$–10, $6^{a}4$, $10^{b}12$–18, 13–15, and 26–28. This repeated concern with human "whiteness" also appears in *On Interpretation*, beginning with $18^{a}15$–20 and $20^{b}35$–40.

7. R. K. Sinclair (197–202) offers a good summary of the debate over the

number of slaves as does Finley in both *The Ancient Economy* and *Ancient Slavery* (especially 67–93).

8. For other discussions of this term, see Thompson 197 and Sagan 261. The Macedonians did not, of course, invent the act of razing a city and enslaving its population. One need do no more than read Thucydides accounts of the way Athens treated the Mitylenians, the Melians, and the Scionaeans to see that the Athenians were as adept at destroying and enslaving as any political entity in the Mediterranean world.

9. One can easily see the sort of apologies this kind of thinking leads to. The third sentence in Oxford University Press's brochure advertising Kennedy's new translation of the *Rhetoric* reads as follows: "[Kennedy] eliminates euphemistic and sexist language (which Aristotle did not use)." While it is true that some of the older translations use masculine pronouns where Aristotle's Greek does not absolutely require them, the suggestion that Aristotle was not sexist—a suggestion that this sentence clearly makes— is both ridiculous and dangerous. Anyone who reads the *Politics* knows that no translator does Aristotle a disservice by using exclusive (and frequent!) masculine pronouns. Pretending somehow that the *Rhetoric* is not a sexist document embedded deeply in a sexist culture does, however, do us a disservice because it helps us blind ourselves to things that we prefer not to see.

10. Aristotle and his students gathered at least 158 different constitutions for *The Athenian Constitution* and the *Politics*. This process of gathering every available piece of evidence, organizing and synthesizing all the evidence, summarizing it, and then critiquing it, really is the beginning of scholarship. See Sagan (310) and Kagan (*Great* 199). (Throughout my text, I will treat *The Athenian Constitution* as an Aristotelian text even though that assumption is disputed.)

11. Aristotle certainly knew that many slaves became slaves because their ancestors prior to Solon had taken mortgages on their own bodies that they failed to pay. In *The Athenian Constitution*, after all, Aristotle explains Solon's abolition of "loans secured on the person." For whatever reason, Aristotle chooses not to mention this form of generational enslavement.

12. This argument in which some "men" are clearly more "men" than others does not seem to bother Aristotle, even though he spends considerable time in *Categories* (2^b1–4^b19) and *Metaphysics* (1006^a1–1007^b18) arguing that "man" is by definition "man" and cannot be less than "man." In point of fact, however, it turns out that "man" really means only aristocratic, philosophical "man," for nonaristocratic, nonphilosophical "man" is clearly a notch down; works-for-a-living "man" is two notches down; woman is three notches down; and slave is really nothing more than an animal in man form. David Ross (160) and Abram Shulsky (93–94) discuss this same problem.

13. For other treatments of the νοῦς, see Martha Nussbaum (251) and Kagan (*Pericles* 24–25).

14. Quoted in Chroust (1.233). In an endnote to the passage, Chroust traces this notion throughout the Aristotelian canon.

15. The Greek that I am translating as "wiser and superior to" reads as follows: "σοφὸν καὶ διαφέροντα τῶν ἄλλων." I am translating the participle as meaning "going beyond" in a categorical, escatological way, hence "superior being."

16. It would be hard to overstate the degree of Aristotle's class prejudice. One need not accept de Ste. Croix's Marxism to see it glaringly. Abram Shulsky's (75–89) explication of the Aristotelian derogatory noun χρηματιστικός shows Aristotle's contempt for those who had to make a living in any way other than owning land. Finley ("Aristotle" 18) argues that Aristotle's insistence on the unnaturalness of commercial trade prevents him from examining the mechanics of economics. Joseph Schumpeter makes the same case, arguing that Aristotle operated "in the light of the ideological preconceptions to be expected in a man who lived in, and wrote for, a cultured leisure class, which held work and business pursuits in contempt and, of course, loved the farmer who fed it and hated the money lender who exploited it" (60). Christian Meier and A. H. M. Jones repeat this formulation, with Jones contending that Plato and Aristotle were gentlemen who "despised workers and justified their contempt by asserting that manual work deformed the body and the soul" ("Economic" 29) and Meier contending that Aristotle, like others in "affluent circles," had "contempt for work" (145).

17. In *Metaphysics* (1075ᵃ12–1076ᵃ4) Aristotle sets up the same sort of world view. In *Nicomachean Ethics* he divides the soul in a similar way (1139ᵃ).

18. I recognize that Aristotle treats the practical and productive as mutually exclusive. In chapter 2 below, I deal with the way in which Aristotle's rhetoric violates the law of noncontradiction.

19. I treat this history in more detail in a forthcoming essay ("Degradation"), but anyone can read the essays by W. T. Hewett, H. C. G. Brandt, James Morgan Hart, F. V. N. Painter, Theodore W. Hunt, Henry R. Lang, John G. R. McElroy, and A. Marshall Elliott that appeared in the very first issue of *PMLA*. The essays by James MacAlister and Henry E. Shepherd in volume 3 as well as the essay by Morton W. Easton in volume 4 also bear scrutiny. The way literature created itself by degrading composition is astonishing, even to someone who remembers what it was like before "composition studies" existed as a professional designation.

2. *Metaphysics* and the Demonstration of Rhetoric

1. Carl Classen's description of rhetoric ("Ars Rhetoric" 9) articulates clearly the conception of rhetoric I mean in this paragraph.

2. See the first four chapters of *Plato, Derrida, and Writing*.

3. Lawrence Green summarizes the latitude in the term *counterpoint* as follows: "it can mean whatever each of us needs it to mean. . . . It can mean (1) that X is a mirror image of Y, or (2) that X is the proportional

opposite of Y, or (3) that X is an exact parallel of Y, or (4) that X-in-its-context is the same as Y-in-its-context, or (5) that X and Y (like yin and yang) fit together in such a way as to make a whole, and so forth" (22–23).

4. Green (12–15) summarizes the two other traditions of interpreting ἀντίστροφος between Alexander and the Renaissance. In general, Green argues that the relationship between rhetoric and dialectic can be seen in one of three ways: opposite, similar, or convertible.

5. For a cautionary warning against seeing ἀντίστροφος as a rehabilitation of rhetoric as well as an introduction to the history of that claim, see Green (24–25).

6. Green (8) attempts to refute this idea.

7. The verb form of this term, παραφύομαι, has only a passive form and means "to grow beside or at the side of." Aristotle uses a different form of the term παραφύομαι in Nicomachean Ethics (1096ᵃ23) to explain how the "relative" relates to the absolute. In this case the term suggests that the relative is an offshoot or accident of true 'being'.

8. Grimaldi (Studies 54) offers a rather unusual translation of lines 30–33: "Rhetoric is, as it were, a constitutive part of dialectic and is similar to dialectic, as I said at the beginning, insofar as neither rhetoric nor dialectic is a science (episteme) concerned with the specific and determinate nature of any subject matter. They are rather faculties (dynameis), so to speak, for providing reasonable explanations." In my opinion Grimaldi is so eager for rhetoric to be intellectually respectable that he stretches the Greek to fit his needs.

9. The Greek verb ὑποδύομαι has the sense of one entity entering into another, especially the sense of an actor taking on a character in a play "because the actor's face was put under a mask" (Liddell and Scott).

10. For a close and thorough analysis of the way Aristotle equates ἐπιστήμη with the process of pure science, see Nussbaum (290ff.).

11. In his new translation of the Rhetoric Kennedy approaches this passage in a way quite different from mine. He sees Aristotle as trying to argue that both the rhetorician and the dialectician need to be able to differentiate valid and fallacious arguments. I do not disagree with his translation, but I think he elides the loss of moral purpose implied in the configuration Aristotle gives rhetoric in this passage.

12. Aristotle articulates this law as the foundation of his philosophy in Metaphysics (especially 1005ᵇ5–1011ᵇ23).

13. I choose these two because each is a "famous philosopher" whose work has been used to offer a theoretical matrix for the teaching of writing.

14. Cicero argues the point I am making here as well as anyone (De Inventione 2.2.8) when he says that Aristotle's school was "busy with philosophy, but devoting some attention to the art of rhetoric as well." Cicero places ultimate blame for the split between philosophy and the resulting degradation of rhetoric on Socrates, who, according to Cicero (De Oratore 3.16.59–60),

separated the science of wise thinking from that of elegant speaking, though in reality they are closely linked. . . . This is the source from which has sprung the undoubtedly absurd and unprofitable and reprehensible severance between the tongue and the brain, leading to our having one set of professors to teach us to think and another to speak.

Of course, anyone who reads Aristotle would know right away that he thought of himself as one who taught thinking, not one who taught speaking.

15. I have tried to argue this point at length in *Plato, Derrida, and Writing*, and thus I will not take it up here.

16. According to David Ross (5), Aristotle taught not only rhetoric, but also sophistic and politics in the afternoons when larger, less intellectually gifted audiences could join in the strolls through the Lyceum.

17. Lunsford and Ede ("Classical" 86–88), who are among the most distinguished scholars in composition studies, cite Rosenfield (1–16) and Johnstone both to argue that one must read the *Rhetoric* in the context of the entire Aristotelian opus and to argue that Aristotle's *Rhetoric* is rather kinder and gentler than I find it to be.

18. Short and Price make essentially the same kind of point, paralleling *Rhetoric* with *Topics* and *Analytics* to create theoretical, practical, and productive "antistrophic arts" that share common formal patterns.

19. Ingemar Düring had already made essentially the same case in 1966 (*Aristoteles* 139ff.), but at least in 1966 the power of rhetoric had not been reasserted as it had been by the time Annas wrote. More importantly, however, Annas waves rhetoric away with a sniff in a cultural document like *The Oxford History of the Classical World*, and she does it in full confidence that no one who knows anything at all would presume to differ with her.

20. Vickers offers an excellent summary of the history of rhetoric (see especially 197–209 and 283–84, where he complicates Walter Ong's history of Ramism, and 460–61, where he picks up Nietzsche's reply to the devaluation of rhetoric in the modern period). Chaim Perelman ("Rhetoric" 129–30) also offers a concise and useful history of the decline of rhetoric to little more than "mere figures." Ernesto Grassi spreads the blame for the decline of rhetoric much broader than I do: "The theory of the preeminence of logic and therefore of rational language—implying the exclusion of rhetorical language from the field of speculation—characterizes Western thought and leaves its seal upon it; from Plato with *Gorgias*, from scholasticism to Cartesian rationalism, up until German idealism from Kant to Hegel, with its total devaluation of rhetoric" (68). Kate Ronald, in contrast, takes issue with claims made by Robert Connors and S. Michael Halloran that classical rhetoric was constructed in such a way as to guarantee its demise in the modern period. And both Vickers (199) and James Zappen try to show the rhetoricity of early modern texts that use rhetorical strategies to attack

rhetoric. In short, any good Aristotelian rhetorician should know how to make a case opposite to the one I am making.

21. See *Rhetoric* 1403ᵇ14–24, where Aristotle foregrounds the "naturalness" of his separation of the "thought element" in rhetoric from such external matters as style, delivery, and arrangement.

22. The term ἀπόδειξις appears in several places throughout the *Rhetoric*. When it does, given the nature of the way the Aristotelian system works, it creates real problems for those who wish to see the Aristotelian vocabulary as consistent throughout both the *Rhetoric* and the entire canon. Grimaldi (*Studies* 139–41) points out all the places where ἀπόδειξις appears in *Rhetoric* and in each case has an explanation why the term should be there and how it does nothing to obscure the clarity of Aristotle's system.

23. "The invention of the syllogism, or rather the systematic treatment of the laws of inference, was," according to Tredennick, "Aristotle's greatest and most original achievement" (182).

24. For an explanation that Aristotle, working on a hint from Plato, created the syllogism, see Ross 32. So powerful is the Aristotelian syllogistic process that Forster translates συλλογισμός into English with the term *reasoning* (*Topics* 100ᵃ25, *Sophistical Refutations* 165ᵃ1).

25. Chroust (1.239) uses *Posterior Analytics* 71 and 99–100, which he dates prior to 350, and *Nicomachean Ethics* 1140–41, which he dates after 335 to argue that "Aristotle consistently adhered to a single conception of the scientific method and scientific knowledge."

26. For a description of the syllogism's various figures and moods, a detailed explanation of assertoric, apodeictic, and problematic syllogisms, and an explanation of where premises can be found, see *Prior Analytics* 24ᵇ18–46ᵃ30.

27. For Aristotle's notions about the gradual, inexorable progress of science, see *Topics* 151ᵇ12, *Sophistical Refutations* 183ᵇ17, *Meteorology* 351ᵇ25, *Metaphysics* 993ᵃ30, and *Nicomachean Ethics* 1098ᵃ23.

28. In *Categories* (2ᵃ11–4ᵇ19) Aristotle explains the essence of true, primary substance by using "man," particularly "white man," as his primary example.

29. For a slightly different formulation of this mantra, see *Topics* 105ᵃ34–ᵇ2.

30. Kennedy has also argued that demonstration is superior to dialectic and that dialectic is more like rhetoric than it is like demonstration (*Classical* 65).

31. For Aristotle's explanation that scientific knowledge can be both taught and learned, see *Nicomachean Ethics* 1139ᵇ25.

32. For a similar ranking of syllogism and enthymeme, see Crem, who clearly finds the enthymeme to be secondary and imperfect (59).

33. Grimaldi (*Studies* 85) points to *Topics* 162ᵃ15, where Aristotle discusses demonstrative, dialectical, sophistical, and contradictorily dialectical syllogisms, calling them, in order, a philosopheme, an epichireme, a sophism, and an aporeme. Grimaldi contends that Aristotle had not yet thought

of the enthymeme, but if he had it would be the name for a rhetorical syllogism. Ryan (38–40), like McBurney (119–20), links the dialectical and rhetorical syllogisms based on the points of departure. He argues that the category shift occurs between demonstration and dialectic and that once one gives up the absolute premise, there is little difference between the rhetorical and dialectical syllogisms. Obviously I differ. It seems clear to me that dialectic shares the rigor of syllogism with demonstration, a rigor that rhetoric is freed from. Ross (38–41) seems to agree with me, that the enthymeme is not so rigorous as the syllogism and that there is a clear three-tiered theory, which Ross calls scientific, dialectical, and rhetorical. The sort of hierarchy I see is an almost exact copy of the way Aristotelian metaphysics were read in the Middle Ages (see Wallace for a clear and useful overview of medieval notions of Aristotelian metaphysics).

34. Even the three kinds of rhetoric (deliberative, forensic, and epideictic) are determined by the hearer (*Rhetoric* 1358^{a}36).

35. Though I am sure that Ryan would oppose my reading of the *Rhetoric* at every turn, he seems to agree with me about the sort of audience for which Aristotelian rhetoric is appropriate: We see "from the description of rhetoric's function," he writes

> that Aristotle is thinking of listeners who have some difficulty keeping their minds on the speaker's business, are easily distracted, tend to forget what has gone before, are not absorbed with abstract ideas, etc. Nor are these people apt subjects for instruction or education; one would not try to share with them scientific or causal knowledge. (156; see also 47–48)

Other, more traditional, rhetoricians also agree with me. See, for example, Kennedy (*Classical* 71) and Grimaldi (*Studies* 88).

36. In *Metaphysics* 1064^{a}10–16 Aristotle explains that the "object" of scientific, demonstrative study is the source of its own motion. He then goes on to contrast this sort of object with the results of the practical and productive intellects. The source of motion in productive arts is the producer, not the thing produced; the source of motion in prudential endeavors is the agent, not the thing acted upon.

37. This tripartite descent is so clear in Aristotle that one sees vestiges of it on every page. For those who would like a specific point of departure, I recommend comparing *Posterior Analytics* 71^{b}9–24 with *Topics* 105^{b}30–32 and then with *Rhetoric* 1355^{a}5–7 and 1403^{a}10–15. See also Grimaldi, *Studies* 92. One can, of course, read this system quite differently from the way I do. For an example of how to do this, see Larry Arnhart's defense of the *Rhetoric* (12–53, 72–73). In fact, Arnhart tries to save rhetoric by arguing that there is one thing worse, sophistry. He offers an elaborate analysis of the Aristotelian system in order to show that one does not reach bottom with rhetoric; one reaches bottom only with sophistry. My response would be that sophistry exists outside the Aristotelian system because Aris-

totle makes no place for it. One can only elevate rhetoric in the Aristotelian system, in my opinion, by arguing that sophistry is present in Aristotle by its absence.

38. One page later (29), Cole offers a Kuhnian reading in which Plato and Aristotle mount a type of Kuhnian revolution. This allows them to reconfigure all their precursors as minor forerunners rather than serious intellectuals who had genuine influence on the Academic revolution.

39. Both Schiappa and Cole argue that Plato created the term ῥητορική early in the fourth century as a way of distinguishing his enterprise from that of those he wished to oppose. Poulakos ("Interpreting") has argued against the etymological history and Schiappa ("History") has responded (see also Schiappa's "Sophistic Rhetoric").

40. Aristotle makes essentially the same division in *On the Soul* 433^{a}14–15.

41. I recognize that I am offering a fairly loose translation of 1139^{b}14–17. The reference of the dative plural relative pronoun (οἷς) is, for me at least, ambiguous at best.

42. For other discussions of Aristotle's division of intellectual activity into theoretical, practical, and productive aspects, see Kennedy, *Classical* 62–63; Ross 20; and Grimaldi, *Studies* 25 and 137.

43. A host of scholars use the theoretic-practical-productive hierarchy as a way of claiming Aristotle's greatness as a rhetorician. Lois Self offers an excellent survey of the literature on rhetoric as a practical or productive faculty, and she concludes that Aristotle saves rhetoric, making it not only necessary but also worthwhile, by making the rhetorician a model of human virtue, a "man of practical wisdom" (130–45). Nussbaum also offers a compelling argument for Aristotle's genius in allotting rhetoric to the practical intellect" (301–14), as do Grimaldi (*Studies* 26), Perelman ("Rhetoric" 133), Paul Schollmeier (97), and Donald Cushman and Phillip Tompkins (43). Thomas Farrell sums up the various arguments for rhetoric as the method of the practical intellect with two arguments: (1) "that classical rhetoric offers us a practical ideal of the appropriate . . . [and] provides us with a kind of overarching form of reasoning with *doxa*"; and (2) that "within the context of classical theory, rhetoric is an art of practice to be developed in real-life settings, where matters are in dispute and there are no fixed or final criteria for judgment" (187). Janet Atwill and Janice Lauer, in a carefully argued analysis of the passages having to do with theoretic, practical, and productive faculties, try to show that rhetoric has often been trapped in a theory-practice split; unlike those cited above, Atwill and Lauer offer the productive intellect as a "third kind of knowledge" through which rhetoric escapes the theory-practice trap. Like Self and Nussbaum, Atwill and Lauer offer a thorough study of the literature about the passages in question; they are especially thorough in their critiques of Grimaldi, Cope, and Kennedy. I have no interest in arguing with any of these excellent analyses. I would, however, like to point out that after Aristotle, such "things" as practical, theoretic, and productive intellects "exist" and can be argued for or against.

My hunch is that Aristotle would not care how the three are interpreted or even ranked just so long as the arguments continue to be conducted in his vocabulary.

44. Ross goes on to explain the sterile and unsatisfactory notion of God that this generates, and he summarizes some of the attempts to try to rectify or pass over it.

45. I cannot resist noting that according to ancient tradition Plato referred to Aristotle as the νοῦς. On those occasions when Aristotle was late to class, Plato would make the other students wait. Then when Aristotle arrived, he would say, "read now, the Mind is present" (Chroust 1.11, 104).

3. Aristotle's Beard, Or S(h)aving the Face of Professional Discourse

1. See Tredennick (183) for a poignant lament about the state of the text of *Prior Analytics*.

2. To read the full range of Kennedy's notion, see *Art* 82–114, *Classical* 61–79, and *Aristotle* 299–305.

3. In *Classical Rhetoric* (63–64), Kennedy does warn that because "the *Rhetoric*, like Aristotle's other treatises, is a developing work, we should avoid imposing an artificial consistency on it."

4. In *Classical Rhetoric* (77) Kennedy argues that Book III does not constitute an illogical step and that we should not see it as a late addition after Plato's influence had faded.

5. Neither Düring nor Zürcher has "carried the day," but their work demands that we remember just how speculative anything we try to say about Aristotle must be. Chroust (1.257, n. 1) offers an extended catalog of those who rushed to dispute Zürcher. Düring appears in almost every major study of Aristotle, usually as being refuted or wrong.

6. While I have not tried to catalog the places where Grimaldi says that the *Rhetoric* is Platonic, the claim does appear on the following pages (*Studies*): 2, 17, 21, 86, 151.

7. Rosalind Gabin has offered an interesting and provocative commentary on Grimaldi's attempt and the response it generated. In particular, she explores the play of meanings around the word "unity" (see especially 172–73).

8. For the hunch that Aristotle came to Athens at age eight rather than age eighteen as well as a general set of guidelines for guessing when Aristotle did in fact arrive there for the first time, see Chroust (1.92).

9. For the standard version in which Isocrates is described condescendingly as "a born educationalist, the most tedious writer Athens ever produced, who unfortunately lived to the age of ninety-eight," see Oswyn Murray's "Life and Society in Classical Greece" in *The Oxford History of the Classical World*, the same volume in which Julia Annas's essay discussed above appears. According to Murray, Isocrates made sophistic education "training in technique without content." His "theories lacked any incentive

to serious thought. They were therefore eminently suited to become the standard pattern for organized higher education." Murray gives Isocrates credit only for serving as the foil for Plato and Aristotle (30).

In light of Murray's safe and secure history of the West, it seems only fair to offer Isocrates a chance to reply, which I do by offering a brief quotation from *Panathenaicus* (18–20). Given the setting of the story Isocrates tells, one cannot help thinking of Aristotle as the speaker in question, even though Aristotle would have been away from Athens at the time Isocrates wrote this passage and would not set up his "school" in the Lyceum for another six years:

> some of my friends met me and related to me how, as they were sitting together in the Lyceum, three or four of the sophists [without question, Isocrates would have referred to Aristotle as a sophist] of no repute—men who claim to know everything and are prompt to show their presence everywhere—were discussing the poets, especially the poetry of Hesiod and Homer, saying nothing original about them, but merely chanting their verses and repeating from memory the cleverest things which certain others had said about them in the past. It seems that the bystanders applauded their performance, whereupon one of these sophists, the boldest among them, attempted to stir up prejudice against me, saying that I hold all such things in contempt and that I would do away with all the learning and the teaching of others, and that I assert that all men talk mere drivel except those who partake of my instruction.

10. As with everything about Aristotle, Green's notion of his influence on Alexander is disputable. Chroust, for example, includes an entire chapter in which he summarizes all the reasons for doubting whether Aristotle ever taught Alexander at all, concluding that the whole tradition "is by no means so firmly established as some people would like us to believe" (1.125-32). The whole myth, Chroust continues after having summarized the flimsiness of its sources in ancient literature, may be "just one of those stories which suddenly arise and for some reason become widespread, but whose origins are impossible to ascertain."

11. To Aristotle, the phrase, "extreme democracy" meant "working people are in a majority and can hold office, and the people is sovereign" (A. Jones 72, 149). Aristotle discusses "extreme democracy" throughout *Politics*; see especially 1277^b, 1296^b, 1298^a, 1312^b, 1313^b, and 1320^a.

12. Herodotus makes clear that he can see the value of ἐλευθερία (freedom) in Book V (78), where he praises the Athenian soldiers who did not make effective fighters until after "the yoke [of despotism] was flung off." While he clearly sees and argues that advantage, one must remember both that the freedom he discusses was limited to those few who occupied hoplite status or above, which constitutes a kind of oligarchy, and that he did not see the democracy as a sound way to make political judgments, only as a

sound way to field soldiers who had a personal and economic stake in the outcome of a war.

13. For a much fuller account of Thucydides' bias against democracy, see Jones (*Athenian* 62–69), Kagan (*Pericles* 212–42), and P. Jones (30).

14. Ignoring Isocrates' later work in which he repeatedly called for Philip to serve as a Greek king, Vickers describes Isocrates as a democrat. For a concise argument, see Hornblower (142) who calls Isocrates "a spokesman for the propertied class." Kagan (*Great* 142) explains that Isocrates did not begin as a monarchist, but that he gradually moved to monarchy as he grew older. Peter Green (47–49; 82–83) paints a rather chilling picture of Isocrates' notion of monarchy. Green claims that it began with Gorgias, was seconded by Lysias, and then picked up again by Isocrates. In *Address to Philip* Isocrates asks for a campaign that, in modern terms, amounts to little more than a race war.

15. For the problems with dating the Old Oligarch, see Cole (101–4).

16. For different treatments of Aristotle's attempts to be fair with democracy, see Jones (411) and Sinclair (68).

17. The noun δημοκρατία appeared first in the 420s in the texts of Herodotus and Xenophon.

18. For the passages quoted here, see 1292ª18–32, 1319ª26–1320ᵇ19.

19. Donald Kagan (*Great* 200–202) tries to draw a clearer distinction between Platonic oligarchy and Aristotelian oligarchy that I have done. Kagan calls Aristotle a "moderate oligarch" in the tradition of Theramanes and tries to articulate Aristotle's politics in contradistinction to Plato's.

20. For an argument that only the most radical of the Greeks differed with Aristotle, see Barker 297. I respond to this defense in two ways: first, the defense proves yet again that the case opposite to Aristotle's was being made in Athens, and thus he cannot have been ignorant of it; second, defending Aristotle by placing him in the majority is an odd strategy, given his attitude toward majorities.

21. Elisabeth Alford argues that Thucydides' description of the plague in 430 is the first extant effort at scientific writing and that this passage constitutes a striking rhetorical difference from the epideictic "Funeral Oration" by Pericles that follows it.

22. Sinclair summarizes the ancient literature to show the general distrust of elite men's clubs after 411 (142), and Sagan offers a whole chapter on clubs and the aristocratic clubbing instinct (159ff.)

23. See, for example, 1291ᵇ14–30, where Aristotle takes up the kinds of oligarchies.

24. Throughout the fifth and fourth centuries there was a shorthand vocabulary of social distinction. Sinclair offers an excellent introduction to the polarized Greek language that separated the rich from everyone else (15–16, 121). Strauss (214), Kagan (*Great* 120), and Vickers (88–90) also foreground this vocabulary.

25. Euripides *Suppliants* (404–8 and 433–41) and his *Phoenician Women* (535) also praise democracy at least through the word "equality" (ἰσότης).

26. See Starr (*Birth* 16) as well as R. A. de Laix, who doubts this law, and G. Busolt, who accepts it.

27. See Sinclair (23) for an introduction to the literature on the "colossal statue" the Athenian citizenry set up for democracy in 333–32, shortly after Aristotle returned to Athens.

28. Though he is more circumspect and considerably kinder (e.g., "today's fool can correct the errors of yesterday's genius"), Strauss also argues that Aristotle and his teachers were wrong about both Athenian institutions and the people who ran them (212–33).

29. For the charge that the leaders after Pericles were power-seeking demagogues, see Aristophanes' *Knights* 178–93 and 733–40 and *Frogs* 727–37, and Aristotle's *Politics* 1274ª14–15 and *Athenian Constitution* 28. See Sagan (105) for an explanation of the neologism νεόπλουτος (*nouveau riche*), which the Athenian intellectuals invented as a way of degrading the leaders after Pericles by implying that these leaders had earned, rather than inherited, their money.

30. For an introduction to the debate over whether to read Aspasia's speech as parody, see Kennedy (*Art* 158–64), Vickers (136–37), and Michael Carter (218-31).

31. Kagan does briefly hint at the dark side to democracy (*Pericles* 188).

4. In the Heart of the Heart of the *Rhetoric*

1. *New York Times*, 22 July 92, A10.

2. I do not think I am stretching the Greek (ἐν τοῖς νόμοις ἔγραψε λόγων τέχνην μὴ διδάσκειν) in offering this summary. Vickers (7) translates the passage as forbidding rhetoricians to work, and Marchant (27), in a footnote to his Loeb translation of Xenophon's *Memorabilia*, glosses the passage as forbidding the practice of "making the worse appear the better argument." While the language does lump philosophy, sophistry, eristic, and rhetoric all into one loose category, it seems that Critias wanted to shut the mouths of all the intellectuals, whatever their methodology or affiliation.

3. I had to omit the letter "i" because I could not readily think of anyone whose last name begins with "i" and who has published an argument claiming that Aristotle is the most influential rhetorician. I looked quickly through what I have by Bill Irmscher, but to no avail.

4. Richard Enos replies to Conley, accusing him of a "country club mentality." Enos sees Conley as a wrathful guardian of "Lady Rhetoric," who "overextends the point by implying that only researchers who master Greek thoroughly can contribute to, and enrich us in, Hellenic rhetoric." Enos suggests that the "first-order" scholarship demanded by Conley is only one sort and that it is not in any way superior to "second-order" scholarship that tries to apply classical rhetoric ("Classical" 284–88).

5. As one would expect inside any professional discourse, de Romilly, because her work has been widely read, is often recast, often refuted, and often critiqued. Ward, for example, offers a careful and enlightening reading

in which he chastens de Romilly's vocabulary, arguing that her notion of a pendulum swing from rhetoric as magic spell before Aristotle to rhetoric as intellectualized technique after Aristotle is too simple. Finding de Romilly's polarity too reductive, he suggests that rhetoricians see the history of rhetoric as a kind of "simultaneous peaking" of control and disruption (57–64, 116–18).

6. Kathleen Welch makes a similar point in arguing that since Corax and Tisias there have been the sort of atheoretical, technical rhetorics scorned by Plato, Aristotle, and George Kennedy (*Classical* 106). These rhetorics "offer the lure of enabling one to manipulate language more effectively" ("Ideology" 278). Cole offers a similar definition. He argues that rhetoric in its "narrowest and most conventional sense" is persuasion; it is not eloquence and not "an overall science of discourse or an art of practical reasoning and deliberation" (ix).

7. Cole also makes this point, arguing that Plato and Aristotle changed rhetoric's focus "from manner to matter"; after Plato and Aristotle, Cole argues, understanding of content and purpose "precede instruction in oratorical method" (24).

8. Given the volume of literature on enthymeme, it is not difficult to discover a doorway into the arena of debate. For those new to the field, however, in addition to Hood's bibliography and Conley's essay on enthymeme, I would recommend the following as covering most of the arguments: Grimaldi (*Studies* 70–78), Ryan (29–35), and Kennedy (*Classical* 70–71). These seventeen pages of professional discourse will satisfy all but those who wish to become ἐνθυμηματικός, which is always and forever a process of becoming anyway.

9. Phillip Arrington, for example, not only sees Aristotle's *Rhetoric* as reductive, temporal, causal and mechanistic but also argues that it is an art (τέχνη), not a faculty (δύναμις) (326). The Baumlins, in contrast, go to Freud for a set of labels through which they can align logos with ego, pathos with id, and ethos with superego. That done, they can explain how Aristotle rescues rhetoric from Plato and conclude that Aristotle "defines rhetoric not as a *techne* or impersonal craft but as a *dynamis* or human faculty" dependent on mind.

10. See Lois Self for a thorough introduction to the debate over φρόνησις and the scholarly apparatus that has grown up around it.

11. See Arnhart (15) and D. S. Hutchinson for an introduction to the scholarly debate over ἕξις.

12. No doubt others have entered the fray on the site of this term; these eight essays merely happen to be the ones I have read.

13. In light of the point I am making, it is worth rereading *Politics* 1253ᵃff., where Aristotle describes the "body politic." I would press my point here by arguing that, for the polis, the necessary organs are the leisure classes; farmers, workers, and artisans are merely contributory. The leisure classes constitute the heart, brain, and lungs of the body politic; those who work constitute its hands and feet.

14. For a slightly more extended explanation of the generality of both rhetoric and dialectic, see *Sophistical Refutations* 170ª37–172ᵇ11.

15. The notion of a clever speaker, a speaker with a sharp enough intellect to deceive an audience, was a tricky issue in fifth- and fourth-century Athens. As Cleon tries to get his way in the Mitylene debate (he wanted the first decision, the one condemning the Mitylenes to death and slavery, to stand), he uses the rhetorical ploy of accusing his adversaries of being "clever speakers."

16. While I do not wish to offer examples, I would like to call attention to the frequency with which books and articles about rhetoric adopt a "saving the maiden" tone. Rhetoric appears in its own discourse as a misunderstood, maligned, and abused fragility that needs to be saved by having the world understand its true nature better.

17. Plato, in my opinion, had set the tone for Aristotle's discussion of the proofs. In *Gorgias* (454ᵈ–455ª) Plato distinguishes between πίστις, which can be either true or false, and ἐπιστήμη, which can only be true. Both Michael Carter (220) and Vickers (92) also discuss this passage from *Gorgias* in relation to Aristotle's use of the term πίστις in the *Rhetoric*.

18. For a reading of the proofs that is the reversal of mine, see Kennedy (*Classical* 67). As I do, Kennedy sees the proofs as "the essence of rhetoric." In contrast, however, he does not use "essence" either ironically or comically. Grimaldi (as ever) goes farther. He takes up the forty-one appearances of the term *pistis* in the *Rhetoric* and then claims that in all forty-one cases the text provides sufficient evidence for its own exegesis (*Studies* 57).

19. All seven of the following quotations are my translations.

20. I assume that Aristotle is writing about rhetoric in the abstract. It seems to me that Athens was small enough that few speakers could get away with trying to generate an ethos radically at odds with their lived lives. On those occasions when the Pnyx was full, however, perhaps there was more anonymity than I imagine.

21. For a very different treatment of the transition from invention to arrangement and style, see Fortenbaugh (242–46).

22. For a catalog of quotations from Demosthenes claiming that "Rhetoric *is* delivery," see Nadeau (53–54).

23. Ryan (152) argues that the traditional translation of λέξις as "style" creates too narrow a notion of the term, which includes a whole speech, a way of speaking, and even a certain turn of phrase.

24. See 11 and 122. See also 136–38 where Cole traces the solidification of the separation of style and arrangement from substance.

25. As I will argue later, his theory of style for demonstration and dialectic opposes the theory of style for rhetoric. Appropriate style changes when one moves from one form of intellectual inquiry to another.

26. Aristotelian logic, David Ross explains, is not a study of words but of the thought words represent. Aristotelian logic seeks to determine the success of thought in attaining truth; such logic wishes to know how close it has come to apprehending the nature of things. In effect Plato's *Cratylus*

works through this whole metaphysics in exploring what a "word" tells us "about the object it applies to."

27. De Romilly sees Aristotle's repeated use of πρέπω as part of his gradual reduction of style—a process that was, she argues, necessary if he was to strip rhetoric of its magical, spellbinding qualities (72–74). Kennedy (*Classical* 78) in writing about the demands for clarity in *Poetics* 1458ª15 makes a similar point in saying that "the irrational powers of language have no attraction for" Aristotle. While I do not differ with de Romilly and Kennedy, I do think they fail to note that Aristotle is not describing a style that has inherent virtue or even inherent logocentrism. Rather, he is explaining how the *logos* goes about making itself presentable to the masses. For an introduction to the influence of Aristotle's demands for correctness, see Vickers (64).

28. In treating Aristotle's terms for clarity, appropriateness, and purity, Scaglione argues that Aristotle equates style with virtue. For Aristotle, he writes, clarity "was the main requisite, the only one truly deserving the name of 'virtue' " (15–16). As I argue below, I think that Aristotle is not describing a style that is in and of itself virtuous. Rather, he is describing a style that will *seem* virtuous to the audience and thus generate a comfortable solidarity in their minds.

29. Cole (79) contends that Timaeus in the third century was the first to associate Gorgias with the figuration now known as Gorgianic. Such elaborate figuration, Cole argues, "could have been simply a prominent feature of Gorgias's written demonstration pieces that became linked with his name only when the memory of the oral performances on which his reputation was chiefly based had largely disappeared." In the (to me) unlikely event that Cole is correct, it would not matter to the point I am making, for this sample of style calls attention to itself regardless of who wrote it or what other things he may have written or spoken.

30. Cole describes Aristotle's theory of style as "the result of a series of calculated deviations from the everyday" (14).

31. In both places (1412ª18 and 1413ª120) where Aristotle explains the lively quality that metaphor supplies to the logos, he uses the term ἀστεῖος, which has as a "first meaning," "of the city." See also Jordan (236–47).

32. Like everything else about the *Rhetoric*, metaphor has been a site for professional dispute. Cope (*Introduction* 374ff.) provides a good starting place for anyone interested in tracing the filiations of analysis since the nineteenth century. For those who have read this far and find my own treatment inappropriate or unbelievable, Ryan (157–72) and Eden (73–75) offer detailed antidotes, as does D'Angelo, who offers a straightforward explanation of the ways in which Aristotelian metaphor works ("Tropics" 102). One can use Vickers (451–53 and 464–70) for an attack on the ways in which deconstruction has treated metaphor, and then use Vickers's ample and useful set of citations to discover the places where the voice of deconstruction speaks itself. A good "entry point" into this subdispute over the term *metaphor* inside the inside of the interpretive field of the *Rhetoric* is

Samuel Levin's 1982 essay, which responds to Christine Brooke-Rose and W. Bedell Stanford, who argue that Aristotle's theory of metaphor is useless, unsystematic, careless, biased, and incomplete. In the absolutely necessary professional response, Levin sets out to show "that Aristotle's theory of metaphor is in fact consistent," that Aristotle's purpose "is to explain how metaphor promotes to consciousness an awareness of relations that subsist between the objects and concepts that make up our universe," and that Aristotle's explanation of metaphor "takes the form it does under the influence of his preoccupation with the teaching function of metaphor" (25). In the remainder of his essay, Levin offers a careful, often diagrammatic working through of Aristotle's four types of metaphor.

33. As Classen has pointed out, Aristotle was not alone in attributing rhetorical skill to natural talent; it was an idea widely shared among ancient rhetoricians (9). The whole notion of an aristocratic, gifted person, someone blessed at birth with the knowledge of how to succeed in society, was fairly commonplace in ancient Greece. Writing a century before Aristotle wrote the *Rhetoric*, Thucydides treats this notion using the term γνώμη. See, for example, his treatment of Pericles, the paradigmatic possessor of γνώμη (ii.65). Kagan (*Great* 110) articulates the notion quite well.

34. Oddly enough, even though Richards contends with Aristotle about this notion, Richards quotes the notion from the *Poetics* not from the *Rhetoric*.

35. In a vein similar to Richards's, Seitz asks the field of composition studies how long the field will "continue simply to mention metaphor as something one might occasionally 'use' in the service of 'stability' and 'clarity' " (297).

36. For an overview of Aristotle's teleological notions of all things, see *On the Heavens* (288^{a}2), *Physics* (198^{b}10–200^{b}7), *Metaphysics* (1045^{b}35–1050^{b}2), and *Parts of Animals* (641^{a}32-^{b}37).

5. The Composition of Sophistry and the Sophistry of Composition

1. Actually, the MLA's categories suggest that 24.5 percent of the jobs are in writing, but 6.5 percent of that number are for creative writers, and I do not consider creative writers or creative writing part of rhet/comp. In *Plato, Derrida, and Writing* I have tried to explain the separation between "creative" writing and "all other kinds." In my opinion, it is not a useful distinction, but when one speaks of "jobs," it is foolish to pretend that "creative writing" falls into the same category as "the teaching of writing," which is still the phrase used to described the rhet/comp enterprise within MLA.

2. In addition to the symposium in the October 1992 *CCC*, see also the following works, all of which, in one way or another, reiterate the ways in which composition as "woman" is both silenced and marginalized: Batson,

Bauer, Bennett, Bizzell ("Power"), Brodkey ("Picturing" and "Transvaluing"), Flynn ("Composing" and "Composing 'Composing' "), Holbrook, Hunter, and Miller.

3. On first reading, I thought Merrill's essay, like Bloom's, was something of a hoax or parody, but I have finally decided that Merrill's argument is a face-value, genuine statement of his opinions.

4. Plato and Isocrates, for example, each called the other a sophist and himself a philosopher. See Lloyd (94, n. 153).

5. R. K. Sinclair, for example, estimates that Isocrates' school cost about 1,000 drakhmai, about thirty months' total wages for a working Athenian of the thetic class (193). For an introduction to Lasthenia and Axiothea as well as a fictional dialogue between Plato and Lasthenia on the subject of women in the Academy, see the Hackett Publishing Company's fall 1992 catalog and C. D. C. Reeve's "The Naked Old Women in the Palaestra: A Dialogue Between Plato and Lasthenia of Mantinea," which is reprinted there (33–42).

6. I have made a similar point before ("Where").

WORKS CITED

Aeschines. *The Speeches of Aeschines*. Trans. Charles Darwin Adams. Loeb. Cambridge, MA: Harvard Univ. Press, 1919.

Alford, Elisabeth M. "Thucydides and the Plague in Athens: The Roots of Scientific Writing." *Written Communication* 5 (1988): 131–53.

Annas, Julia. "Classical Greek Philosophy." In *The Oxford History of the Classical World*. Ed. John Boardman et al. New York: Oxford Univ. Press, 1986. 234–53.

Aristotle. *Ars Rhetorica*. Ed. W. D. Ross. New York: Oxford Univ. Press, 1959.

———. *The "Art" of Rhetoric*. Trans. John Henry Freese. Loeb. Cambridge, MA: Harvard Univ. Press, 1991.

———. *The Art of Rhetoric*. Trans. Hugh Lawson-Tancred. New York: Penguin, 1991.

———. *The Athenian Constitution, The Eudemian Ethics, On Virtues and Vices*. Trans. H. Rackham. Loeb. Cambridge, MA: Harvard Univ. Press, 1981.

———. *The Categories, On Interpretation, Prior Analytics*. Trans. Harold P. Cooke and Hugh Tredennick. Loeb. Cambridge, MA: Harvard Univ. Press, 1983.

———. *The Complete Works of Aristotle: The Revised Oxford Translation*. 2 vols. Ed. Jonathan Barnes. Princeton, NJ: Princeton Univ. Press, 1984.

———. *The Metaphysics I–IX*. Trans. Hugh Tredennick. Loeb. Cambridge, MA: Harvard Univ. Press, 1989.

———. *Metaphysics X–XIV, Oeconomica, Magna Moralia*. Loeb. Cambridge, MA: Harvard Univ. Press, 1977.

———. *Minor Works*. Trans. W. S. Hett. Loeb. Cambridge, MA: Harvard Univ. Press, 1980.

———. *The Nicomachean Ethics*. Trans. H. Rackham. Loeb. Cambridge, MA: Harvard Univ. Press, 1990.

———. *On Rhetoric: A Theory of Civic Discourse*. Trans. George A. Kennedy. New York: Oxford Univ. Press, 1991.

————. *On Sophistical Refutations, On Coming-to-Be and Passing-Away.* Trans. E. S. Forster and D. J. Furley. Loeb. Cambridge, MA: Harvard Univ. Press, 1978.

————. *On the Soul, Parva Naturalia, On Breath.* Trans. W. S. Hett. Loeb. Cambridge, MA: Harvard Univ. Press, 1986.

————. *Politics.* Trans. H. Rackham. Loeb. Cambridge, MA: Harvard Univ. Press, 1977.

————. *Posterior Analytics, Topica.* Trans. Hugh Tredennick and E. S. Forster. Loeb. Cambridge, MA: Harvard Univ. Press, 1989.

————. *Problems XXII–XXXVIII, Rhetorica Ad Alexandrum.* Trans. W. S. Hett and H. Rackham. Loeb. Cambridge, MA: Harvard Univ. Press, 1983.

————. *The Rhetoric of Aristotle.* Trans. Lane Cooper. New York: Prentice Hall, 1960.

————. *Rhetoric, Poetics.* Trans. W. Rhys Roberts and Ingram Bywater. New York: Modern Library, 1954.

Arnhart, Larry. *Aristotle on Political Reasoning: A Commentary on the "Rhetoric".* De Kalb: Northern Illinois Univ. Press, 1981.

Arrington, Phillip K. "Tropes of the Composing Process." *College English* 48 (1986): 325–38.

Atwill, Janet, and Janice Lauer. "Refiguring Rhetoric as an Art: Aristotle's Concept of *Techne*." Unpublished manuscript, 1990.

Baker, Sheridan. *The Practical Stylist.* New York: Harper & Row, 1973.

Barker, Ernest. *Greek Political Theory.* London: Methuen, 1977.

Batson, Lorie Goodman. "A Reprint: Defining Ourselves as Women in the Profession." *Pretext* 10 (1989): 117–22.

Bauer, Dale M. "The Other 'F' Word: The Feminist in the Classroom." *College English* 52 (1990): 385–96.

Baumlin, James S., and Lita French Baumlin. "Psyche/Logos: Mapping the Terrains of Mind and Rhetoric." *College English* 51 (1989): 245–61.

Benjamin, Jessica. *The Bonds of Love.* New York: Pantheon, 1988.

Bennett, S. K. "Student Perceptions and Expectations for Male and Female Instructors: Evidence Relating to the Question of Gender Bias in Teaching Evaluation." *Journal of Educational Psychology* 74 (1982): 170–79.

Benoit, William Lyon. "Aristotle's Example: The Rhetorical Induction." *Quarterly Journal of Speech* 66 (1980): 182–92.

————. "On Aristotle's Example." *Philosophy and Rhetoric* 20 (1987): 261–67.

Berkenkotter, Carol. "Paradigm Debates, Turf Wars, and the Conduct of Sociocognitive Inquiry in Composition." *College Composition and Communication* 42 (1991): 151–69.

Berlin, James. "Aristotle's *Rhetoric* in Context: Interpreting Historically." Unpublished manuscript, 1990.

————. "Rhetoric and Ideology in the Classroom." *College English* 50 (1988): 477–94.

Bitzer, Lloyd. "Aristotle's Enthymeme Revisited." *Quarterly Journal of Speech* 45 (1959): 141–55.

———. "Rhetoric and Public Knowledge." In *Rhetoric, Philosophy, and Literature*. Ed. Don Burks. Lafayette, IN: Purdue Univ. Press, 1978. 67–93.

Bizzell, Patricia. "Power, Authority, and Critical Pedagogy." *Journal of Basic Writing* 10 (1991): 54–70.

———. "Review of *The Social Construction of Written Communication*." *College Composition and Communication* 40 (1989): 483–86.

Bizzell, Patricia, and Bruce Herzberg. *The Rhetorical Tradition: Readings from Classical Times to the Present*. Boston: Bedford, 1990.

Blettner, Elizabeth. "One Made Many and Many Made One: The Role of Asyndeton in Aristotle's Rhetoric." *Philosophy and Rhetoric* 16 (1983): 49–54.

Bloom, Lynn Z. "I Want a Writing Director." *College Composition and Communication* 43 (1992): 176–79.

———. "Why Don't We Write What We Teach? And Publish It?" *Journal of Advanced Composition* 10 (1990): 87–100.

Brodkey, Linda. "Picturing Writing: Writers in the Modern World." In *Academic Writing as Social Practice*. Philadelphia: Temple Univ. Press, 1987. 54–86.

———. "Transvaluing Difference." *College English* 51 (1989): 597–601.

Brooks, Cleanth, and Robert Penn Warren. *Understanding Poetry*. 3d ed. New York: Holt, Rinehart, 1970.

Brummett, Barry. "A Eulogy On Epistemic Rhetoric." *Quarterly Journal of Speech* 76 (1990): 69–72.

Bryant, Donald C. "Rhetoric: Its Function and Scope." In *The Province of Rhetoric*. Ed. Joseph Schwartz and John A. Rycenga. New York: Ronald, 1965. 3–36.

Burstein, Stanley M. "Greek Class Structures and Relations." In *Civilization of the Ancient Mediterranean*. Vol. 1. Ed. Michael Grant and Rachael Kitinger. New York: Scribner, 1988. 529–48.

Busolt, G. *Griechische Staatskunde*. Munich, 1926.

Cahn, Michael. "Reading Rhetoric Rhetorically: Isocrates and the Marketing of Insight." *Rhetorica* 7 (1989): 121–44.

Carleton, Walter M. "What Is Rhetorical Knowledge? A Reply to Farrell—And More." *Quarterly Journal of Speech* 64 (1978): 313–28.

Carter, Michael F. "The Ritual Functions of Epideictic Rhetoric: The Care of Socrates' Funeral Oration." *Rhetorica* 9 (1991): 209–32.

Carter, Michael. "*Stasis* and *Kairos*: Principles of Social Construction in Classical Rhetoric." *Rhetoric Review* 7 (1988): 97–112.

Cherwitz, Richard A., and James W. Hikins. "Burying the Undertaker: A Eulogy for the Eulogists of Rhetorical Epistemology." *Quarterly Journal of Speech* 76 (1990): 73–77.

———. "Rhetoric as a 'Way of Knowing': An Attenuation of the Epistemological Claims of the 'New Rhetoric.' " *Southern Speech Communication Journal* 42 (1977): 207–19.

———. "Toward a Rhetorical Epistemology." *Southern Speech Communication Journal* 47 (1982): 135–62.

Chroust, Anton-Hermann. "Aristotle and Athens: Some Comments on Aristotle's Sojourns in Athens." *Laval Theologique et Philosophique* 22 (1966): 186–96.

———. *Aristotle: New Light on His Life and on Some of His Lost Works.* 2 vols. Notre Dame, IN: Univ. of Notre Dame Press, 1973.

Cicero. *Cicero on Oratory and Orators.* Trans. J. S. Watson. Carbondale: Southern Illinois Univ. Press, 1970.

Classen, Carl Joachim. "Ars Rhetorica: L'essence, Possibilities, Gefahren." *Rhetorica* 7 (1988): 7–19.

———. "The Speeches in the Courts of Law: A Three-Cornered Dialogue." *Rhetorica* 9 (1991): 195–207.

Claster, Jill N. *Athenian Democracy: Triumph or Tragedy.* New York: Holt, Rinehart, 1967.

Coe, Richard M. "Defining Rhetoric—and Us." *Journal of Advanced Composition* 10 (1990): 39–52.

Cole, Thomas. *The Origins of Rhetoric in Ancient Greece.* Baltimore: Johns Hopkins Univ. Press, 1991.

Conley, Thomas M. "Aristotle's *Rhetoric* in Byzantium." *Rhetorica* 8 (1990): 29–44.

———. "The Enthymeme in Perspective." *Quarterly Journal of Speech* 70 (1984): 168–87.

———. "Kennedy on the History of Rhetoric." *Quarterly Journal of Speech* 67 (1981): 206–9.

———. "The Greekless Reader and Aristotle's *Rhetoric.*" *Quarterly Journal of Speech* 65 (1979): 74–79.

Connor, Robert W. *The New Politicians of Fifth-Century Athens.* Princeton, NJ: Princeton Univ. Press, 1971.

Connors, Robert J. "Personal Writing Assignment." *College Composition and Communication* 38 (1987): 166–82.

———. "The Rhetoric of Explanation: Explanatory Rhetoric from Aristotle to 1850." *Written Communication* 1 (1984): 189–210.

Consigny, Scott. "Dialectical, Rhetorical, and Aristotelian Rhetoric." *Philosophy and Rhetoric* 22 (1989): 281–87.

———. "The Rhetorical Example." *Southern Speech Communication Journal* 41 (1976): 121–32.

Cope, Edward M. *An Introduction to Aristotle's Rhetoric.* New York: Macmillan, 1867.

———. *The Rhetoric of Aristotle with a Commentary.* 3 vols. Ed. John E. Sandys. Cambridge: Cambridge Univ. Press, 1877.

Corbett, Edward P. J. "Teaching Composition: Where We've Been and Where We're Going." *College Composition and Communication* 38 (1987): 444–52.

Corder, Jim W. "Hunting for *Ethos* Where They Say It Can't Be Found."
    Rhetoric Review 7 (1989): 299–316.
Crem, Theresa. "The Definition of Rhetoric According to Aristotle. "In
    Aristotle: The Classical Heritage of Rhetoric. Ed. Keith V. Erickson.
    Metuchen, NJ:Scarecrow, 1974. 52–71.
Croasmun, Earl, and Richard A. Cherwitz. "Beyond Rhetorical Relativism."
    Quarterly Journal of Speech 68 (1982): 1–16.
Crowley, Sharon. "Derrida, Deconstruction, and Our Scene of Teaching."
    Pretext 8 (1987): 170–83.
———. "A Plea for the Revival of Sophistry." *Rhetoric Review* 7 (1989):
    318–34.
———. "Rhetoric, Literature, and the Dissociation of Invention." *Journal
    of Advanced Composition* 6 (1986): 17–32.
Cushman, Ronald P., and Phillip K. Tompkins. "A Theory of Rhetoric for
    Contemporary Society." *Philosophy and Rhetoric* 13 (1980): 43–67.
D'Angelo, Frank J. "Tropics of Arrangement: A Theory of *Dispositio*." *Jour-
    nal of Advanced Composition* 10 (1990): 101–9.
Dasenbrock, Reed Way. "J. L. Austin and the Articulation of a New Rheto-
    ric." *College Compostion and Communication* 38 (1978): 291–305.
Decker, Randall E. *Patterns of Exposition*. 3d ed. Boston: Little, Brown,
    1970.
de Laix, R. A. *Probouleusi at Athens*. Berkeley: Univ. of California Press,
    1973.
Demosthenes. *De Corona and De Falsa Legatione*. Trans. C. A. Vince and
    J. H. Vince. Loeb. Cambridge, MA: Harvard Univ. Press, 1953.
———. *Funeral Speech, Erotic Essay, Exordia, and Letters*. Trans. Norman
    W. De Witt and Norman J. DeWitt. Loeb. Cambridge, MA: Harvard
    Univ. Press, 1949.
———. *Medias, Androtion, Aristocrates, Timocrates, Aristogeiton*. Trans.
    J. H. Vince. Loeb. Cambridge, MA: Harvard Univ. Press, 1935.
———. *Olynthiacs, Philippics, Leptines, Etc*. Trans. J. H. Vince. Loeb.
    Cambridge, MA: Harvard Univ. Press, 1930.
de Romilly, Jacqueline. *Magic and Rhetoric in Ancient Greece*. Cambridge,
    MA: Harvard Univ. Press, 1975.
Dover, K. J. *Lysias and the Corpus Lysiacum*. Berkeley: Univ. of California
    Press, 1968.
Düring, Ingemar. *Aristotles*. Heidelberg: Carl Winter, 1966.
Eden, Kathy. "Hermeneutics and the Ancient Rhetorical Tradition." *Rheto-
    rica* 5 (1987): 59–86.
Eichhorn, Jill, et al. "A Symposium on Feminist Experiences in the Compo-
    sition Classroom." *College Composition and Communication* 43 (1992):
    297–322.
Elbow, Peter. "Closing My Eyes as I Speak: An Argument for Ignoring
    Audience." *College English* 49 (1987): 50–69.
Engstrom, Timothy H. "Philosophy's Anxiety of Rhetoric: Contemporary
    Revisions of a Politics of Separation." *Rhetorica* 7 (1989): 209–38.

Enos, Richard Leo. "The Art of Rhetoric at the Amphiareion of Oropos: A Study of Epigraphical Evidence as Written Communication." *Written Communication* 3 (1986) 3–14.

———. "The Classical Tradition(s) of Rhetoric: A Demur to the Country Club Set." *College Composition and Communication* 38 (1987): 283–90.

———. "Review of *Rhetoric and Praxis.*" Ed. Jean Diety. *Rhetoric Society Quarterly* 17 (1987): 97–100.

Farrar, Cynthia. *The Origins of Democratic Thinking.* New York: Cambridge Univ. Press, 1988.

Farrell, Thomas B. "From the Parthenon to the Bassinet: Death and Rebirth along the Epistemic Trail." *Quarterly Journal of Speech* 76 (1990): 78–84.

———. "Knowledge, Consensus, and Rhetorical Theory." *Quarterly Journal of Speech* 62 (1976): 1–14.

———. "Practicing the Arts of Rhetoric: Tradition and Invention." *Philosophy and Rhetoric* 24 (1991): 183–212.

———. "Social Knowledge II." *Quarterly Journal of Speech* 64 (1978): 329–34.

Finley, M. I. *The Ancient Economy.* Berkeley: Univ. of California Press, 1973.

———. *Ancient Slavery and Modern Ideology.* New York: Viking, 1980.

———. *Democracy Ancient and Modern.* Rev. ed. New Brunswick, NJ: Rutgers Univ. Press, 1973; 1985.

Fish, Stanley. *Doing What Comes Naturally.* Durham, NC: Duke Univ. Press, 1989.

Flower, Linda. "Cognition, Context, and Theory Building." *College Composition and Communication* 40 (1989): 282–311.

———. "The Construction of Purpose in Writing and Reading." *College English* 50 (1988): 528–50.

Flynn, Elizabeth A. "Composing as a Woman." *College Composition and Communication* 39 (1988): 423–35.

———. "Composing 'Composing as a Woman': A Perspective on Research." *College Composition and Communication* 41 (1990): 83–89.

Fortenbaugh, William W. "Aristotle's Platonic Attitude Toward Delivery." *Philosophy and Rhetoric* 19 (1986): 242–53.

Fowler, Alastair. "Apology for Rhetoric." *Rhetorica* 8 (1990): 103–18.

Gabin, Rosalind J. "Aristotle and the New Rhetoric: Grimaldi and Valesio." *Philosophy and Rhetoric* 20 (1987): 171–82.

Gage, John T. "Teaching the Enthymeme: Invention and Arrangement." *Rhetoric Review* 2 (1983): 38–50.

Gaines, Robert N. "Aristotle's Rhetorical Rhetoric?" *Philosophy and Rhetoric* 19 (1986): 194–200.

Garver, Eugene. "Aristotle's *Rhetoric* as a Work of Philosophy." *Philosophy and Rhetoric* 14 (1986): 1–23.

———. "Aristotle's *Rhetoric* on Unintentionally Hitting the Principles of the Sciences." *Rhetorica* 6 (1988): 381–393.

Grassi, Ernesto. "Why Rhetoric Is Philosophy." *Philosophy and Rhetoric* 20 (1987): 68–78.

Green, Lawrence D. "Aristotelian Rhetoric, Dialectic, and the Traditions of *Antistrophos*." *Rhetorica* 8 (1990): 5–27.

Green, Peter. *Alexander of Macedon: A Historical Biography*. 1974. Reprint. Berkeley: Univ. of California Press, 1991.

Grimaldi, William M. A. *Aristotle, Rhetoric I: A Commentary*. Bronx, NY: Fordham Univ. Press, 1980

———. *Aristotle, Rhetoric II: A Commentary*. Bronx, NY: Fordham Univ. Press, 1988.

———. *Studies in the Philosophy of Aristotle's Rhetoric*. Wiesbaden: Steiner, 1972.

Halloran, S. Michael. "Rhetoric in the American College Curriculum: The Decline of Public Discourse." *Pretext* 3 (1982): 245–69.

———. "Tradition and Theory in Rhetoric." *Quarterly Journal of Speech* 62 (1976): 234–41.

Hansen, M. H. "The Number of *Rhetores* in the Anthenian *Ecclesia*: 355–22 B.C." *Greek, Roman and Byzantine Studies* 25 (1984): 123–55.

———. "*Rhetores* and *Strategoi* in Fourth-Century Anthens." *Greek, Roman and Byzantine Studies* 24 (1983): 151–80.

Hauser, Gerard A. "The Example in Aristotle's Rhetoric: Bifurcation or Contradiction?" *Philosophy and Rhetoric* 1 (1968): 78–89.

———. "Reply to Benoit." *Philosophy and Rhetoric* 20 (1987): 268–73.

Havet, É. *Étude sur la Rhétorique d'Aristote*. Paris: Presses Universitaires de France, 1846.

Heidegger, Martin. *An Introduction to Metaphysics*. Trans. Ralph Mannheim. Landover Hills, MD: Anchor, 1961.

Holbrook, Sue Ellen. "Women's Work: The Feminizing of Composition." *Rhetoric Review* 9 (1991): 201–29.

Holmberg, Carl B. "Dialectical Rhetoric and Rhetorical Rhetoric." *Philosophy and Rhetoric* 10 (1977): 232–44.

Hornblower, Simon. "Greece: The History of the Classical Period." In *The Oxford History of the Classical World*. Ed. John Boardman et al. New York: Oxford Univ. Press, 1986. 125–55.

Horney, Karen. "The Dread of Women." *International Journal of Psychoanalysis* 13 (1932): 348–60.

Hull, Glynda, et al. "Remediation as Social Construct: Perspectives from an Analysis of Classroom Discourse." *College Composition and Communication* 42 (1991): 299–329.

Hunter, Susan. "A Woman's Place *Is* in the Composition Classroom: Pedagogy, Gender, and Difference." *Rhetoric Review* 9 (1991): 230–45.

Hutchinson, D. S. *The Virtues of Aristotle*. London: Routledge and Kegan Paul, 1986.

Irmscher, William F. "Finding a Comfortable Identity." *College Composition and Communication* 38 (1987): 81–88.

Isocrates. *Isocrates In Three Volumes.* Trans. George Norlin and Larue Van Hook. Loeb. Cambridge, MA: Harvard Univ. Press, 1928–45.

Jacoli, Martin J. "Using the Enthymeme as a Heuristic in Professional Writing Courses." *Journal of Advanced Composition* 7 (1987): 41–51.

Jarratt, Susan C. "Feminism and Composition: The Case for Conflict." In *Contending with Words: Composition in a Postmodern Era.* Ed. Patricia Harkin and John Schilb. New York: Modern Language Association, 1991. 105–25.

———. *Rereading the Sophists: Classical Rhetoric Refigured.* Carbondale: Southern Illinois Univ. Press, 1991.

Johnstone, Christopher Lyle. "An Aristotelian Trilogy: Ethics, Rhetoric, Politics, and the Search for Moral Truth." *Philosophy and Rhetoric* 13 (1980): 1–24.

Joint Association of Classical Teachers. (See Jones, Peter V.)

Jones, A. H. M. *Athenian Democracy.* Oxford: Basil Blackwell, 1957.

———. "The Athenian Democracy and Its Critics." *Cambridge Historical Journal* 11 (1953): 1–26.

———. "The Economic Basis of the Athenian Democracy." In *Athenian Democracy, Triumph or Travesty.* Ed. Jill Claster. New York: Holt, Rinehart, 1967. 25–33.

Jones, Peter V., et al., eds. *The World of Athens: An Introduction to Classical Athenian Culture.* New York: Cambridge Univ. Press, 1984.

Jordan, William J. "Aristotle's Concept of Metaphor in Rhetoric." In *Aristotle: The Classical Heritage of Rhetoric.* Ed. Keith V. Erickson. Metuchen, NJ: Scarecrow, 1974. 235–50.

Kagan, Donald. *The Great Dialogue: History of Greek Political Thought from Homer to Polybius.* New York: Free Press, 1965.

———. *Pericles of Athens and the Birth of Democracy.* New York: Free Press, 1991.

Kane, Francis I. "Peitho and the Polis." *Philosophy and Rhetoric* 19 (1986): 99–124.

Kauffman, Charles. "Poetic as Argument." *Quarterly Journal of Speech* 67 (1981): 407–15.

Kennedy, George. *The Art of Persuasion in Greece.* Princeton, NJ: Princeton Univ. Press, 1963.

———. *Classical Rhetoric and Its Christian and Secular Tradition from Ancient to Modern Times.* Chapel Hill: Univ. of North Carolina Press, 1980.

Kent, Thomas. "Beyond System: The Rhetoric of Paralogy." *College English* 51 (1989): 492–507.

———. "On the Very Idea of a Discourse Community." *College Composition and Communication* 42 (1991): 425–45.

Kinneavy, James L. "The Process of Writing: A Philosophical Base in Hermeneutics." *Journal of Advanced Composition* 7 (1987): 1–9.

———. *A Theory of Discourse.* New York: Norton, 1980.

———. "William Grimaldi—Reinterpreting Aristotle." *Philosophy and Rhetoric* 20 (1987): 183–98.

Knoblauch, C. H. "Rhetorical Construction: Dialogue and Commitment." *College English* 50 (1988): 125–40.

Knoblauch, C. H., and Lil Brannon. *Rhetorical Traditions and the Teaching of Writing.* Upper Montclair, NJ: Boynton/Cook, 1984.

Kostelnick, Charles. "Process Paradigms in Design and Composition: Affinities and Directions." *College Composition and Communication* 40 (1989): 267–81.

Lamb, Catherine E. "Beyond Argument in Feminist Composition." *College Composition and Communication* 42 (1991): 11–24.

Lawson-Tancred, Hugh. Introduction to *Aristotle: The Art of Rhetoric.* Trans. Hugh Lawson-Tancred. New York: Penguin, 1991. 1–61.

Leff, Michael C. "In Search of Ariadne's Thread: A Review of Recent Literature on Rhetorical Theory." *Central States Speech Journal* 29 (1978): 73–91.

Levi, Albert William. "Love, Rhetoric, and the Aristocratic Way of Life." *Philosophy and Rhetoric* 17 (1984): 189–208.

Levin, Samuel R. "Aristotle's Theory of Metaphor." *Philosophy and Rhetoric* 15 (1982): 24–46.

Liddell, Henry George, and Robert Scott. *A Greek-English Lexicon.* Oxford: Oxford Univ. Press, 1940.

Lunsford, Andrea, and Lisa Ede. "Classical Rhetoric, Modern Rhetoric, and Contemporary Discourse Studies." *Written Communication* 1 (1984): 78–100.

———. "On Distinctions Between Classical and Modern Discourse." In *Essays on Classical Rhetoric and Modern Discourse.* Ed. Robert Connors et al. Carbondale: Southern Illinois Univ. Press, 1984. 37–49, 265–67.

Lysias. *Lysias.* Trans. W. R. M. Lamb. Loeb. Cambridge, MA: Harvard Univ. Press, 1930.

McBurney, James H. "The Place of the Enthymeme in Rhetorical Theory." *Speech Monographs* 3 (1936): 49–74.

MacIntyre, Alasdair. *After Virtue; A Study in Moral Theory.* Notre Dame, IN: Univ. of Notre Dame Press, 1981.

Mackin, James A., Jr. "Schismogenesis and Community: Pericles' Funeral Oration." *Quarterly Journal of Speech* 77 (1991): 251–62.

Meier, Christian. *The Greek Discovery of Politics.* Cambridge, MA: Harvard Univ. Press, 1990.

Merlan, Philip. "Isocrates, Aristotle, and Alexander the Great." *Historia* 3 (1954): 60–81.

Merrill, Robert. "Against the 'Statement.'" *College Composition and Communication* 43 (1992): 154–58.

Miller, Susan. "The Feminization of Composition." In *The Politics of Writing Instruction: Postsecondary.* Ed. Richard Bullock and John Trimbur. Upper Montclair, NJ: Boynton/Cook, 1991. 39–53.

Mulgan, R. G. *Aristotle's Political Theory*. New York: Oxford Univ. Press, 1977.

Murphy, James J., ed. *Demosthenes' On the Crown*. Trans. John J. Keaney. Davis, CA: Hermagoras, 1983.

———. *The Rhetorical Tradition and Modern Writing*. New York: Modern Language Association, 1982.

Murray, Donald M. "All Writing Is Autobiography." *College Composition and Communication* 42 (1991): 66–74.

Murray, Oswyn. "Greek Historians." In *The Oxford History of the Classical World*. Ed. John Boardman et al. New York: Oxford Univ. Press, 1986.

———. "Life and Society in Classical Greece." In *The Oxford History of the Classical World*. Ed. John Boardman et al. New York: Oxford Univ. Press, 1986.

Myres, John L. *The Political Ideas of the Greeks*. Nashville, TN: Abingdon, 1927.

Nadeau, Ray. "Delivery in Ancient Times: Homer to Quintilian." *Quarterly Journal of Speech* 50 (1969): 53–60.

Neel, Jasper P. "The Degradation of Rhetoric, Or Dressing Like a Gentleman, Speaking Like a Scholar." In *Rhetoric/Sophistry/Neopragmatism*. Ed. Steven Mailloux. New York: Cambridge Univ. Press, forthcoming.

———. *Plato, Derrida, and Writing*. Carbondale: Southern Illinois Univ. Press, 1988.

———. "Where Have You Come From, Reb Derissa, and Where Are You Going." *Journal of Advanced Composition* 10 (1990): 387–93.

North, Stephen M. *The Making of Knowledge in Composition: Portrait of an Emerging Field*. Upper Montclair, NJ: Boynton/Cook, 1987.

Nussbaum, Martha C. *The Fragility of Goodness: Luck and Ethics in Greek Tragedy and Philosophy*. New York: Cambridge Univ. Press, 1986.

Orr, C. Jack. "How Shall We Say: 'Reality Is Socially Constructed Through Communication?' " *Central States Speech Journal* 29 (1978): 263–75.

Perelman, Chaim. "Rhetoric and Politics." *Philosophy and Rhetoric* 17 (1984): 129–34.

Perrine, Laurence. *Story and Structure*. 4th ed. New York: Harcourt Brace, 1974.

Plato. *Euthyphro, Apology, Crito, Phaedo, Phaedrus*. Trans. Harold N. Fowler. Loeb. Cambridge, MA: Harvard Univ. Press, 1982.

———. *Lysis, Symposium, Gorgias*. Trans. W. R. M. Lamb. Loeb. Cambridge, MA: Harvard Univ. Press, 1983.

———. *Republic I–V*. Trans. Paul Shorey. Loeb. Cambridge, MA: Harvard Univ. Press, 1982.

———. *Republic VI–X*. Trans. Paul Shorey. Loeb. Cambridge, MA: Harvard Univ. Press, 1987.

———. *Statesman, Philebus, Ion*. Trans. Harold N. Fowler and W. R. M. Lamb. Loeb. Cambridge, MA: Harvard Univ. Press, 1990.

———. *Theaetetus, Sophist*. Trans. Harold N. Fowler. Loeb. Cambridge, MA: Harvard Univ. Press, 1977.

————. *Timaeus, Critias, Cleitophon, Menexenus, Epistles.* Trans. R. G. Bury. Loeb. Cambridge, MA: Harvard Univ. Press, 1939.

Poulakos, John. "Argument, Practicality, and Eloquence in Isocrates' *Helen.*" *Rhetorica* 4 (1986): 1–19.

————. "Giorgias *Encomium* and *Helen* and the Defense of Rhetoric." *Rhetorica* 1 (1983), 1–15.

————. "Interpreting Sophistical Rhetoric: A Response to Schiappa. *Philosophy and Rhetoric* 23 (1990): 218–28.

————. "Toward a Sophistic Definition of Rhetoric." *Philosophy and Rhetoric* 16 (1983): 35–48.

Price, Robert. "Some Antistrophes to the *Rhetoric.*" *Philosophy and Rhetoric* 1 (1968): 145–64.

Raphael, Sally. "Rhetoric, Dialectic, and Syllogistic Argument: Aristotle's Position in *Rhetoric I–1.*" *Phronesis* 19 (1974): 153–67.

Recchio, Thomas E. "A Bakhtinian Reading of Student Writing." *College Composition and Communication* 42 (1991): 446–54.

Reeve, C. D. C. "The Naked Old Women in the Palaestra: A Dialogue Between Plato and Lasthenia of Mantinea." In *Hackett Works in the Humanities: Fall 1992 Complete Catalogue.* Indianapolis, IN: Hackett, 1992. 33–42.

Reynolds, John Frederick. "Motives, Metaphors, and Messages in Critical Reception of Experimental Research." *Journal of Advanced Composition* 10 (1990): 110–16.

Rist, John M. *The Mind of Aristotle: A Study in Philosophical Growth.* Toronto: Univ. of Toronto Press, 1989.

Roemer, Marjorie, et al. "Portfolios and the Process of Change." *College Composition and Communication* 42 (1991): 455–69.

Ronald, Kate. "A Reexamination of Personal and Public Discourse in Classical Rhetoric." *Rhetoric Review* 9 (1990): 36–48.

Rose, Mike. "Narrowing the Mind and Page: Remedial Writers and Cognitive Reductionism." *College Composition and Communication* 39 (1988): 267–302.

Rosenfield, L. W. "Rhetorical Criticism and an Aristotelian Notion of Process." *Speech Monographs* 33 (1966): 1–16.

Ross, David. *Aristotle.* London: Methuen, 1949.

Royer, Daniel J. "New Challenges to Epistemic Rhetoric." *Rhetoric Review* 9 (1991): 282–97.

Russell, David R. *Writing in the Academic Disciplines, 1870–1990: A Curricular History.* Carbondale: Southern Illinois Univ. Press, 1991.

Ryan, Eugene E. *Aristotle's Theory of Rhetorical Argumentation.* Montreal: Lés Éditions Ballarmin, 1984.

Sagan, Eli. *The Honey and the Hemlock: Democracy and Paranoia in Ancient Athens and Modern America.* New York: Basic Books, 1991.

Ste. Croix, G. E. M. de. *The Class Struggle in the Ancient Greek World.* Ithaca, NY: Cornell Univ. Press, 1981.

Scaglione, A. *The Classical Theory of Composition from Its Origins to the* focus

Present: A Historical Survey. Chapel Hill: Univ. of North Carolina Press, 1972.

Schiappa, Edward. "History and Neo-Sophistic Criticism: A Reply to Pou-lakos." *Philosophy and Rhetoric* 23 (1990): 307–15.

———. "Neosophistic Rhetorical Criticism in the Historical Reconstruction of Sophistic Doctrines?" *Philosophy and Rhetoric* 23 (1990): 192–217.

Schmandt-Besserat, Denise. "The Origins of Writing: An Archaeologist's Perspective." *Written Communication* 3 (1986): 31–45.

Schollmeier, Paul. "Practical Intuition and Rhetorical Example." *Philosophy and Rhetoric* 24 (1991): 95–104.

Schrag, Calvin O. "Communicative Rhetoric and the Claims of Reason." The Van Zelst Lecture in Communication: Northwestern University School of Speech, May 1989.

———. "Rhetoric Resituated at the End of Philosophy." *Quarterly Journal of Speech* 71 (1985): 164–74.

Schumpeter, Joseph A. *History of Economic Analysis*. Ed. Elizabeth B. Schumpeter. New York: Oxford Univ. Press, 1954.

Scott, Robert L. "On Viewing Rhetoric as Epistemic." *Central States Speech Journal* 18 (1967): 9–18.

———. "On Viewing Rhetoric as Epistemic: Ten Years Later." *Central States Speech Journal* 27 (1976): 258–66.

Seitz, James. "Composition's Misunderstanding of Metaphor." *College Composition and Communication* 42 (1991): 288–98.

Self, Lois. "Rhetoric and Phronesis: The Aristotelian Ideal." *Philosophy and Rhetoric* 12 (1979): 130–45.

Short, Bryan C. "The Temporality of Rhetoric." *Rhetoric Review* 7 (1989): 367–79.

Shulsky, Abram N. "The 'Infrastructure' of Aristotle's *Politics*: Aristotle on Economics and Politics." In *Essays on the Foundation of Aristotelian Political Science*. Ed. Carnes Lord and David K. O'Conner. Berkeley: Univ. of California Press, 1991. 74–111.

Sinclair, R. K. *Democracy and Participation in Athens*. New York: Cambridge Univ. Press, 1988.

Sloane, Thomas O. "Reinventing *Inventio*." *College English* 51 (1989): 461–73.

Solmsen, Friedrich. "The Aristotelian Tradition in Ancient Rhetoric." *American Journal of Philology* 62 (1941):35–50, 169–90.

Sommers, Nancy, and Donald McQuade, eds. *Student Writers at Work and in the Company of Other Writers: The Bedford Prizes, Second Series*. Boston: Bedford, 1986.

Starr, Chester G. *The Ancient Greeks*. New York: Oxford Univ. Press, 1971.

———. *The Birth of Athenian Democracy: The Assembly in the Fifth Century B.C.* New York: Oxford Univ. Press, 1990.

Strauss, Barry, S. "On Aristotle's Critique of Athenian Democracy." In *Essays on the Foundations of Aristotelian Political Science*. Ed. Carnes

Lord and David K. O'Connor. Berkerley: Univ. of California Press, 1991. 212–33.

Thompson, George. *The First Philosophers*. London: Laurence & Wishart, 1955.

Thompson, Lester, and A. Craig Baird. *Speech Criticism*. New York: Ronald, 1948.

Thucydides. *History of the Peloponnesian War*. Trans. Rex Warner. New York: Penguin, 1972.

Vickers, Brian. *In Defense of Rhetoric*. New York: Oxford Univ. Press, 1988.

Vitanza, Victor J. "Rhetoric's Past and Future: A Conversation with Edward P. J. Corbett." *Pretext* 8 (1987): 247–64.

Wallace, William A. "Aristotelian Science and Rhetoric in Transition: The Middle Ages and the Renaissance." *Rhetorica* 7 (1989): 7–21.

Wallbank, Frank W. "Political Equality: An Arrested Development." In *Athenian Democracy*. Ed. Jill Claster. New York: Holt, Rinehart, 1967. 47–59.

Ward, John D. "Magic and Rhetoric from Antiquity to the Renaissance: Some Ruminations." *Rhetorica* 6 (1988): 5–14.

Welch, Kathleen E. *The Contemporary Reception of Classical Rhetoric*. Hillsdale, NJ: Erlbaum, 1990.

———. "Electrifying Classical Rhetoric: Ancient Media, Modern Technology, and Contemporary Composition." *Journal of Advanced Composition* 10 (1990): 22–38.

———. "Ideology and Freshman Textbook Production: The Place of Theory in Writing Pedagogy." *College Composition and Communication* 38 (1987): 269–82.

———. "The Platonic Paradox: Plato's Rhetoric in Contemporary Rhetoric and Composition Studies." *Written Communication* 5 (1988): 3–21.

Witte, Stephen P. "Pre-Text and Composing." *College Composition and Communication* 38 (1987): 397–425.

Xenophon. *Anabasis IV–VII, Symposium, and Apology*. Trans. Carleton L. Brownson and O. J. Todd. Loeb. Cambridge, MA: Harvard Univ. Press, 1947.

———. *Hellenica, Books I–V*. Trans. Carleton L. Brownson. Loeb. Cambridge, MA: Harvard Univ. Press, 1930.

———. *Hellenica, Books VI and VII, Anabasis, Books I–III*. Trans. Carleton L. Brownson. Loeb. Cambridge, MA: Harvard Univ. Press, 1950.

———. *Memorabilia and Oeconomicus*. Trans. E. C. Marchant. Loeb. Cambridge, MA: Harvard Univ. Press, 1953.

———. *Scripta Minora*. Trans. E. C. Marchant. Loeb. Cambridge, MA: Harvard Univ. Press, 1925.

Zappen, James P. "Aristotelian and Ramist Rhetoric in Thomas Hobbs *Leviathan*: Pathos Versus Ethos and Logos." *Rhetorica* 1 (1983): 65–91.

Zürcher, Joseph. *Aristotles Werk and Geist*. Paderborn: Verlag, 1952.

INDEX

English Terms

Agon, 121–23, 201–6
Analyst, 177
Appearances, 54, 204. *See also* Reality
Aristotelianism: deception of, 204; determinism of, 31; foundation of, 54; as origin of professional discourse, 13–15; pure philosopher in, 29–32; and superior beings, 29–31; triumph of, 195; versus pedagogy, 144
Aristotle: and Alexander, 102–3; as alien, 100–101; behavior of, 97–99; biography of, 97–100; canon of, 100, 126; as creator of research, 20–21; as definer of rhetoric, 141; democracy to, 107–9, 218n.11; elitism of, 96; enigma of, 98; as founder of intellectual inquiry, 20–22; as human being, 93; as Isocrates' student, 101; language theory of, 170–71; logic of, 222n.26; and oligarchy, 111–15; pedagogy of, 202–4; personality of, 97–98; as Plato's student, 101; politics of, 16–18, 98–100; racial theories of, 25; and relativism, 55; not a rhetorician, 143; as savior of rhetoric, 53; as site of excava-

tion, 1, 7; situation of, 101, 184; and slavery, 19–25; social theories of, 211n.16; system of, 26, 53–73, 179, 215n.37; as teaching assistant, 48–53; texts of, 48, 90–94; voice of, 90–94; wealth of, 97–98; why read, 5–9; works by, 94; world of, 103–4; writing process of, 90–94
Athens, 103–23. *See also* Democracy; Slavery
Audience, 156, 168, 215nn.34, 35. *See also* Delivery; Pathos
Authorship, 177. *See also* Writing, situation of teachers of

Canons, 14–15, 209n.4
Chaos, 1, 97
Clarity, 175–79. *See also* Style
Commonplaces, 14–15
Communication, 50
Composition studies: agon of, 190; alienation of, 57–58; and Aristotle, 105, 181; as backside, 205; beginnings of, 132–33; canon of, 74–75; degraded nature of, 36–40; entry into, 37–40; history of, 33–34, 211n.19; and literary studies, 38; location of, 58–59; metaphysics of, 73; and moralizing, 125–26; obligations of, 134–35; ontogeny of, 6–9, 201–6; phylog-

241

text of, 91–94; and teachers of writing, 96–97; as theoretical-practical-productive, 216n.43; unity of, 91–96; writing process of, 97

Rhetorician: abilities of, 153–54; and demonstration, 73; not a speaker, 152

Rogerian argument, 26

Science: Aristotelian, 212n.8, 214n.25; methods and origins of, 61; most noble, 66–67; progress of, 214n.27; purity of, 61; and rhetoric, 151; and Supreme Scientist, 61; voice of, 85–86

Self-presence, 170–71

Sexism, 189–90, 202, 210n.9

Situation: of author, 1; of student writers, 26–27, 86–89; of writing, 88–90

Slavery: in ancient Athens, 19–21; Aristotle's justification of, 15–25; in *Economics*, 209n.6

Sophist, 1, 192

Sophistry: as antidote, 203–4; Aristotelian, 190–96; in Aristotelianism, 55; aversion to knowledge of, 194; as derogatory term, 225n.4; effects of, 192; elitism of, 225n.5; and feminism, 191; happiness of, 205–6; and Isocrates, 217n.9; life of, 198; methods of, 193–94; and moral purpose, 46; motives of, 193; opposition to slavery of, 21–24; Plato's, 191–92; playfulness of, 205; as process, 198; risks of, 195–96; terror of, 202; and the truth, 186–87; uncertainty of, 191; unlike rhetoric, 43; usefulness of, 126

Soul, 16–19; of discourse, 24; five operations of, 67; hierarchy of,

32, 66–68; landscape of, 67–70; security of, 168; and society, 68

Speech, 170

State, 25–26

Strange attractor, 1, 91

Style: as adornment, 24; clarity of, 171; contrived nature of, 174; deceptiveness of, 173; Gorgian, 172–73, 223n.29; as guardian of proofs, 171; metaphysics of, 171–72; ordinariness of, 172; as part of ethos, 174; plain, middle, 176–77; poetic vs. rhetorical, 174–75

Superior being, 34

Syllogism: in demonstration, 56–58; and ethymeme, 63–65; form of, 56; invention of, 214n.23; and student writing, 57–58

Taxonomy: and composition studies, 181–90; effect of, 24; and historicism, 198; and rhetoric, 153

Teleology: Aristotelian, 224n.36; of democracy, 107; effects of on composition, 28; operation of, 184; and politics, 108; of rhetoric, 154, 168, 180

Theoretical life, 30–31. *See also* Science: and Supreme Scientist

Theory: desire for, 32; interpretation as, 182–84; opposition to, 197; role in Aristotelianism, 30–31; sophistry as, 190–96; and truth, 66. *See also* Sophistry

Truth, 65

University, 202

West, 20–22

Writing: education of teachers of,

JASPER NEEL is a professor of English at Vanderbilt University. Since 1990 he has served as director of the College Writing Program, a program that includes faculty from all disciplines in the College of Arts and Science; in fall 1994 he began a term as chair of the English department. Before joining the faculty at Vanderbilt, Professor Neel held appointments at the University of Waterloo (Canada), Northern Illinois University, Francis Marion College (South Carolina), New York University, the Modern Language Association, and Baylor University.

Professor Neel's 1988 book, *Plato, Derrida, and Writing* (also published by SIU Press), received the Mina Shaughnessy Prize from the Modern Language Association, and his 1992 essay, "Dichotomy, Consubstantiality, Technical Writing, Literary Theory: The Double Orthodox Curse," received the James Kinneavy Prize, which is awarded jointly by the *Journal of Advanced Composition* and the Association of Teachers of Advanced Composition. Professor Neel's research interests range from the history of rhetoric to classroom pedagogy, from critical theory to academic administration. He is currently at work on two books: the first, a study of process pedagogy in North American university English departments; the second, a history of Anglo-American critical theory before 1900.